The Hollywood Tutor's

AMERICAN ENGLISH
Book Two

THE HOLLYWOOD TUTOR'S AMERICAN ENGLISH ©Copyright 2020 Mitch Rubman. All rights reserved. No part of this publication may be reproduced or distributed in any form or by any means without the written permission of the copyright owner

The Hollywood Tutor's
AMERICAN ENGLISH

How to lose an accent in 7 lessons while learning American English, Book Two

Mitch Rubman, M.A.
Hollywood, CA

7 Complete lessons

A Modern American Hollywood (hol-ee-wood) Experience.

Pronunciation, Vocabulary, Sentences, Dialogues, Citizenship, Covid-19, BLM: Racism and Discrimination, American Heroes, an ESL reader

From basic sounds to conversations, for beginners to the advanced.

Foreword by Danny Hutton, Three Dog Night

ISBN:978-1-7333110-2-1

© 2020 Mitch Rubman
All rights reserved.
Rights for permission to reproduce material from this work should be sent to mrubman@gmail.com
Published by The Hollywood Tutor
Mitch Rubman Publishing
first

No part of this publication may be reproduced or distributed in any form or by any means without the written permission of the copyright owner. All rights reserved.
Cover photo by M. Rubman

Hollywood, California

Dedications and Acknowledgments

My special thanks to:

In memory of my parents, Sol and Sarah Rubman, who kept saying to me, write a book.

My sister Randee Sullivan, thank you for camping out all night to get tickets for us to see Led Zeppelin at Madison Square Garden.

The many excellent New York City public school teachers, from P.S. 169, Ms. Friedman, Ms. Soberman, Ms. Weinstein, Ms. Seibold, Ms. Christie, and Ms. Scher.

Mr. Lutvak from I.S. 25, for those many moments of inspection.

The Bronx High School of Science, Mr. Harrison, Mr. Stark, and Ms. Strauss.

Antioch University, where I received a Master's degree in clinical psychology, thank you for creating a school without exams.

Boston University, where I studied with Elie Wiesel, a Holocaust survivor and a Nobel laureate, a scholar who shook my hand and told me that I would be a teacher.

B.U. Astronomy Department, Prof. W. Jeffrey Hughes.

Barbara, Jennifer, and Jama and GoFundMe.

My cousins, David, Lou, and Devorah, for their help.

Kimberly and the team at LAC + USC Medical Center for fixing my broken right elbow.

M. Cohen and T. Tannenbaum for hometown inspiration.

Jonathan, Gregg, and Tom, from college days.

Mucci and Devin, for their many years of friendship and support.

Betsy Blank, in memory of her kindness, laughter, and love of life.

Sondra Lynn, for sharing croissants and the French language.

Boris Leskin, and that remarkable year of study.

Julie Ariola, dear friend, and acting teacher.

Maureen for her compassion and kindness, with love and support.

Thank you to my many accent reduction students who inspired me with tales from the Earth's four corners.

Contents

Dedications and Acknowledgments	v
Contents	244
Foreword by Danny Hutton	248
Preface	250
Introduction to Book Two	252

Lesson 8 254
Vowels, Weather and Difficult words 254

8.1	Pronunciation Key 12	254
8.2	Long and short vowels in words.	257
8.3	How is the weather?	258
8.4	Synonyms 6	259
8.5	Contractions with sentences	260
8.6	Difficult words and sentences 1	261
8.7	Dialogue: Shopping at the Flea Market	263
8.8	Fashion: Styles, and Trends	265
8.9	Complex Colors	267
8.10	Dialogue: Buying a slice of Pizza	269
8.11	Dialogue: Ordering at a Delicatessen	270
8.12	Antonyms 3	272
8.13	Compare and Contrast 3	274
8.14	Dialogue: Tony, the Car Mechanic	278
8.15	Coffee Bar Drinks	279
8.16	Conditional Sentences	280

Lesson 9 281
Covid-19, Sports, Cliches, Chess 281

9.1	Pronunciation Key 13	281
9.2	COVID-19 and related terms	282
9.3	Dialogue: COVID-19 Emergency Room	284
9.4	COVID-19 Symptoms	285
9.5	COVID-19 Warning signs	285
9.6	Tongue Twisters 4	286
9.7	Clichés, Idiomatic expressions and Proverbs 2[B-G]	287
9.8	American Football	289
9.9	American Soccer	290
9.10	Badminton	291
9.11	Baseball	292
9.12	Basketball	293
9.13	Bicycle Parts	295
9.14	Boxing	295
9.15	Fitness, Workout and Nutrition terms	296
9.16	Golf	298
9.17	Gymnastics, Track & Field	300
9.18	Ping Pong	301
9.19	Pool: Eight ball	302
9.20	Sailing and Nautical terms	302
9.21	Surfing	303
9.22	Swimming	304
9.23	Yoga Postures	305
9.24	Tennis	306
9.25	Chess	307

Lesson 10 310
BLM: American Heroes, Anatomy, Astrology 310

10.1	Pronunciation Key 14	310

The Hollywood Tutor's AMERICAN ENGLISH © 2020 Mitch Rubman. All rights reserved. No part of this publication may be reproduced or distributed in any form or by any means without the written permission of the copyright owner

10.2	Black Lives Matter: American Heroes	312
10.3	Human Anatomy	324
10.4	Difficult words and sentences 2	328
10.5	Tongue Twisters 5	331
10.6	Synonyms 7	332
10.7	Compare and Contrast 4	334
10.8	Prefixes, Suffixes and Roots 2	338
10.9	Noun suffixes	344
10.10	Common Root Words	346
10.11	Onomatopoeias	346
10.12	Astrology	347

Lesson 11 348

Antonyms, Mortgages, Business English 348

11.1	Pronunciation Key 15 with sentences	348
11.1	Pronunciation Key 16	351
11.2	Dialogue: Mortgage Refinance	352
11.3	Antonyms 4	354
11.4	William Shakespeare	355
11.5	Difficult words and sentences 3	356
11.6	Clichés, Idiomatic expressions and Proverbs 3[G-M]	359
11.7	Compare and Contrast 5	362
11.8	Business English	364
11.9	Difficult words and sentences 4	367
11.10	Composers and Musicians	372

Lesson 12 375

The Internet, Computers, Jobs, Cover letter 375

12.1	Pronunciation Key 17 with sentences	375
12.2	The Internet: Technology, Social Media, Computers	376
12.3	Difficult words and sentences 5	383
12.4	Dialogue: At the Yogurt Shop	385
12.5	Synonyms 8	387
12.6	Dialogue: Grocery Shopping	388
12.7	Dialogue: A Job interview	390
12.8	Dialogue: The Florist Shop	392
12.9	Difficult words and sentences 6	393
12.10	Dialogue: Cover letter for Resume	395
12.11	Difficult words and sentences 7	396
12.12	Bartender: Mixed drinks, beers, alcohol, and supplies	398
12.13	Prefixes, Roots and Suffixes 3	401

Lesson 13 405

The Moon, Polygons, Prefixes, Hybrids 405

13.1	Pronunciation Key 18	405
13.2	Abbreviations, acronyms, mnemonics	407
13.3	The Four Seasons of the Year	410
13.4	Moon notes	410
13.5	Moon idiomatic expressions	411
13.6	Numbers 6: Polygons	411
13.7	Numbers 7: Volume 3D shapes	412
13.8	Numbers 8: The Decimal point	412
13.9	Periodic Table of Elements	414
13.10	The Solar System	416
13.11	Cloud types	416
13.12	Scientific and Meteorological Terms	417
13.13	Chemistry Laboratory	420
13.14	Aviation and aerospace	421
13.15	Difficult words and sentences 8	421

13.16	Dialogue: At the Post Office	425
13.17	The Internal Combustion Gas Engine	427
13.18	Electric and Hybrid Cars	431
13.19	Compare and Contrast 6	433
13.20	Clichés, Idiomatic expressions and Proverbs 4[M-S]	443

Lesson 14 446

Beauty Salon, Jazz, Cliches, Derivatives 446

14.1	Pronunciation Key 19 and sentences	446
14.2	Pronunciation Key 20	449
14.3	Irregular plural nouns	451
14.4	Dialogue: The Beauty Salon	452
14.5	Difficult words and sentences 9	453
14.6	Slang Spoken Contractions:	457
14.7	Clichés, Idiomatic expressions and Proverbs 5 [S-W]	457
14.9	Word Derivatives and Root forms	461
14.10	World list of 194 Countries	463
14.11	Prefixes, Roots and Suffixes 4	473

Bibliography 475

INDEX	477

The Hollywood Tutor's AMERICAN ENGLISH © 2020 Mitch Rubman. All rights reserved. No part of this publication may be reproduced or distributed in any form or by any means without the written permission of the copyright owner

Foreword by Danny Hutton

I have been going to the same coffee shop across from the DGA in West Hollywood for years. After a while, you start to see some of the same faces, you start saying hi, you get used to seeing the regulars with their newspaper or laptop. But for this one man that I saw almost every day, I couldn't tell what the heck he was doing. He had a book in front of him – self printed, spiral bound – called *American English*. He was joined by people – a young woman or an older man, a lot of hip looking guys and girls – and he was teaching them from this book, across the table, while drawing all over sheets of paper. Diagrams and arrows and certain words or letters. Weird way to learn English, but okay…

Eventually I realized that these people already knew English. What he was teaching them was more specific: it was to speak it without an accent getting in the way of being understood. He was an Accent Eliminator!

After many years in the music business, singing, performing, songwriting and producing, I have heard dozens of instruments and hundreds of trained and untrained vocalists. Every one of them – including my own band Three Dog Night – is always reaching for a sound that will connect with the audience. The one that will make them feel the music with you. The one perfect note that blends with the others and lets the audience members close their eyes and disappear into the song. Artists work all their lives to find that one perfect sound.

Well—I realize that speaking heavily accented English is a little like playing guitar with a cast on one arm: it's just not going to sound right. Only in this case, the people didn't even know the notes because some of them don't exist in other languages. Imagine coming to Los Angeles to sell your script or your song, or even just cashier at the coffee shop, and all your Ws or Vs or your Rs and Ls are scrambled. It'd be hard to be understood, but it would also set up a wall between you and your dreams. Mitch Rubman's students had done the hard work of learning English, but there was a final step that no one had told them about that would make them understood, that would help them belong: they were going to have to pronounce it. Beyond speaking words like Won and One, or Colonel or Yacht, he helped them with idioms. Imagine being in a meeting and having an exec start to say "I'm going to have to take a raincheck. "Huh?

I'd pop in for a coffee and hear him helping these people find the sounds for the first time. Then they'd start to relax, laugh and have fun. Using our idioms correctly was a lot like getting a song memorized. And speaking unaccented American English was like a piano in tune instead of out of it. It wasn't natural for everyone, but it was something that could be learned. And Mitch helps his students do it. Year after year, he does it over a cup of coffee and a spiral bound textbook. He's a confidence builder and provides what I call Accent Relief. This is one man who knows what he's doing.

Danny Hutton
Three Dog Night
Hollywood, California.

Preface

Before I authored this book, I had been teaching English to students using dictionaries, tongue twisters, flashcards, and handouts. I quickly started to realize that I needed to craft a book based on my methods and ideas in teaching accent reduction and learning English. I reviewed many English books, going back to the 1800s. In those early English books, there are a lot of stories about horses and building the country. In this book, you will find the Internet, sports and COVID-19.

These old English textbooks inspired me to think that I, too, should author a book. Slowly I began, assembling general topics. As I continued teaching, I would add new exercises on different subjects. Sometimes a student would ask for a particular topic say, for example, baseball. Later that night I would research the topic and write the section. But really what would happen is that after I wrote the baseball section I thought I needed to add Football, Soccer, Badminton, Baseball, Basketball, Bicycle Parts, Boxing, Fitness, Golf, Gymnastics, Ping Pong, Pool, Sailing, Surfing, Swimming, Tennis, and ending with relaxing with Yoga. That's how some of the lessons developed.

The purpose of this book is to help a person learn English pronunciation at the same time that they are learning new words and expressions. Ten years after I began teaching, I have created a book that has been tried and tested by hundreds of students from around the globe. This book is going to make you feel smarter and sound smarter, you will see. Enjoy. Take a deep breath. Go ahead, you first.

Introduction to Book Two

As American English grew over the years, I soon noticed that many students got nervous as the book expanded from 50 pages to 200 to 350 and finally 475 pages. I would see students leaf through the pages when I stood up to get a cup of coffee. I would mention that we did not have to complete the book, but still a large textbook makes people nervous. So, I split the book into two halves' hence books one and two and the consecutive exercises with lesson numbers starting at lesson eight.

Since the beginning of time, people have struggled to pronounce the English language correctly. Even native-born speakers can be confused by the many sounds and variations in pronunciation. What is the secret to learning English? The answer is the purpose of this book and my quest for the last ten years. How to make English accessible to all.

The approach is to begin each lesson by reciting a pronunciation key with anchor words. This is critical to success. These anchor words contain a small singular phoneme that represents one of the different sounds in American English. By repeating them, specific muscles become stronger and more elastic. For some students, this might be the first-time certain sounds have ever been spoken. You might feel your muscles stretch as you study the lessons and articulate new words. Don't be too hard on yourself, if the jaw starts to hurt, take a break. I generally gave two-hour lessons, which can be exhausting. That's a good length for a real workout, especially if it is all out loud.

In addition to improving your English, you are going to feel smarter. Here is why. Recent studies indicate that different sounds of speech are formed in various locations in the brain. The [ch] or [d] sound is not made next to the [th] or [k] sound but at another location. Because sounds are recorded at various locations, the more vocalization the student makes, the more neurons and synapses are connected, the smarter the student will become. As a result of reading the pronunciation tables, brain plasticity occurs.

The day after a lesson, students reported that they felt a bit sharper, brighter. For long-term students, they noticed that their memory improved. To friends, students start to sound different, clearer with a louder voice. By using phonetic spellings instead of symbols, the student gains confidence quicker and becomes more understandable sooner. As the student reads through this book, they will discover synonyms, antonyms, homonyms, and get practice by reciting dialogues and conversations from everyday American situations.

This book is based on experiences as a teacher for more than a dozen years. No matter what country the student is from, no matter how little English they spoke, this book is a life-changer.

People at the café, where I sometimes tutored, often told me of their glimpses of students before and after a lesson. Observers noted a change in the way the student sounded, stood, and moved. It took just one lesson to start the shift from fear into confidence. The pronunciation keys with sentences, the lists, the dialogues with phonetic spellings are going to make a difference. This book is designed from the inside out.

Why wait? Just read aloud and practice the first few exercises. The idea is to start with pure basic sounds, then words, phrases, sentences, and finally dialogues. But of course, words are needed to explain everything, so the first few chapters have basic directions to use. Then the lessons progress in difficulty. However, at the front of the book, there are several brief conversations on daily life based on the fact that students will often have to jump right in. If these are too difficult, skip them and return after reviewing the first two chapters.

There are also newly written sections on COVID-19, including vocabulary and conversations on treating the virus and how to stay safe.

As I was editing this book, the death of George Floyd occurred. This senseless moment has affected the entire planet, with protests still continuing. There is a need to be able to talk about George Floyd. I have therefore added a section on American Heroes involved with fighting racial injustice, bigotry, and discrimination in America.

This book is very flexible and can be used to focus on specific problem sounds. For example, a student was unable to pronounce [th] sounds properly. Instead of doing a regular lesson with everything, we read and practiced different pronunciation keys and lists that focused on the [th] sound. This redundancy allows for focused work on problem sounds. There are surprises too. Many students have told me that it was the first time they had heard and seen a word together — a phrase like hors' d' oeuvres(awr-durvz), or the word chorus(kawr-uhs) are two prime examples of vocabulary that students might encounter.

As the author, I recommend that the student read the book from cover to cover. If the sentences are too complicated, skip over them and practice words from the many lists and then return to the sentences later.

Enjoy the vastness and depth of the hundreds of exercises.

Take a breath, listen, think, learn, and speak.
Mitch Rubman,
Los Angeles,
December 21, 2020.

Lesson 8

Vowels, Weather and Difficult words

8.1 Pronunciation Key 12

These are all the sounds of the English language using different key words.

Practice until they are easy. Say the key word and the sentence that follows.

Exercise 1: Repeat the words aloud.
Exercise 2: Create an original sentence for each word.

Key Word (phonetic spelling)	Phonetic Sound	Example sentence
Asia (ey-zhuh)	Long a	The seven continents (kon-tn-uhnts) are: Africa (af-ri-kuh), Antarctica (ant-ahrk-ti-kuh), Asia (ey-zhuh), Australia (aw-streyl-yuh), Europe (yoor-uh), North America (uh-mer-i-kuh) and South America.
Actor (ak-ter)	Short a	The actor went early to the audition (aw-dish-uhn).
Airplane (air-pleyn)	Air	Did you see the (wurld) World War II (two) airplane?
Arctic (ahrk-tik)	Ar	The Arctic (ahr-tik) expedition (ek-spi-dish-uhn) will be returning in two months.
August (aw-guhst)	Aw	In August, record temperatures were blamed for the blackout.
Bald (bawld)	B	The Bald (bawld) Eagle, America's national emblem (em-bluhm) since 1782, is a bird of prey in North America that builds the largest tree nest of any species (spee-sheez).
Black (blak)	Bl	Don't fall into a black hole.
Branch (brahnch)	Br	That branch is from an Apple tree.
Cabin (kab-in)	Hard c and k	Did you see the log cabin by the lake?
Cloud (kloud)	Cl	Doesn't that cloud (kloud) look like a swan?
Crab (krab)	Cr	The hermit crab uses discarded shells from other animals for its home.
Queen (kween)	Qu	Is the Queen in her castle (kas-uhl)?
Chair (chair)	Ch	The Queen sits in her chair, called the throne (throhn).
Daffodil (daf-uh-dil)	D	These daffodil flowers are a beautiful yellow color.
Drum (druhm)	Dr	How many pieces in that drum set?
Equal (ee-kwuhl)	Long e	Four plus three equals seven.

Egg (eg)	Short e	How many eggs are in the omelet (om-lit)?
Ear (eer)	Eer	In acupuncture (ak-yoo-puhngk-cher), the ear represents the entire body.
Photo (foh-toh)	F and ph	Did you get the photo?
Flipper (flip-er)	Fl	Seals (seelz), whales (weylz) and turtles (tur-tls) have flippers for swimming and navigating.
Frame (freym)	Fr	Did you buy a frame with the painting?
Gold (gohld)	Hard g	Is that a gold watch?
Glass (glas)	Gl	The glass in the front window of your car is called the windshield (wind-sheeld).
Gray (grey)	Gr	The sky is looking very gray today.
Hand (hand)	H	Are you righthanded, left-handed, or ambidextrous (am-bi-dek-struhs)?
Icicle (ahy-si-kuhl)	Long i	An icicle is a mass of ice formed by dripping water.
India (in-dee-uh)	Short i	It's monsoon (mon-soon) season in India.
Geology (jee-ol-uh-jee)	J and soft g	Have you studied Geology before?
Laundry (lawn-dree)	L	Can't we do the laundry after getting coffee?
Mask (mahsk)	M	Remember, no Halloween (hal-uh-ween) masks in the bank.
Nail (neyl)	N	Use a toenail clipper to trim your nails.
Ocean (oh-shuhn)	Long o	Did life start in the ocean?
Orca (awr-kuh)	Or	The Orca (awr-kuh), a killer whale, is also a very smart marine mammal (mam-uhl).
Oil (oil)	Oy	It sounds like you can use a little oil on that hinge (hinj).
Olive (ol-iv)	Short o	How many kinds of olives can you name?
Owl (oul)	Short ow	The barn owl (oul) caught the mouse with its talons (tal-uhnz).
Painting (peyn-ting)	P	I think that painting is counterfeit, its provenance (prov-uh-nuhns) is not known.
Planet (plan-it)	Pl	The nine planets in the solar system are Mercury(mur-kyuh-ree), Venus(vee-nuhs), Earth(urth), Mars(mahrz), Jupiter(joo-pi-ter), Saturn(sat-ern), Uranus(yoor-uh-nuhs), Neptune(nep-toon), and Pluto(ploo-tuh). To remember their names, try this mnemonic (ni-mon-ik) device. My Very Excellent Mother Just Sent Us Nine Pies.
Prime (prahym)	Pr	A prime number is only divisible by itself and one, for example, the following numbers are prime: 2, 3, 5, 7, 11, 13, 17, and 19
Radar (rey-dahr)	R	The radar (radio detection and ranging) has found a UFO.
Cent (sent)	S/ soft c	I spent every cent on that car for repairs.
Skin (skin)	Sk	I like the salmon (sam-uhn) skin roll at the sushi bar.
Screw (skroo)	Skr/scr	Just screw the cap off.
Square (skwair)	Squ	The square root of 16 is four.

Slice (slahys)	Sl	Just a slice of cheese pizza (peet-suh).
Smile (smahyl)	Sm	Don't you ever smile?
Snow (snoh)	Sn	It never snows in Southern California.
Spiral (spahy-ruhl)	Sp	DNA is shaped like a double spiral.
Split (split)	Spl	Let's split dessert (dih-zurt).
Spring (spring)	Spr	Spring is right around the corner.
Stamp (stamp)	St	The forever stamps are good forever.
Strawberry (straw-ber-ee)	Str	Which berry do you prefer, strawberries, blueberries, boysenberries, or raspberries?
Sphere (sfeer)	Sph	The equation for the volume of a sphere is four-thirds pi (pie)- times [r] cubed(kyoobd).
Swan (swon)	Sw	Swans usually mate for life, although divorce (dih-vawrs) sometimes happens.
Shoe (shoo)	Sh	Does the shoe fit?
Shrimp (shrimp)	Shr	I'd like to order the shrimp with lobster sauce.
Talk (tawk)	T	Listen, and then talk.
Three	Th	Three Dog Night (1967-) American Rock band. Three founding members include Danny Hutton, Cory Wells, and Chuck Negron.
Train (treyn)	Tr	Take the last train to Clarksville (klahrks-vil) is a hit song by the Monkees.
Twist (twist)	Tw	The chassis got twisted in the wreckage (rek-ij).
Third (thurd)	Th	I used to play third base in little league (leeg).
Thread (thred)	Thr	Are your eyes good enough to thread (thred) a needle?
Unicorn (yoo-ni-kawrn)	Long u	Her workspace was covered with stickers of unicorns (yoon-e-korn).
Umbrella (uhm-brel-uh)	Short u	No umbrella is necessary for Los Angeles today.
Earth (urth)	Ur	The Earth's equatorial (ee-kwuh-tawr-ee-uhl) diameter is approximately 7,900 miles.
Verb (vurb)	V	The verb oversees the sentence.
One (wuhn)	W	The one and only.
Whale (hweyl)	Wh	Let's go whale watching.
Yellow (yel-oh)	Y	I'd like the yellow curry.
Zebra (zee-bruh)	Z	The lions sleep near the zebras so that they can have fast food.

8.2   Long and short vowels in words.

The English language is composed of words with long and short vowels. Please review the following examples.

Exercise 1: Practice aloud the following examples of long and short vowels.

Long vowel	Short vowel
Child (chahyld) n. She is just a child.	Children (chil-druhn) n. The children's department is on the right.
Divine (dih-vahyn) adj. That chocolate is divine.	Divinity (dih-vin-i-tee) n. They both went to divinity school.
Mine (mahyn) prn.n. That's mine.	Mineral (min-er-uhl) n.adj What mineral is that?
Serene (suh-reen) adj. The courtyard is very serene.	Serenity (suh-ren-i-tee) n. I was seeking serenity.
Dream (dreem) n. This was in a dream	Dreamt (dremt) v. I dreamt I was on the Tonight Show.
Nation (ney-shuhn) n. This is a great nation.	National (nash-uh-nl) adj. They ran a national presidential campaign.
Sane (seyn) adj. That's a very sane idea.	Sanity (san-i-tee) n. His sanity was in question.
Goose (goos) n. Where is that goose from?	Gosling (goz-ling) n. That gosling is very young.
School (skool) n. He was real old school.	Scholarly (skol-er-lee) adj. That scholarly research can be done in the library.
Holy (hoh-lee) adj. The relics were considered holy.	Holiday (hol-i-dey) n. When does the holiday start?
Cone (kohn) n. I'll have the ice cream in a cone.	Conical (kon-ik-kal) adj. The front of the space craft had a conical shape.
Know (noh) v. Do you know the answer?	Knowledge (nol-ij) n., They had that knowledge at one time.
South (south) n.adj.adv. San Diego is south of Los Angeles.	Southern (suth-ern) adj. They ordered the Southern Fried Chicken.
Pronounce (pruh-nouns) v. How do you pronounce choir?	Pronunciation (pruh-nuhn-see-ey-shuhn) n. Practicing the pronunciation keys are the quickest way to improve your articulation.

8.3 How is the weather?

In Los Angeles, the weather is usually beautiful, however some days it might be pouring rain with mud slides, stormy. Not to mention earthquakes. Talking about the weather is always good way to start a conversation. Here are a variety of responses.

Exercise 1: Repeat the following questions and answers with a partner, switch sides repeat.

Question: What's the weather(weth-er) outside?
Answer: It's breezy, better wear a light coat.
Question: How's the weather outside?
Answer: It's cloudy, it might rain. I've got a hat and a raincoat.
Question: What's the weather like outside?
Answer: It's hailing, look out some of the hailstones(heyl-stohns) are the size of a baseball. I've got an umbrella.
Question: What's the weather outside?
Answer: It's lightning(lahyt-ning) better come inside.
Question: What's the weather like outside?
Answer: Very hot.
Question: How's the weather outside?
Answer: It's been raining for hours everything is flooded.
Question: What's the weather like outside?
Answer: It's flooding.
Question: What's the weather like outside?
Answer: Look, it's 105 degrees outside; I hope you have water.
Question: What's the weather like outside?
Answer: Let me look out my window — another sunny day in Los Angeles.

8.4 Synonyms 6

Exercise 1: Repeat each word aloud, going across the row of synonyms.
Exercise 2: Compose a sentence for each word.

Word	Synonym	Synonym
1. compensate (kom-puhn-seyt)	2. balance(bal-uhns)	3. recompense (rek-uhm-pens
4. competent (kom-pi-tuhnt)	5. able(ey-buhl)	6. capable (key-puh-buhl)
7. conceive (kuhn-seev)	8. design(dih-zahyn)	9. plan(plan)
10. confirmation (kon-fer-mey-shuhn)	11. acknowledgement (aknol-ij-muhnt)	12. proof(proof)
13. contradict (kon-truh-dikt)	14. deny(dih-nahy)	15. oppose(uh-pohz)
16. contribution(kon-truh-byoo-shuhn)	17. donation (doh-ney-shuhn)	18. grant(grahnt)
19. courteous (kur-tee-uhs)	20. polite(puh-lahyt)	21. well-mannered
22. craving (krey-ving)	23. desire (dih-zahyuhr)	24. longing (lawng-ing)
25. credulous (krej-uh-luhs)	26. confident (kon-fi-duhnt)	27. trustful(truhst-fuhl)
28. damp(damp)	29. moist (moist)	30. wet(wet)
31. dare(dair)	32. challenge(chal-inj)	33. defy(dih-fahy)
34. decay(dih-key)	35. decline(dih-klahyn)	36. rot(rot)
37. decent(dee-suhnt)	38. honorable (on-er-uh-buhl	39. pure(pyoor)
40. dense(dens)	41. filled(fild)	42. packed(pakt)
43. designate (dez-ig-neyt)	44. name(neym)	45. select(si-lekt)
46. detain(dih-teyn)	47. hold(hohld)	48. keep(keep)
49. disclose (dih-sklohz)	50. announce (uh-nouns)	51. reveal(ri-veel)

8.5 Contractions with sentences

In American English, contractions are used in informal writing and casual conversations. Remember when reading the contraction do not undo the contraction, an apostrophe replaces the letter or word.

Exercise 1: Practice saying each sentence aloud.
Exercise 2: Create a simple sentence for each contraction.

[KEY]
Contraction (phonetic spelling) (pre-contraction): used in sentence.

1.	Can't (kant)(cannot): I can't believe it; I won(wuhn) the Powerball lottery.
2.	Couldn't (kood-nt) (could not): Thanks for your help, I couldn't have done it by myself.
3.	Didn't (did-nt) (did not): Didn't she make a beautiful bride?
4.	Doesn't (duhz-uhnt) (does not): Doesn't that sound familiar?
5.	Don't (dohnt) (do not): Don't use water on that electrical fire.
6.	Hadn't (had-nt) (had not): He hadn't been interviewed until yesterday?
7.	Hasn't (haz-uhnt) (has not): She hasn't been to France.
8.	Haven't (hav-uhnt) (have not): They haven't had a quiet night since the move.
9.	He'd (heed) (he had, he would): He'd rather sit in the window seat.
10.	He'll (heel) (he will): He'll be early, you'll see.
11.	He's (heez) (he is, he has): He's in hot water, isn't he?
12.	Here's (heerz) (here is): Here's the new Mayor.
13.	How's (houz) (how is): How's that Ferrari on gas mileage?
14.	I'd (ahyd) (I would, I had): I'd rather fly first class.
15.	I'll (ahyl) (I will, I shall): But I'll fly coach this time.
16.	I'm (ahym) (I am): I'm all in.
17.	I've (ahyv) (I have): I've had enough of your shenanigans (shuh-nan-i-guhns).
18.	Isn't (iz-uhnt) (is not): Isn't that a mistake?
19.	It's (its) (it is, it has): It's the butler.
20.	Let's (lets) (let us): Let's go rollerblading.
21.	Mustn't (muhs-uhnt) (must not): She mustn't be late.
22.	Needn't (need-nt) (need not): You needn't add salt to the soup.
23.	She'd (sheed) (she had, she would): She'd be home if she took the freeway.
24.	She'll (sheel) (she will, she shall): She'll be back for the Holidays, don't worry.
25.	She's (sheez) (she is, she has): She's in a lot of trouble, I bet.
26.	Shouldn't (shood-nt) (should not): Shouldn't we take the 101?
27.	That's (thats) (that is, that has): That's a bad idea, the freeway is jammed.
28.	There's (thairz) (there is, there has): There's no more paint left.

29. They'd (theyd) (they had, they would): They'd be home by now if they took the short cut.
30. They'll (theyl) (they will, they shall): They'll be on time, don't worry.
31. They're (thair) (they are): They're on the earlier flight.
32. They've (theyv) (they have): They've done this before, don't worry.
33. Wasn't (wuhz-uhnt) (was not): There wasn't anyone home, I checked.
34. We'd (weed) (we had, we would): We'd do better if we had five guys.
35. We'll (weel) (we will): We'll be there in half an hour, hold your horses.
36. We're (weer) (we are) I told you we're early, look-- no cars in the parking lot.
37. We've (weev) (we have): We've got one more ride to try.
38. Weren't (wurnt) (were not): Weren't you supposed to be the employee of the month?
39. What's (hwuhts) (what is): What's up?
40. Where's (hwairz) (where is): Where's that chocolate chip cookie?
41. Who'd (hood) (who had, who would): Who'd be into driving up the coast?
42. Who'll (hool) (who will, who shall): Who'll pick up the slack after the layoff?
43. Who's (hooz) (who is, who has): Who's in charge?
44. Won't (wohnt) (will not): That won't work here, they check ticket stubs.
45. Wouldn't (wood-nt) (would not): Wouldn't you like to go on a long weekend?
46. You'd (yood) (you had, you would): You'd be better off with the salmon.
47. You'll (yool) (you will, you shall): You'll miss me when I'm gone.
48. You're (yoor) (you are): You're under arrest.
49. You've (yoov) (you have): You've arrived too late, breakfast is finished.

8.6 Difficult words and sentences 1

This is a list of common tricky words and sentences, take some time. Look up new words that you are not sure of.

Exercise 1: Repeat the words aloud and the sentences that follow.
Exercise 2: Create a new sentence using the words below. Repeat aloud.

Afternoon(af-ter-noon):	I know it's my first day, but can I have the afternoon off?
Arm(ahrm):	How did you break your arm?
Bargain (bahr-guhn):	I enjoy shopping for bargains, how about you?
Basically(bey-sik-lee):	Basically, everyone enjoys looking for bargains.
Biscuit (bis-kit):	Careful those biscuits are hot.
Budge(buhj):	He would not budge on his decision.
Business(biz-nis):	It's good to own your own business in America.
Buzzing (buhz-ng) That bee was buzzing around.

Candidate(kan-di-deyt):	Are you a candidate for the office of President of the United States?
Catastrophic (kat-uh-strof-ik):	A catastrophic earthquake struck the center of the city.
Circulate(sur-kyuh-leyt):	The blood circulates through the body.
Colonel (kur-nl):	The Colonel is a commissioned officer.
Consistent(kuhn-sis-tuhnt):	It was consistent with what he said it would be.
Crocodile (krok-uh-dahyl):	Even the late, great comedian Robin Williams was petrified(pe-truh-fahd) of the crocodile in the film Peter Pan.
Dawn:	Venus rises just before dawn.
Desperate(des-per-it):	During the drought (drout), they were desperate for water.
Deterioration (dih-teer-ee-uh-rey-shuhn):	It is difficult to see the deterioration of the rain forests.
Development(dih-vel-uhp-muhnt):	The development of new technology has allowed us to receive information very quickly.
Disastrous (dih-zas-truhs):	The storm was disastrous to the yachts (yotz) in the dock.
Disease(dih-zeez):	The hospital was for infectious diseases.
Euphoria (yoo-fawr-ee-uh):	After I won(wuhn) the Powerball lottery, I was filled with euphoria.
Exclamation (ek-skluh-mey-shuhn):	One exclamation mark is enough to get your point across!
Exist(ig-zist):	I never knew this restaurant existed.
Foliage(foh-lee-ij):	Beautiful foliage at Big Sur.
Get:	Let me get you some water.
Impunity(im-pyoo-ni-tee):	That dictator functioned with impunity.
It:	At first, it seemed like a good idea.
Little(lit-l):	If you practice, your English will improve little by little.
Mass(mas):	Force equals mass multiplied by acceleration or F=ma.
Pause (pawz):	There was a pause during the song.
Perk(purk):	One of the perks of the job is free food.
Phrase (freyz):	That's a great phrase.
Physician (fi-zish-uhn):	Where did the physician go to Medical School?
Pollute(puh-loot):	Don't pollute, recycle that garbage.
Praise(preyz):	All he had was praise for the employee.
Pronunciation (pruh-nuhn-see-ey-ehuhn):	At first, you must work hard at pronunciation.
Quit(kwit):	Did you quit or get fired?
Realtor (ree-uhl-ter):	Did you use Mimi and Kevin the realtor to find this house?
Recur (ri-kur):	I have this recurring dream about going up a bridge and then falling backward, what do you think it means?
Relevant(rel-uh-vuhnt):	Please provide the relevant details.
Results(ri-zuhlts):	Did they post the results of the exam?

Silicon(sil-i-kuhn):   They found a moon of Jupiter that is filled with silicon(sil-i-kuhn) oceans (oh-shuhnz).
Sneaked (sneekd):   The kids sneaked out after curfew.
Spay(spey):   Don't forget to spay your pets.
Stir(stur):   Stir not shaken is a famous line from James Bond.
Transition(tran-zish-uhn):   Tell them all about the transition from scene to scene.
Twilight (twahy-lahyt):   Twilight occurs from sunset to nightfall.
Unfortunate(uhn-fawr-chuh-nit):   It is unfortunate that the weather has delayed our trip.
Up(uhp):   Kara got up every morning, had iced coffee, and then went on her run through the Malibu Mountains.
Zealous (zel-uhs):   They were zealous about the song.

8.7   Dialogue: Shopping at the Flea Market

The flea market or bazaar is a great place to buy used clothing, books, shoes, and antiques cheaply. In Hollywood there is fun flea market on Sundays at Fairfax and Melrose.

Exercise 1: Repeat aloud the following dialogue. Practice with a friend. Repeat.
Exercise 2: Visit a Flea Market, write about the experience.

Buyer: How much is this?
Seller: For you, ten dollars.
Buyer: But it's missing a stone.
Seller: Okay, then eight.
Buyer: Never mind. How much is this watch?
Seller: Which watch?
Buyer: Which wristwatches are Swiss wristwatches (rist-wochs)?
Seller: Here, these watches are Swiss wristwatches?
Buyer: I'll give you ten.
Seller: How bout eighteen?
Buyer: How about fifteen?
Seller: Okay, deal, here.
Buyer: Look a vintage clothing booth. Come on.
Seller: How can I help you?

Buyer: I'm just browsing. Is that skirt (skurt) pleated (pleetd)? That's a beautiful blouse (blous) with the polka dots (poh-kuh-dots), how much is it?
Seller: For you fifteen dollars ($15.00).
Buyer: Hmmm. Lovely gown (goun). I wonder if it will fit over my cotton stretch (kot-n strech) pants.
Seller: Try it on. It looks good on you.
Buyer: How much are these overalls (oh-ver-awls) and these boots?
Seller: The suede (sweyd) boots are fifty-five dollars. The overalls are twenty.
Buyer: How about forty-five for the boots?
Seller: Deal.
Buyer: Here's fifty.
Seller: Here's five. Do you want a bag, or are you going just to wear them?
Buyer: I'll just wear them.
Seller: They look great on you.
Buyer: Thanks
Seller: I'm happy they found a right home.
Buyer: What are these paisley stretch pants made from? Are they Dacron (dak-ron), rayon (rey-on), nylon (nahy-lon), polyester (pol-ee-es-ter) or cotton (kot-n)? What about these argyle socks?
Seller: The argyle socks are all cotton, the stretch pants well…here's the label.
Buyer: How much is this enamel brooch (ih-nam-uhl brohch)?
Seller: That's made of sterling silver and it's forty.
Buyer: How about thirty?
Seller: Thirty-five.
Buyer: Deal. Here you go.
Seller: Have a great day.
Buyer: Is that a neoprene (nee-uh-preen) survival suit?
Seller: Yes, it provides buoyancy (boi-uhn-see) and insulation (in-suh-ley-shuhn) in case you fall overboard while filming in Alaska.

Buyer: How much?	
Seller: For you, $100.00(one hundred dollars).	
Buyer: Next time.	
Seller: Seventy –five dollars.	
Buyer: Really? How about seventy?	
Seller: Sold. Do you want a bag, or are you going to wear it now?	
Buyer: Funny. Here you go.	
Seller: Thank you. Have a great day.	

8.8 Fashion: Styles, and Trends

Styles change so quickly, here are some fashion standards to review.

Exercise 1: Repeat the following names for pieces of clothing aloud.
Exercise 2: Create a sentence and a drawing for each phrase.
Exercise 3: Add your favorite piece of clothing to the list.

1. Acetate(as-i-teyt)
2. Acrylic(uh-kril-ik)
3. Alpaca(al-pak-uh)
4. Angora(ang-gawr-uh)
5. Batik design (buh-teek)
6. Beret(buh-rey)
7. Black Belt (belt)
8. Black tie
9. Blend(blend)
10. Blue blazer with brass buttons (bley-zer)
11. Bow tie (bou-tahy)
12. Burlap(bur-lap)
13. Button down collar (buht-n) (doun) (kol-er)
14. Buttonhole (hohl)
15. Cashmere(kazh-meer)
16. Chamois(sha-mwah)
17. Checkered shirt (chek-erd) (shurt)
18. Chenille robe (shuh-neel)

19. Chesterfield velvet lapelled (chester-feeld)
20. Chiffon(shi-fon)
21. Chintz(chints)
22. Corduroy pants (kawr-duh-roi)
23. Cotton(kot-n)
24. Crew neck t-shirt (kroo) (nek)
25. Crushed velvet sofa (kruhshd) (vel-vit)
26. Cummerbund (kuhm-er-buhnd)
27. Dacron(dak-ron)
28. Denim jeans (den-uhm)
29. Derby (dur-bee) hat
30. Double breasted suit (duhb-uhl) (bres-tid)
31. Embroidered uniform (em-broi-derd)
32. Fedora hat (fi-dawr-uh)
33. Floral design (flawr-uhl)
34. Hemp(hemp)
35. Herringbone (her-ing-bohn)

36. High heeled shoes (heeld)	65. Short sleeves (shawrt) (sleevs)
37. Kiltie fringed shoe(kil-tee) (frinjd)	66. Silk ascot (askuht)
38. Laces (leys-ez)	67. Single breasted suit (sing-guhl) (bres-tid)
39. Leather slacks (leth-er)	
40. Linen(lin-uhn)	68. Speckled overcoat (spek-uhld)
41. Loafer shoes (loh-fer)	69. Sports jacket (spawrts)
42. Long sleeves (sleevs)	70. Striped jump suit (strahyptd)
43. Mohair sweater (moh-hair)	71. Suede shoes (sweyd)
44. Neck (nek)	72. Taffeta(taf-i-tuh)
45. Nylon(nahy-lon)	73. Tartan plaid (tahr-tan)
46. Open necked shirt	74. Terry cloth robe (ter-ee)
47. Oxford (oks-ferd) shoe	75. Thick soled shoes (sohld)
48. Paisley dress shirt (peyz-lee)	76. Tie with a Windsor knot (tahy)
49. Panama hat (pan-uh-mah)	77. Tie dyed shirt (dahy)
50. Patchwork quilt (pach-wurk)	78. Tights (tahyts)
51. Patent leather (pat-nt)	79. Top pocket handkerchief (pok-it)
52. Pencil skirt (pen-suhl) (skurt)	80. Trench coat
53. Pinstripe (pin-strahyp)	81. Tuxedo(tuhk-see-doh)
54. Plaid luggage (plad)	82. Tweed (tweed)
55. Plain white t shirt (pleyn)	83. V neck t shirt
56. Polka dot skirt (pohl-kuh)	84. Velour(vuh-loor)
57. Polyester(pol-ee-es-ter)	85. Velvet(vel-vit)
58. Rayon(rey-on)	86. Waist coat (weyst)
59. Satin(sat-n)	87. Wingtip shoes
60. Scarf (skahrf)	88. Wool(wool)
61. Seam (seem)	89. Woolen (wool-uhn)
62. Seersucker(seer-suhk-er)	90. Worsted (woos-tid)
63. Semi-formal event	91. Yarn(yahrn)
64. Shirtless (shurt-les)	92. Zig zag pattern

8.9 Complex Colors

When another term is introduced the number of colors or flavors increases dramatically. This is a short example of some complex colors. See how many colors you can name. They are used often in advertising or interior design.

Exercise 1: Repeat the following color phrases.
Exercise 2: Create a flavor or color example.

Colors of the Spectrum: Red, Orange, Yellow, Green, Blue, Indigo, Violet
Santa's suit red
Blood(bluhd) red
Valentine(val-uhn-tahyn) red
Red parrot(par-uht)
Cherry red
Burnt(burnt) orange(awr-inj)
Sunset(suhn-set) orange(awr-inj)
Pineapple orange
Yellow(yel-oh) lilies(lil-eez)
Yellow roses
Yellow hibiscus(hahy-bis-kuhs)
Lemon(lem-uhn) yellow(yel-oh)
Lemon(lem-uhn) grass
Forest(fawr-ist) green
Grass(gras) green
Leaf(leef) green
Lime(lahym) green
Parrot(par-uht) green
Spring(spring) green
Mint green
Ice(ahys) blue(bloo)
Lunar (loo-ner) blue (bloo)
Midnight(mid-nahyt) blue(bloo)
Navy(na-vy) blue (bloo)
Peacock(pee-kok) blue(bloo)
Sky(skahy) blue(bloo) ice(ahys)

Fluorescent(floo-res-uhnt) indigo(in-di-goh)
Electric indigo
Bright indigo

Violet(vahy-uh-lit)sparkle
French violet
Violet mist

Nantucket(nan-tuhk-it) gray (grey)
Smoking(smohk-ng) gray
Steel(steel) gray

Obsidian(uhb-sid-ee-uhn) black(blak)
Ebony (eb-uh-nee) black
Onyx(on-iks) black
Black licorice (lik-uh-rish)

Brilliant white
Chantilly(shan-til-ee) lace
Winter white

Indigo Dark Royal Purple(pur-puhl)
Light purple
Medium purple
Rebecca purple
Purple grape

Cotton (kot-n) candy (kan-de)
Mountain (moun-tn) mist (mist)

Shocking(shok-ing) pink(pingk)
Pink(pingk) panther(pan-ther)
Petunia(pi-oo-nyuh) pink
Pink ribbon(rib-uhn)
Pink corsage(kawr-sahzh)
Pink bubble-gum

8.10 Dialogue: Buying a slice of Pizza

Pizza is a favorite dish, usually starting with a piece of flat round dough, covered with Italian tomato sauce made with mozzarella cheese, and cooked in a high-temperature oven. Sicilian pizza is made with a thick rectangular dough instead of the flat round shape found in a regular pizza.

Exercise 1: Repeat aloud the following dialogue. Practice with a friend, switch characters.
Exercise 2: Order a pizza over the phone. See if they understand.

Chef:	How may I help you?
Customer:	I'd like a slice of pizza.
Chef:	What kind would you like?
Customer:	I was thinking of a slice of vegetarian. What's in that?
Chef:	It has mushrooms, peppers, garlic, spinach (spin-ich), artichoke (ahr-ti-chohk) hearts, onions, and tomatoes (tuh-mey-tohs), or should I say tomatoes (tuh-mah-tohs).
Customer:	No cheese?
Chef:	Of course, it has Mozzarella (mot-suh-rel-luh) cheese.
Customer:	Do you have Sicilian?
Chef:	Yes, right over here.
Customer:	Can I get a slice of each? I want that one.
Chef:	Would you like a drink?
Customer:	Yes, here one of these, and can I also get a salad?
Chef:	Green or Caesar
Customer:	What's in the green salad?
Chef:	It has avocado (av-uh-kah-doh), mushrooms, croutons (kroo-tons), cheese, bell peppers, broccoli (brok-uh-lee), cauliflower (kaw-luh-flou-er), dried cranberries, lettuce, tomatoes, and chickpeas. Did you know that avocadoes are also known as alligator pears?
Customer:	No. Really? That's fine, with Italian dressing, please.
Chef:	Alright, and you, what can I get you?
Customer:	Two slices of the meat lover's pizza.
Chef:	The one with pepperonis, sausage, and salami?
Customer:	Yes, that sounds good.

Chef:	Salad?
Customer:	No. I'll share it.
Chef:	Cannoli's (kuh-noh-lees)?
Customer:	Yes, I almost forgot to order Cannoli's.

8.11   Dialogue: Ordering at a Delicatessen

A Delicatessen sells everything from sandwiches to soups, salads, and cakes. Canters, a deli on Fairfax is a favorite spot to eat. They are open until late at night.

Exercise 1: Repeat aloud the following dialogue. Practice, switch characters. Insert your favorite sandwich.

Glenn:	I'm hungry.
Barry:	Me, too.
Glenn:	Where would you like to go?
Barry:	I'm thinking of Italian food.
Glenn:	Not in the mood. How about Greek?
Barry:	No, How about Mexican?
Glenn:	Had that last night.
Barry:	Glenn, what are you thinking?
Glenn:	Let's get a corned (kawrnd) beef sandwich (sand-wich).
Barry:	Ok, where do we go?
Glenn:	Let's go to the Delicatessen (del-i-kuh-tes-uhn).
Barry:	Sounds great.
Host:	How may I help you?
Lisa:	We'd like a booth, please.
Host:	Please follow me.
Barry:	Thank you. Where's the bathroom?
Host:	That way. Here we go… a cozy booth (booth) and some menus.
Jen:	Thank you. We'd like to order.

Waiter:	Hello, everyone. Can I get you some drinks?
Jen:	Vodka (vod-kuh) cranberry (kran-ber-ee).
Waiter:	And you?
Barry:	Can I get a glass of red wine? Do you have a Bordeaux (bawr-doh)?
Waiter:	Yes, got it, one Bordeaux. And you, Miss?
Lisa:	White dry wine like a Chablis (sha-blee) or a Pinot (pee-noh) Grigio (gri-jee-oh) and a glass of water.
Waiter:	Got it. And you, sir?
Glenn:	Can you uncork this?
Waiter:	There's a five-dollar corkage (kawr-kij) fee. I'll be right back.
Glenn:	Thanks. That's fine.
Glenn:	What are you getting?
Lisa:	Steak, and you?
Glenn:	Sandwich (sand-wich).
Lisa:	What kind?
Glenn:	Triple layer. Roast beef, corned beef, and tongue (tuhng).
Lisa:	Glenn.
Waitress:	I got your drinks, here we go. Are you ready to order?
Lisa:	I'd like steak and eggs.
Waitress:	How would you like it?
Lisa:	Medium (rair) with vegetables and sparkling water. No peas, please, and the eggs over hard.
Waitress:	Got it, and you?
Jen:	Can I have a vegetarian (vej-i-tair-ee-uhn) melt on whole-wheat toast with coleslaw and a pickle and an iced tea.
Waitress:	Got it, and you?
Glenn:	I'd like a triple-layer sandwich on pumpernickel (puhm-per-nik-uhl) and a black cherry soda.

Waitress:	Right. And you?
Barry:	I'd like to order a turkey cutlet with pasta and just water with ice.
Waitress:	Right. Be right back.
Glenn:	The triple-layer, impressive. I love this place.
Jen:	It still has the original ceiling.
Lisa:	I used to come here in High School.
Waiter:	Okay, here we are. Steak, there. Sandwiches over here, and this here.
Waitress:	You guys all set?
Barry:	Oh, yes.
Waitress:	Enjoy. Let me know if you need anything else.

8.12   Antonyms 3

Studying antonyms is always a good method in learning vocabulary. Lookup one word and now you know two, the word and its opposite.

Exercise 1: Practice saying aloud the following antonyms. Go across and then down the row to see the opposites.
Exercise 2: Create a sentence for each word.

1. easy(ee-zee)	2. difficult (dif-i-kuhlt)
3. ebb(eb)	4. flow(floh)
5. east(eest)	6. west(west)
7. economize(ih-kon-uh-mahyz)	8. waste(weyst)
9. encourage(en-kur-ij)	10. discourage(dih-skur-ij)
11. entrance(en-truhns)	12. exit(eg-zit)
13. employer(em-ploi-er)	14. employee(em-ploi-ee)
15. empty(emp-tee)	16. full(fool)
17. excited(ik-sahy-tid)	18. calm(kahm)
19. end(end)	20. beginning(bih-gin-ing)

21. expand(ik-spand)	22. contract(kon-trakt)
23. expensive(ik-spen-siv)	24. cheap(cheep)
25. export(ik-spawrt)	26. import(im-pawrt)
27. exterior(ik-steer-ee-er)	28. interior(in-teer-ee-er)
29. external(ik-stur-nl)	30. internal(in-tur-nl)
31. fail(feyl)	32. succeed(suhk-seed)
33. false(fawls)	34. true(troo)
35. feeble(fee-buhl)	36. powerful(pou-er-fuhl)
37. foolish(foo-lish)	38. wise(wahyz)
39. fast(fahst)	40. slow(sloh)
41. few(fyoo)	42. many(men-ee)
43. famous(fey-muhs)	44. unknown(uhn-nohn)
45. forelegs(fawr-legz)	46. hind legs (hahynd-legz)
47. fat(fat)	48. thin(thin)
49. find(fahynd)	50. lose(looz)
51. first(furst)	52. last(lahst)
53. freedom(free-duhm)	54. captivity(kap-tiv-i-tee)
55. fold(fohld)	56. unfold(uhn-fohld)
57. frequent(free-kwuhnt)	58. seldom(sel-duhm)
59. forget(fer-get)	60. remember(ri-mem-ber)
61. found(found)	62. lost(lawst)
63. fresh(fresh)	64. stale(steyl)
65. friend(frend)	66. enemy(en-uh-mee)
67. fortunate(fawr-chuh-nit)	68. unfortunate(uhn-fawr-chuh-nit)
69. get on	70. get off

71. limited(lim-i-tid)	72. unlimited(uhn-lim-i-tid)
73. odd(od)	74. even(ee-vuhn)
75. one(wuhn)	76. many(men-ee)
77. pick up	78. drop off
79. put on	80. take off
81. rest(rest)	82. motion(moh-shuhn)
83. run after	84. run away
85. straight(streyt)	86. curved(kurvd)
87. light(lahyt)	88. dark(dahrk)
89. good(good)	90. bad(bad)
91. square(skwair)	92. oblong(ob-lawng)
93. right(rahyt)	94. left(left)
95. speed up	96. slow down
97. indelible(in-del-uh-buhl)	98. erasable(ih-reys-ey-buhl)

8.13 Compare and Contrast 3

Here's a quick review. Check the phonetic spelling of the word if you are unsure how the word sounds. Some words are included as a point of comparison.

Exercise 1: Review the following sentences aloud.

Homograph: A word with the same spelling but with a different meaning and a different pronunciation. For example: [(lead the way) (lead the element)], [(wind the watch), (feel that wind)] [(bowl of food), and to (bowl a game)].
Homonym: A word with the same sound and spelling but different meaning. For example, [duck (kind of bird), duck (look out for object)], [(bark of a tree), and the (bark of a dog)], (lock of hair) or (open the airlock)].
Homophone: A word with the same sound but different spelling and meaning: For example: [(so, sew), (to, too, two), (ad, add)].

Berry (ber-ee):	Have you tried the iced Swedish Berry Tea?
Bury (ber-ee):	Let's bury the hatchet, what do you say?

Bare (bair):	Be careful you don't sunburn (suhn-burn) those bare legs.
Beer (beer):	Beer and kimchee go well together.
Bear (bair):	There are many distinct species (spee-sheez) of bears (bairz) such as Grizzly bears (bairz), Giant Panda bears (bairz), and Polar bears (bairz).
Billed (bild):	The top partner at the law firm billed at $1200 per hour.
Build (bild):	He could build quite a profitable practice.
Chews (chooz):	The termite chews wood.
Choose (chooz):	What name did you choose?
Gene (jeen):	I chose (chohz) Gene as a name.
Jean (jeen):	Nice pair of jeans, are those vintage (vin-tij)?
Gored (gawr):	The elephant gored the hunter.
Gourd (gawrd):	Did you eat that gourd?
Jam (jam):	Is that strawberry or grape jam?
Jamb (jam):	Did you order the new mahogany jambs with the door?
Worn (wawrn):	He had worn both of his suits.
Warn (wawrn):	There is a giant warning sign in front of the Lion's cage.
Bass (beys):	Did you see the stand-up bass?
Base (beys):	Can you play first base?
Weather (weth-er):	Let's check on the weather.
Whether (hweth-er):	Do you know whether the film has started?
Cell (sel):	Have you taken Cell Biology?
Sell (sel):	Let's sell it at the Flea market.
Toe (toh):	I heard a rumor that Marilyn Monroe had six toes.
Tow (toh):	Can you tow the car to Dover Hall?
Scent (sent):	Dogs are curious to scent.
Cents (sents):	There are one hundred cents to a dollar.
Sent (sent):	They got sent home after the earthquake.
Sense (sens):	The five senses are sight, hearing, taste, touch, and smell.

Coarse (kawrs):	Order the coarse sandpaper and not the medium sandpaper.
Course (kawrs):	The Captain asked the Navigator to change the course.
Suite (sweet):	The office is in suite 200.
Sweet (sweet):	Let's get some sweets.
Steel (steel):	That refrigerator (ri-frij-uh-rey-ter) is made of stainless steel so that magnets won't stick.
Steal (steel):	Did you see the seagull steal the hamburger?
Still (stil):	Remain still while they take your headshot.
Deer (deer):	Let's get up early and look for deer.
Dear (deer):	She called me Dear.
Sale (seyl):	Can we have a yard sale?
Sail (seyl):	Is it too windy to go sailing?
I (ahy):	I must start cooking dinner.
Eye (ahy):	The Ophthalmologist (of-thuhl-mol-uh-jist) examined my eyes.
Mail (meyl):	Did you check the mail?
Male (meyl):	The male lion is larger than the female lion and has a mane.
Close (klohz):	Close the airlock quickly.
Clothes (klohz):	Did you see the Emperor's new clothes?
Flower (flou-er):	I picked a flower for you.
Flour (flou-er):	Is that whole wheat or corn flour?
Hole (hohl):	You will need an electric drill to make a hole in the mahogany (muh-hog-uh-nee).
Whole (hohl):	You ate the whole thing?
Maid (meyd):	What time is the maid expected?
Made (meyd):	Forget about it, it's made in America and guaranteed for life.
One (wuhn):	There can only be one winner.
Won (wuhn):	I heard you won the Marathon, congratulations.

Peace (pees):	A toast to World Peace.
Piece (pees):	Can I have a piece of chocolate?
Profit (prof-it):	The business showed a continuous profit that made Wall Street investors very happy.
Prophet (prof-it):	The prophet predicted future events, read minds, and interpreted dreams.
Son (suhn):	He had three sons.
Sun (suhn):	Don't stare directly into the sun during the eclipse (ih-klips).
War (wawr):	Have you seen the film World War Z with Brad Pitt?
Wore (wawr):	The soap opera star wore Valentino at the event.
Patience (pey-shuhns):	Please have some patience; you are next in line.
Patients (pey-shuhnts):	This doctor is always accepting new patients.
Wood (wood):	There's plenty of wood to burn.
Would (wood):	Would you go outside and get the wood it's by the shed.
Hour (ouuhr):	At what hour does the flight arrive?
Our (ouuhr):	That's our table over there.
Which (which):	Which way is the Empire State building?
Witch (wich):	How many witches are in classic film, The Wizard of Oz?
Board (bawrd):	Can we buy a wood board to fix that hole?
Bored (bawrd):	You looked bored in your Physics class.
Poor (poor):	You are not poor, just low on cash.
Pour (pawr):	Please pour me a glass of water.
Pore (pawr):	I need a skin treatment to cleanse my pores.

8.14 Dialogue: Tony, the Car Mechanic

A good mechanic is hard to find, as the idiomatic expression goes.
Exercise 1: Repeat aloud the following dialogue. Practice with a friend. Switch characters.
Exercise 2: What skills must a mechanic have? Create a list.

Jessy, Car owner: It won't start. Can you fix my car?
Tony, the Car Mechanic: What's wrong with it?
Jessy: It makes a funny sound.
Tony: That is not a good sign.
Jessy: Is it the carburetor(kahr-buh-rey-ter)?
Tony: Not sure.
Jessy: Is it the alternator (awl-ter-ney-ter)? Or maybe the generator (jen-uh-rey-ter)?
Tony: Does it start?
Jessy: Not anymore. I just made it over here.
Tony: Is that it with the smoke?
Jessy: It also has a leak in the radiator(rey-dee-ey-ter).
Tony: How long has it been on fire?
Jessy: Just started.
Tony: Let me put that out. Be right back.
Jessy: I think it might be the water pump(puhmp).
Tony: Alright do you have the key?
Jessy: Here's the key.
Tony: Hold on.
Jessy: How long?
Tony: It's on fire!
Jessy: Can you detail it?
Tony: Let me get to the flames first.

Jessy: I see, but how long? Can you fix that front tire?
Tony: We need to call the Fire Department.

8.15   Coffee Bar Drinks

Knowing how to make a special coffee beverage is always fun.

Exercise 1: Repeat the following coffee drinks aloud.
Exercise 2: Write a sentence about which drink is your favorite and why.

1.	Americano(uh-mer-i-kan-oh): Espresso brewed to the top of the cup with added boiling water.
2.	Brewed(broo-d) coffee: Using water between 195-205 degrees Fahrenheit(far-uhn-hahyt) to make the perfect cup.
3.	Café au lait (oh-ley): Brewed coffee with steamed milk and foam.
4.	Café caramel(kar-uh-muhl): Brewed coffee with caramel, steamed milk, and foam.
5.	Café latte(lah-tey): Espresso with steamed milk and foam.
6.	Café mocha(moh-kuh): Brewed coffee with chocolate, steamed milk, and foam.
7.	Café vanilla(vuh-nil-uh): Brewed coffee with vanilla, steamed milk, and foam.
8.	Cappuccino (kap-oo-chee-noh): Espresso with foam and steamed milk.
9.	Caramel latte (lah-tey): Espresso with caramel, steamed milk, and foam.
10.	Caramel mocha(moh-kuh) latte: Espresso with chocolate, caramel, steamed milk, and foam.
11.	Chai(chahy) tea latte: Chai tea blend with hazelnut and steamed milk.
12.	Espresso (e-spres-oh): A coffee made by forcing water under pressure through dark roast coffee beans.
13.	Espresso(e-spres-oh) Cubano (kyoo-buhn-oh): Espresso blended with raw sugar.
14.	Hazelnut(hey-zuhl-nuht) latte: Espresso with hazelnut, steamed milk, and foam.
15.	Hot chocolate(chaw-kuh-lit): Steamed milk with chocolate topped with whipped cream.
16.	Macchiato(mah-kee-ott-oo): Espresso topped with foam.
17.	Mocha(moh-kuh) latte: Espresso with chocolate, steamed milk, and foam.
18.	Red eye(ahy): Espresso with brewed coffee.
19.	Snickerdoodle(snik-er-dood-l): Espresso with hazelnut, caramel, chocolate, steamed milk, and foam.
20.	Vanilla chai(chahy) tea(tee) latte(lah-tey): Chai tea with vanilla and steamed milk.
21.	Vanilla(vuh-nil-uh) white(hwahyt) mocha(moh-kuh) latte(lah-tey): Espresso with white chocolate, vanilla, steamed milk, and foam.
22.	White mocha latte: Espresso with white chocolate, steamed milk, and foam.

8.16 Conditional Sentences

Conditional sentences express facts and their implications. A conditional tense is a hypothetical situation with its consequence.

For example. If it rains, the marathon will be canceled.

Exercise 1: Read aloud the following sentences.
Exercise 2: Create a conditional sentence for each example.

There are four main kinds of conditionals:
The Zero Conditional:
(if + present simple, ... present simple)
If you chill water to 32 degrees Fahrenheit, it freezes.
The First Conditional:
(if + present simple, ... will + infinitive)
If it snows tomorrow, we'll go to the ski slope.
The Second Conditional:
(if + past simple, ... would + infinitive)
If I had a lot of time, I would spend the weekend skiing.
The Third Conditional
(if + past perfect, ... would + have + past participle)
If I had gone to the ski lodge early, I would have got breakfast.

Lesson 9

Covid-19, Sports, Cliches, Chess

9.1 Pronunciation Key 13

Exercise 1: Practice saying the list of words and sentences that follow aloud.
Exercise 2: Create a sentence with the list of words.

a	Fate(feyt)	The fate of that winning Powerball ticket is uncertain.
a	Fat(fat)	Where can we trim the fat off the fiscal (fis-kuhl) budget?
a	Fare(fair)	The fare on the Metro needs to be paid in exact change.
a	Father(fah-ther)	Father's Day is celebrated on the third Sunday in June.
e	Me(mee)	Call me when the pizza arrives.
e	Met(met)	They met at a café.
e	Her(hur)	It was her wedding.
i	Bite(bahyt)	I got a bite on that script.
i	Bit(bit)	The word bit is a portmanteau (pawrt-man-toh) of the word binary (bahy-nuh-ree) and digit, meaning only two choices, zero or one. A bit is derived from the contraction b'it, binary digit.
o	Hole(hohl)	Did you see the "hole in one" clip on YouTube?
o	Hot(hot)	With global warming, every year is hotter than the year before.
o	Lost(lawst)	Most large stores have a lost and found department.
oo	Room(room)	Did you get a room with a view?
oo	Foot(foot)	Please put your best foot forward.
u	Pure(pyoor)	The carrot juice is 100% pure.
u	But(buht)	I told Abby not to climb (klahym) on the roof, but she found the ladder.
du	Endure (en-door)	The triathlon (trahy-ath-luhn) tests endurance, patience (pey-shuhns), persistence (per-sis-thuh-ns) and agility (uh-jil-i-tee).
ng	Think(thingk)	Let them think about it, before deciding.

The Hollywood Tutor's AMERICAN ENGLISH © 2020 Mitch Rubman. All rights reserved. No part of this publication may be reproduced or distributed in any form or by any means without the written permission of the copyright owner

th	Breath(breth)	Take a deep breath.
tu	Nature(ney-cher)	I can use more time in nature.

9.2 COVID-19 and related terms

One list of some commonly used terminology.

COVID-19 Virus (vahy-ruhs) Terminology (tur-muh-nol-uh-jee)

Exercise 1: Repeat the following definitions aloud.

Asymptomatic (ey-simp-tuh-mat-ik): Not showing symptoms, even though infected. Let's do a test and see if you are asymptomatic.
Contact tracing: Tracing the potential for a spread of disease by documenting exposed individuals. South Korea did extensive contract tracing to help stop the spread of the virus. This can be done by calling or texting.
COVID-19: The name given to this new disease, Co stands for corona, the shape, like a ring or crown, vi stands for virus and d stands for the disease. The name of the virus responsible for the current pandemic is severe acute respiratory syndrome coronavirus 2, or SARS-CoV-2. The name of the disease caused by SARS-CoV-2 is COVID-19, which stands for coronavirus disease 2019 this name was given by the International Committee on Taxonomy of Viruses (ICTV). This is an airborne virus.
Disease enhancement (en-hans-ment): When antibodies created accidentally make patients worse. Epidemiologists are concerned about disease enhancement while working on the vaccine.
Droplet (drop-lit): Water particles that are breathed out that can lead to the transmission of disease. Droplets can float many feet from the original source.
Emerging disease (dih-zeez): A new disease that strikes an area. Emerging disease research must have fast response.
Epidemic (ep-i-dem-ik): An increase in the number of cases of a disease in a local area. Or an increase in anything in a local area. There was an epidemic of COVID-19 in that city.
False Negative: When a test produces a negative result by mistake. That test produces a 15% false negative.
False Positive: When a test produces a positive result by mistake. That test produces a 5% false positive rate.
Incubation (in-kyuh-bey-shuhn) period: The time observed when a person is first exposed to a disease to the time when the symptoms are observed. He placed himself in incubation for two weeks.
Isolation (ahy-suh-ley-shuhn): Separating patients that are sick from those that are healthy to help reduce the spread of disease. They tried to isolate the sick patients at the Nursing Home.
Monoclonal (mon-uh-klohn-l) Therapy: Cloning specific antibodies from previous sick individuals producing antiviral drugs. That pharmaceutical company utilizes monoclonal therapy in producing vaccines.

Novel (nov-uhl) coronavirus: A strain of a virus that has not been identified before. COVID-19 is a novel coronavirus.
Pandemic (pan-dem-ik): A disease that can spread across continents. That pandemic is an epidemic on steroids.
Polymerase (pol-uh-muh-reys) Chain Reaction (PCR) test: A process called polymerase chain reaction that is used to identify a disease through blood or bodily fluids. Is a PCR test for COVID-19 available?
Quarantine (kwawr-uhn-teen): Separating individuals that might be sick for some time to see if symptoms develop. If exposed to a person who tests positive, quarantine for 10 days is expected.
Remdesivir is viewed as the most promising treatment for COVID-19 and was included among four drugs under evaluation.
Reservoir (rez-er-vwahr): An animal that can serve as a location for a disease to hid for an extended period of time. It is said that coronavirus used a bat as a reservoir.
Resurgence (ri-sur-juhns): When a disease rises and reappears sometime later. They were advised to social distance themselves to avoid a resurgence of the virus.
Screening: A check to see if a person has a disease or antibody. Where do they go for the screening?
Superspreader: A person who transmits a disease to a large number of individuals. See the story of Typhoid Mary. A highly contagious individual. They found the superspreader had taken the last flight out of New York.
Transmission: How disease spreads. Covid-19 is person to person and borne through water droplets. Let me wear a mask and gloves to reduce the transmission of the virus.
Vaccine (vak-seen) any drug used as a preventive inoculation to provide immunity. Who will create the vaccine?
Virologist (vahy-rol-uh-jeest): A person who studies viruses. The virologist researched COVID-19.
Virus: A virus is either DNA or RNA, surrounded by a protein coat. A virus cannot replicate alone; they must infect cells and use components of the host cell to make copies of themselves. The virus spread quickly throughout the world.
Zoonotic (zoh-on-uh-tic): A disease that moves from animals to humans. COVID-19 is said to be a zoonotic disease going from bats to humans.
New Vaccine candidates
Pfizer(fahy-zer)vaccine: The Pfizer vaccine decreased COVID-19 infection(in-fek-shuhn) by 95%(ninety-five per cent) and even though(thoh) it needs to be kept at minus -94 degrees Fahrenheit(far-uhn-hahyt), Pfizer has history and expertise(ek-sper-teez) in cold-chain(cheyn) delivery with an established infrastructure(in-fruh-struhk-cher) to move the vaccine(vak-seen) worldwide.
Moderna vaccine: The Moderna vaccine lowered the percent of Covid-19 infection by 94.5%. Of the 95(ninety-five) cases of Covid among patients in the company's 30,000(thirty thousand)-patient(pey-shuhnt) study. Only five of them developed Covid-19 after receiving the vaccine, mRNA-1273(messenger r.n.a. dash twelve-seventy-three).

9.3 Dialogue: COVID-19 Emergency Room

This is a sample of a possible dialogue. Remember if you are sick, to take care of yourself. There are many resources available.

Exercise 1: Repeat aloud the following dialogue. Practice with a friend.
Exercise 2: Create your own dialogue based upon your last visit.

Nurse: Good afternoon. How may I help you?
Patient: I called earlier, I'm really sick.
Nurse: Have you recently traveled to an area with known local spread of COVID-19?
Patient: No.
Nurse: Have you recently come into contact within six feet with someone who has a confirmed COVID-19 diagnosis in the past fourteen days?
Patient: Yes.
Nurse: Do you have shortness of breath, difficulty breathing or sore throat?
Patient: I can't take a full breath.
Nurse: Are you a first responder, healthcare worker, or employee or attendee of a child or adult care facility?
Patient: I'm not, but my wife is.
Nurse: Are you in pain?
Patient: Yes, right here, my lungs.
Nurse: I'm going to take your temperature.
Patient: Thank you.
Nurse: That's 101.5(one-hundred one point five). I'm going to give you this new mask to put on.
Patient: Thank you.
Nurse: I need to take your blood pressure. Can you roll up your sleeve?
Patient: Yes. One second please.
Nurse: Do you have any chest pain?
Patient: Yes, and difficulty breathing
Nurse: Do you have a shortness of breath
Patient: Yes, and lightheadedness.

Nurse: How long have you felt like this?	
Patient: Three days.	
Nurse: I'm going to move you over here.	
Patient: Thank you.	
Nurse: Please sit in the wheelchair.	
Patient: Thank you for your help.	

9.4 COVID-19 Symptoms

Exercise: Review the following questions and answers regarding COVID-19 aloud.

Q: How does COVID-19 affect different people?

A: COVID-19 affects a variety of people in several ways. Patients report mild symptoms (simp-tuhms) to severe illness.

Q: What are the usual symptoms of COVID-19?

A: The COVID-19 Symptoms that may appear 2(two)-(to) 14(fourteen) days after exposure to the virus are a cough (kawf) and shortness of breath or difficulty breathing. Or having at least two of the following:

Chills (chilz)
Fever (fee-ver)
Congestion (kuh n-jes-chuhn) or runny nose
Nausea (naw-zee-uh) or vomiting
Headache (hed-eyk)
Muscle (muhs-uhl) pain, body aches
Cough (kawf)
Loss of taste or smell
Repeated shaking with chills
Sore (sawr) throat (throht)

9.5 COVID-19 Warning signs

If you develop any of these emergency warning signs for COVID-19, get emergency medical attention immediately either by calling, texting or if necessary, visiting.

1. High temperature.
2. Persistent (per-sis-tuhnt) pain or pressure in the chest.
3. Fatigue (fuh-teeg).
4. New confusion or inability to arouse (uh-rouz).
5. Bluish (bloo-ish) lips or face.

6.	Constant chest pain or pressure.
7.	Severe (suh-veer) difficulty breathing.
8.	Severe shortness (shawrt-nis) of breath.
9.	Severe, constant dizziness or lightheaded (lahyt-hed-id).
10.	Slurred speech.
11.	Extreme difficulty waking up.
12.	Any other extreme or life-threatening symptoms.

9.6 Tongue Twisters 4

This is a challenging set of Tongue Twisters. Take your time and go slowly at first. Phonics have been removed to help the visual continuity.(Makes it easier to see.)

Exercise 1: Repeat the following tongue twisters three times each.
Exercise 2: Create your own tongue twister based on different sounds.

1.	Proper copper coffee pot.
2.	The sixth sitting sheet slitter slit six sheets.
3.	Irish wristwatch, Swiss wristwatch.
4.	There was a minimum of cinnamon in the persimmon cake.
5.	The red beauty bug bled on the black bug's bed.
6.	No sweat, no sweet.
7.	No pain, no gain.
8.	Strike while the iron (ahy-ern) is hot.
9.	He wanted to desert his parfait dessert in the deep dark desert.
10.	Plaid pleated pants, plaid pleated pants, plaid pleated pants, peacefully pressed.
11.	Can you can a can as a canner can can a can?
12.	Three grey geese in green fields grazing.
13.	Silly Sally is shaking some sugar on her shiny silvery silly stiletto shoes.
14.	Don't dilly dally daily in Detroit or disdain your daily duty.
15.	Unique New York, unique New York, unique New York.
16.	Freshly fried flying fish.
17.	Three young rats with black felt hats.
18.	One-one was a space probe. Two, two was one, too. When one one went to space. Two two went too.

9.7 Clichés, Idiomatic expressions and Proverbs 2[B-G]

The list of clichés, idiomatic expressions and proverbs are limitless. These are just a few.

Exercise 1: Repeat the phrase and then the sentence aloud.
Exercise 2: Research the origins of the phrase.

Bottom line: I'll split it with you if the bottom line is good.
Break a leg: It's a tradition in theatre to say, "Break a leg" to the actor before their performance.
Break the ice: Try telling a joke at dinner to break the ice.
Breakneck speed: Those concert tickets sold at breakneck speed.
Brownie points: Helping the teacher clean the classroom will get you plenty of brownie points.
Budding (buhdng) genius: After her violin recital (ri-sahyt-l). She was called a budding genius.
Burn one's bridges: She burned her bridges and was at the point of no return.
Busy as a bee: Sorry I didn't get to it; I've just been busy as a bee.
Butterflies in my stomach: Sometimes, before going on stage, I get butterflies in my stomach.
By leaps and bounds: The understudy's performance was better by leaps and bounds.
The calm before the storm: It's the calm before the storm that worries me.
Camel through the eye of a needle: Quote from the Bible: I tell you; it is easier for a camel to pass through the eye of a needle than for a rich man to enter the kingdom of God.
Carry your heart on your sleeve: Things are bad, she's carrying her heart on her sleeve for everyone to see.
Cat got your tongue: What's wrong? Why don't you comment? Has the cat gotten your tongue?
Catch 22: In the novel by Joseph Heller, a Catch-22 is an infinite loop that can never be attained.
Chalk it up to experience: I rather chalk it up to experience and try again.
Chew the fat: Let's chew the fat and talk about last year.
Climb on the bandwagon: The new company is doing great, join us and climb on the bandwagon.
Close but no cigar: I'm sorry, but that answer is close, but no cigar, next.
Clothes do not make the man: As Juan would ask, is it the cloak that makes the man or the man that makes the cloak.
Coin a phrase: To coin a phrase, by Arnold, I'll be back.
Cold turkey: She suddenly stopped cold turkey and had headaches for days.
Come to think of it: Come to think of it, the dinner starts at six.
Comparing apples to oranges. They're not equal, it's like comparing apples to oranges.
Confide in no one: Don't talk about the case, confide in no one.

Cool as a cucumber (kyoo-kuhm-ber):	That actor was as cool as a cucumber at the audition.
Cost an arm and a leg:	To replace my windshield is going to cost me an arm and a leg.
Cried her eyes out:	After the divorce papers arrived, he cried his eyes out.
Cross your fingers:	For good luck, remember to cross your fingers.
Cry over spilled milk.	No use crying over spilled milk, it won't make any difference.
Curiosity killed the cat:	Curiosity can sometimes be invasive and dangerous.
Cut to the chase:	That is an exciting story but cut to the chase, I got to get home.
Look before you leap:	An idiomatic expression reminding one to think about an action before doing it.
Don't judge a book by its cover:	Books sometimes are very different on the inside than the outside, just like people.
Doom and gloom:	Stop being so full of doom and gloom, the rain will stop, the sun will shine.
Down the drain:	When the computer crashed, all their work went down the drain.
Down the hatch:	My last beer and down the hatch
Easier said than done:	Shooting that chase scene was easier said than done.
Eat humble pie:	You will need to apologize and eat some humble pie.
Excuse my French:	I don't usually curse, so please excuse my French.
Face the music:	Eventually, you will need to go home and deal with the problem.
Familiarity breeds contempt:	Contempt is the emotional reaction to not feeling cared for and perhaps disrespected.
Feel like a million dollars:	Feeling right about something.
Few and far between:	Good mechanics are few and far between.
Fishy:	When something is questionable, it is said to be fishy, implying a smell is emanating.
Fits like a glove:	That wetsuit fits like a glove, tight and secure.
Flake:	Hollywood is filled with flakes, meaning people that don't show up to events.
Fly by the set of your pants:	Idiomatic expression used when things are not planned.
Fly off the handle:	Idiomatic expression meaning to lose one's temper suddenly and unexpectedly.
Foregone conclusion (kuhn-kloo-zhuhn):	It was a foregone conclusion that he would run for office.
Forget about it:	When I asked about the missing chocolate, I was told, forget about it.
Fought like a tiger:	An idiomatic expression meaning someone who fights courageously.
Get down to brass tacks:	Let's get down to brass tacks and start the paper.
Get off someone's back:	An idiomatic expression meaning to stop bothering someone.
Get rid of the evidence:	Don't forget to get rid of that chocolate wrapper.
Get your goat:	Don't let them throw you off your focus or get your goat.
Go postal:	Going postal is when someone gets very upset in an office or work situation and shoots people.

Go the whole hog:	When you are at the buffet, please go the whole hog and try everything.
Go to the dogs: This place is a real mess; it's really going to the dogs.	
Godspeed: I'm wishing you Godspeed; may you have Good luck on the journey.	
Never pass up a good thing: In life remember, never pass up a good thing.	
Good as gold: His word is as good as gold.	
Good riddance to bad rubbish: Tell them to leave, and good riddance to bad rubbish.	
Great talkers are little doers: Idiomatic expression meaning, he talks more than he does.	

9.8 American Football

Football is played on a rectangular field which measures 100 yards by 160 feet.

Exercise 1: Repeat the phrases and definitions aloud.
Exercise 2: Describe and write out one play in a professional football game.

The idea is to carry the football across the end zone to score a touchdown. Each team gets four tries to advance 10 yards. If they move the ten yards, then it's considered a first down and they get four more tries.
A touchdown is worth 6 points, a field goal is worth 3 points, and a try is for an extra 1 or 2 points. A safety is worth 2 points.
Positions: 11 players each team. There is an offensive and a different defensive team. The field is 50 yards long on each side.

Offensive(uh-fen-siv) team

Quarterback(kwawr-ter-bak): The Quarterback calls the plays during the huddle, shouts the signals at scrimmage and receives the ball from the snap.
Halfback(haf-bak): The halfback blocks and carries the ball on running plays.
Fullback(fool-bak): Fullbacks are usually larger than halfbacks and function as blockers.
Center(sen-ter): The Center is the leader of the offensive line, who handles the football on every play. On either side of the center are the guards, while tackles line up outside the guards.
Guard(gahrd): A guard is a blocker whose job it is to protect the Quarterback.
Tackle (tak-uhl): The tackles are the outside two members of the offensive line. A tackle occurs when a player carrying the ball is knocked to the ground by an opposing team member and the play is then considered over.
Tight end: The tight end is both a receiver and a blocker.
Wide receiver (ri-see-ver): The wide receiver is usually the quickest on the offensive team.

Defense (dih-fens) team:
Defensive Line: The defensive line is used to prevent a running play as well as to block passing to receivers. The line has 3-5 players usually including:
Cornerbacks(kawr-ner-baks): Cornerbacks are the wide guards of the field and are opposite offensive receivers. Cornerbacks cover receivers and runners that get missed by the line.
Defensive Tackles(tak-uhls): The defensive tackles are inside the defensive line.
Nose Guard(gahrd): The nose guard is a defensive lineman who is the largest and strongest player who can stop action in the center of scrimmage.
Defensive Ends: The defensive ends job is to sack the quarterback.
Linebackers(lahyn-bak-ers): Linebackers are the main line of defense and are usually fast and very good blockers.
Safety(seyf-tee): The Safety is the last resort defense.
Special teams: Special teams is the name given to the punter, field goal kicker, place holder and snapper.
Punter(puhnt-ur): The punter is a player who can kick punts while moving and during the game. He can usually place the football with great accuracy anywhere on the field.
Fumble(fuhm-buhl): When a team member drops or loses the football.
A safety is when a player allows the ball to go into his own end zone.

9.9 American Soccer

The game of soccer(sok-er) starts with a kick into the opposing team's side.

The object of soccer is to score more goals than the opponent. Only goalies can use their hands. There are 11 total players on the field. The team is made up of the following: one goalie, four defenders, four midfielders, and two strikers.

Exercise 1: Repeat the phrases and definitions aloud.
Exercise 2: Describe one play in a game

1.	Attacker(uh-tak-ur): The attacker is the player that has the ball.
2.	Corner (kawr-ner): A corner is when a player touches the ball last and it travels out of bounds. The game restarts with a kick from the closest corner.
3.	Crossbar (kraws-bahr): A long diagonal pass.
4.	Defenders(dih-fen-derz): The Defenders that stay behind the midline to try and prevent goals from being scored.
5.	Dribble (drib-uhl): Moving the ball forward by using the feet.
6.	Forwards(fawr-werdz): The forwards are the ones kicking the ball into the goal.
7.	Goal (gohl): When a player scores the ball, it is called a goal. All goals under international law must be scored. The size of the goal is 24 feet by 8 feet.

8.	Goalkeeper or Goalie (goh-lee): The Goalie protects the goal and is the only one allowed to use his arms. He must be fast, strong, and smart.
9.	Heading (hed-ng): Using your head to direct the balls flight.
10.	Linesman (lahynz-muhn): An assistant referee.
11.	Midfielders: The Midfielders control most of the motion of the ball through the field.
12.	Obstruction (uhb-struhk-shuhn): A player uses his body to block another player from getting the ball.
13.	Offsides(awf-sahydz): Offsides is called when a player is in front of the ball or in the opponent's half.
14.	Penalty (pen-l-tee) spot: A small spot 12 yards out from the center of the goal where penalty shots are made.
15.	Red card: The final card after two yellow cards throwing the player out of the game.
16.	Send off (send-awf): When the player is removed.
17.	Shielding(sheeld-ng): Shielding is keeping possession of the ball by using your body to block the opponent.
18.	Shot (shot): A shot is when the ball is kicked or headed directly at the net to score a goal.
19.	Tackling (tak-uhl): Tackling is using the feet or the shoulder to get the ball away from the carrier.
20.	Throw-ins: A throw-in is when the ball travels outside the field, the opposing team gets to throw the ball back into the field. Some of the rules for the throw-in include: the player must throw the ball back into the field with both hands over his head and his feet must be on the ground. He must throw the ball from the spot where it went out.
21.	Violations(vahy-uh-ley-shuhns): Violations that result in a red card are tripping a player, kicking a player, charging a player, spitting at a player, handling the ball, illegal blocking, charging the goalkeeper, goalkeeper using his hands when a teammate kicks the ball, wasting time.
22.	Yellow card: A referee issues a yellow card as a warning violation to a player, when the player receives two yellow cards, he issues a red card which removes the player from the game.

9.10   Badminton

Badminton (bad-min-tn) is a sport played by two opposing players across the net that uses racquets (rak-its) to hit a shuttlecock across the net, hoping it will land in the opposing team's court. Developed in the mid-1800s in British India.

Court: Twenty (20) feet wide and approximately forty (44) feet long (depending on if it's set for singles or doubles). The court is divided into two halves.

Exercise 1: Repeat the phrases and definitions aloud.
Exercise 2: Describe one play in a game.

1.	Backhand(bak-hand): When the backside of the racket is used to return the shuttlecock.
3.	Forehand volley(vol-ee): As opposed to a backhand shot, the motion is in the direction of the forehand, and the volley implies that the shuttlecock goes back and forth between players.
4.	Net: The net is 5 ft. 1-inch-high at the edges and 5 ft. High in the center.
5.	Overarm(oh-ver-ahrm): When the racket raises over the head.
6.	Rackets: Badminton rackets are lightweight at between 2.4 oz. to 3.3 oz. Composed of an open face made with string, a shaft, a grip, and a handle.
7.	Scoring: Each game plays to 21 points with players scoring whenever they win a rally regardless of whether they were served.
8.	Shuttlecock(shuht-l-kok), also called a birdie, is a feathered or plastic high drag projectile, open conical shape, used in badminton as the ball in play.
9.	Smash: A smash is when the player comes up close to the net and then strikes the shuttlecock hard over the net, trying to catch the other player off guard.
10.	Underarm serve: The ball is hit by an under arm or the shoulder motion.

9.11 Baseball

Two teams, one's in the field, the other is at-bat. Nine players on each side. There are nine players that take the field. They all wear leather mitts or also called baseball gloves to help them catch the ball

Exercise 1: Repeat the phrases and definitions aloud.
Exercise 2: Write a description of one inning of a baseball game, including a story of each player at bat, what type of pitch was thrown and what the result was.

Baseball (beys-bawl)
Positions: There is an infield and an outfield. The outfield is composed of a left field, center field, and middle field. The diamond includes the pitcher, the catcher, first base, second base, shortstop, and third base.
1. Catcher (kach-er): The catcher catches the ball and sends pitching signals to the pitcher. The catcher also guards the home plate. The catcher uses a catcher's mitt and wears protective gear, including a mask, chest protector, and leg guards.
2. Pitcher (pich-er): The pitcher pitches or throws the ball from the pitcher's mound. He may pitch a fastball, change-up, curveball, slider, knuckleball, or forkball.
3. First base (furst) (beys): The first baseman is responsible for tagging players out at first base. The first baseman also guards the right foul zone.
4. Second base: The second baseman tags players out at second base. They also defend the second base, trying to prevent players from stealing second base. Stealing a base is when a player advances on his own without a hit from a player.
5. Shortstop(shawrt-stop): Shortstop is usually an exceptional fielder since they guard a busy zone of the infield. They stand between second and third base to prevent hits from going into the outfield.

6. Third base: The third base player is responsible for tagging out the runners going to third base and guarding the corridor along the left foul zone.
7. Leftfield: The left-field player is responsible for the left field.
8. Centerfield player: The center field player is responsible for guarding the center area to the back of the wall.
9. Right field player: The right field player is accountable for the right field to the right wall.
The umpire (uhm-pahyuhr): The umpire calls pitches and strikes and determines who's safe at home plate. The umpire stands behind the catcher at home plate.
To score, the batter hits the ball with a bat and runs around the bases. He wears a batter's helmet.
If it's caught like a fly, the batter is out. If a fielder tags the batter, he's out.
When the batter makes it around all the bases and crosses home plate, then it's a run scored.
A double play is when two outs occur on one hit.
A triple play is when three outs occur.
If he hits it out of the park, in fair territory, then it's a home run, and the batter runs around all the bases.
Whoever has the most runs after nine innings wins the game.
In each inning(in-ing), the team returns to bat.
Each side is allowed three outs per inning with as many batters as necessary until the three outs. Each player gets three strikes. When he swings and misses it's a strike if he hits it and it goes into foul territory, then it's a foul and counts as a strike. However, a player can keep hitting fouls and won't be out.
If the pitcher misses the batter's strike zone, then the pitch is called a ball. Four balls and the batter walks to first base.

9.12 Basketball

The regular basketball game is 48 minutes broken down into four (12 minute) quarters. The court is 94'(feet) x 50' having a basket at each end.

In basketball, a five-player team scores points by putting it through the hoop into the basket. Also known as a field goal.

Exercise 1: Repeat the phrases and definitions aloud.
Exercise 2: Observe a game and describe one play.

Positions and basketball terminology:
1. Airball: An airball is when the ball misses the rim and backboard completely.

2. Alley-oop: An alley-oop is a play where a basketball is tossed into the air by one player and slammed into the basket in midair by another.
3. Assist(uh-sist): The last pass, which leads to a field goal with the shooter in motion.
4. Backboard(backboard): The rectangular platform behind the rim.
5. Backcourt(bak-kawrt): The defensive side of the court.
6. Bank shot: In a bank shot, the basketball is first bounced off the backboard before it goes into the basket.
7. Basket(bas-kit): The basket is attached to the backboard; it has a metal rim with an 18" diameter and an 18" corded net. The height of the basket from floor to edge is ten feet (10').
8. Blind pass: The ball is passed to a player predicting where the player will be.
9. Block(blok): To tip or defend a shot, deflecting a pass or a shot into the hoop.
10. Boxing out: A player uses his body to control the court and get rebounds.
11. Center circle: The circular mark at center court where jump balls are given.
12. Center: Tallest player, finds open players in offensive plays.
13. Charging(chahrj-ng): Charging is an offensive foul, whereby a player runs into another player who has already set up a position.
14. Dead ball: When the basketball is no longer in play, for instance, after an official's whistle or if the ball goes out of bounds. Restarted by a free throw, throw-in, or jump ball.
15. Double team: When two players pair up on defense to pressure an opponent (uh-poh-nuhnt).
16. Downtown: A long 3-point shot.
17. Double dribble: Is a violation that occurs when a player uses both hands to dribble or stops and then starts up again. The ball is then turned over to the opposing team, who gets it out of bounds and nearest to where the violation took place.
18. Dribble(drib-uhl): A dribble is when a player bounces the ball with one hand, which is the method used to move the ball, from one end of the court to the other side.
19. Dunk(duhngk): Grabbing the ball and slamming it into the basket.
20. Foul shot: After a foul is called, shots are given at the foul line.
21. Free throw line: The white line where free throws are shot from.
22. Interception(in-ter-sep-shuhn): When a player on the opposing team catches the pass.
23. Jump ball: A referee tosses the ball in the air and players from opposing; teams try to gain possession.
24. Jump shot: The player jumps up and then shoots the ball.
25. Pass: When a player throws the ball to another player on the same team.
26. Pick(pik): When a player tries to block a member from the other side by using a team member's body to gain position or advantage.
27. Point guard: Usually the shortest team member, best passer.
28. Power forward: The power forward catches, passes, and makes the hotshots.
29. Referee(ref-uh-ree): The judges on the court that make sure the rules of the game are followed.
30. Shooting guard: The team's best shooter.
31. Sideline: The edge of the court, inside is fair play and outside, is out of bounds.

> 32. Small forward: Offensive players must score well both inside and outside.

9.13   Bicycle Parts

Exercise 1: Repeat the bicycle part.
Exercise 2: Use in a sentence.

1. Axle(ak-suhl)	13. Hub(huhb)
2. Bell(bel)	14. Pedal(ped-l)
3. Brake(breyk)	15. Air Pump
4. Brake cable	16. Rear light
5. Chain(cheyn)	17. Reflector(ri-flek-ter)
6. Crossbar(kraws-bahr)	18. Saddle(sad-l)
7. Fender(fen-der)	19. Seat(seet)
8. Fork(fawrk)	20. Spokes(spohks)
9. Front light	21. Tire(tahyuhr)
10. Gear level	22. Valve(valv)
11. Grease(grees)	
12. Handlebar(han-dl-bahr)	

9.14   Boxing

Don't get into the ring without first learning these simple boxing terms.

Exercise 1: Repeat the phrases.
Exercise 2: Lookup each term and use in a sentence.

Bob and weave(weev)	Peek a boo(boo)
Bolo punch(puhnch)	Promoter (pruh-moh-ter)
Boxing(bok-sing) gloves(gluhvz)	Punch (puhnch)
Brain fog(fawg)	Rabbit(rab-it) punch
Corner(kawr-ner)	Right(rahyt) hook
Footwork(foot-wurk)	Ring side(sahyd)
Heavy weight(weyt)	Rope and dope(dohp)
Hook(hook)	Ropes(rohps)
Jab(jab)	Southpaw stance(stans)
Knockout(nok-out)	Swing (swing)
Left hook(hook)	Turnbuckle(turn-buhk-uhl)
Light weight(weyt)	Upper cut(kuht)
Manager(man-i-jer)	Weigh(wey) in
Middle weight(weyt)	
Pay per view(vyoo)	

9.15 Fitness, Workout and Nutrition terms

It must be time to work out. Keep moving and burn weight. This list contains terms and vocabulary from exercise, medicinal, herbal, and weight training.

Exercise 1: Practice aloud the words and the definitions that follow.
Exercise 2: Describe a workout.

1. Abductor (ab-duhk-ter): A muscle whose contraction is away from the body.
2. Abdominals(ab-dom-uh-nls): The abdominals are that six-pack look caused by crunches and low body fat.
3. Acetaminophen (uh-see-tuh-min-uh-fuhn): A pain killer, sold under many brand names used instead of aspirin, where stomach issues are concerned.
4. Achilles (uh-kil-eez) tendon: The Achilles tendon connects the heel to the calf muscle.
5. Adenosine triphosphate: ATP is the fuel cell for the body.
6. Aerobic (ai-roh-bik): Exercises that need and utilize large amounts of oxygen.
7. Amino(uh-mee-noh) acids: Amino acids are the fundamental building blocks of protein. The following are the best to consume for exercise: L-leucine (loo-seen), L-isoleucine (ahy-suh-loo-seen), and L-valine (val-een).
8. Aspartame (uh-spahr-teym): Aspartame is an artificial, non-caloric sweetener.
9. Aspirin (as-per-in): Aspirin is a generic term for acetylsalicylic acid, a common over the counter non-steroidal (steer-oidal) anti-inflammatory pain killer. Used as a blood thinner for patients and may be used at times during a heart attack.
10. Barbell(bahr-bel): A barbell is a metal bar 5 to 7 feet in length used to hold weights for lifting, curls, and presses. At the end of both sides are the collars used to hold the weights on the bar.
11. Basal (bey-suhl) metabolic rate: The basal metabolic rate is the daily caloric burn to keep vital functions going, like breathing and keeping warm.
12. Bench press: An exercise device for working the back of the shoulder and arms. The device is available in the incline or straight back positions. The bench helps to work the deltoids (del-toid) and triceps.
13. Bent row: The bent row is lifting barbells or dumbbells to the chest while making an L shape with the body. Especially good for lats and biceps.
14. Biceps(bahy-seps): The bicep is the muscle that flexes the elbow joint.
15. Biceps femoris: The biceps femoris is the large muscle on the back of the thigh.
16. BMI: The body mass index is a ratio of weight to squared height used to decide fat levels or levels of obesity.
17. Bodyweight exercises: Bodyweight exercises use gravity and resistance instead of traditional weights. Like sit-ups, push-ups, and squats (skwots).
18. Breathe (breeth): Typically, a person breathes out when lifting and breathes in when lowering the weights. Take a deep breath (breth).

19. Bulking up: Bulking up occurs when an athlete is gaining size and mass, usually in preparation for a long-distance event.
20. Caffeine(ka-feen): It keeps me up at night. Caffeine is a central nervous system stimulant.
21. Calf (kaf) muscle: The calf muscle is used to move the ankle.
22. Calorie(kal-uh-ree): A calorie is the amount of energy needed to heat one gram of water one degree Celsius (sel-see-uhs).
23. Carbohydrate(kahr-boh-hahy-dreyt): Carbohydrates are digestible food molecules such as starches and sugars that are composed of carbon (kahr-buhn), hydrogen (hahy-druh-juhn), and oxygen (ok-si-juhn) found mostly in vegetables and fruits.
24. Cheat reps: Cheat reps are performed when you have gone past the point of failure but don't want to stop.
25. Circuit(sur-kit) training: Circuit training is working with different exercises, pieces of equipment(ih-kwip-muhnt), and movements for a given period with little or no rest in between. Each set of reps is part of a circuit of exercises.
26. Central Nervous System: The brain and the spinal cord, which contain all that you are, think, and will ever know.
27. Compound exercise: A compound exercise is when you work two muscle groups simultaneously (sahy-muhl-tey-nee-uhs).
28. Concentration(kon-suhn-trey-shuhn) curls: A concentration curl is a curl done one at a time by bending your torso (tawr-so) inward and leaning forward.
29. Deadlift: A deadlift is an exercise whereby you lift the weights straight up and then dropping them on the floor.
30. Deltoids(del-toids): The deltoids are your shoulder muscles.
31. Diuretic (dahy-uh-ret-ik): A diuretic increases the rate at which water (waw-ter) is excreted from the kidneys. Caffeine is a good example of a diuretic.
32. Dumbbell(duhm-bel): A dumbbell is a short metal bar with weights for doing intense arm work, either made of solid metal or with adjustable collars.
33. Ectomorph(ek-tuh-mawrf): An ectomorph is a person with a thin and linear body as contrasting to endomorph (round body type) and mesomorph.
34. Electrolyte(ih-lek-truh-lahyt): Electrolytes are important body minerals(min-er-uhls) such as sodium(soh-dee-uhm), potassium(puh-tas-ee-uhm), magnesium(mag-nee-zee-uhm), and calcium(kal-see-uhm) used for nerve impulses and muscle control.
35. Endocrine(en-duh-krin): The glandular system in the body releasing chemicals into the bloodstream.
36. Enzyme(en-zahym): Enzymes are used to help break down proteins and other substances in the body.
37. Farmer's walk: Homemade weights and a long hike. Try cinderblocks or sandbags.
38. Fat: Food products such as butter, lard, and oils made of fatty acids.
39. Femur (fee-mer): The femur is your thigh bone.
40. Fiber(fahy-ber): A non-digestible part of food found mostly in unprocessed items such as nuts, vegetables, fruits, and grains. An essential part of the diet.

41. Flaxseed(flaks-seed): Flaxseeds are rich in omega-three and should be refrigerated to extend their short shelf life.
42. Flies: To do chest flies, lay back on a bench press with a dumbbell in each hand. Extend them to your sides and then back to your chest. Don't lock the elbows. Go slow; breathe.
43. Free weight: A free weight is the standard type of weight that is unattached to another piece of equipment(ih-kwip-muhnt).
44. Gluteus(gloo-tee-uhs) Maximus: The glutes are the large muscles of the buttocks.
45. Guarana (gwahr-uh-nah): Guarana is an herb (urb) used as a stimulant as it contains large amounts of caffeine.
46. Isolation(ahy-suh-ley-shuhn) Exercise: An isolation exercise works just one muscle group at a time.
47. Negative(neg-uh-tiv): A negative rep is when you lower the weight.
48. Positive(poz-i-tiv): A positive is when you lift the weight.
49. Repetition(rep-i-tish-uhn): One completed motion or movement of an exercise. Like one sit-up.
50. Resistance(ri-zis-tuhns): As usual, the opposing forces of nature. The amount of weight you are lifting or bodyweight exercises.
51. Resistance Bands: The resistance bands come in very different strengths, some are easy to pull apart, and some are impossible.
52. Rest Breaks: While working out, it's important to hydrate and take rest breaks.
53. Set: Each set is a group of reps of any exercise. Can I get in a quick set?
54. Warm-up: Before the exercise or run, stretching, and moving around to get the blood flowing.
55. Workout: A group of exercises or activities that are used to increase cardiovascular fitness.

9.16 Golf

Golf is a sport that uses a variety of different angled clubs to hit balls into a specific number of holes on a specially maintained grass course.

Exercise 1: Repeat the phrases and definitions aloud.
Exercise 2: Review a hole in one video.

1.	Birdie (bur-dee):	A birdie is a score of one under par on an individual hole.
2.	Bogey (boh-gee):	A bogey is a score of one over par on an individual hole.
3.	Bunker (buhng-ker):	A bunker is a hazard made of grass or sand.
4.	Caddie (kad-ee):	The caddie is a worker that carries the golf clubs, offers advice and other assistance.
5.	Cup (kuhp):	The cup is the end place for the golf ball.
6.	Divot (div-uht):	The divot is a piece of lawn that is displaced when the club strikes the grass.
7.	Double eagle (ee-guhl):	A rare double eagle is when a player is 3 under par on a hole.

8.	Drive (drahyv):	The drive is a hit from the tee box down the fairway towards the hole.
9.	Fairway (fair wey):	The fairway is the greenest part of the golf course after the tee off.
10.	Follow-through (fol-oh throo):	The follow-through is a continuous swing through to the end of the stroke
11.	Golf cart (puht-er):	A golf cart is a small vehicle designed to be used on the golf course.
12.	Green (green):	The green is a small area around the hole where the putting is done.
13.	Hazard (haz-erd):	The hazard is an obstacle like a bunker or water that slows down or stops the action.
14.	Iron (ahy-ern):	The iron is a metal club with a flat face that has angles from 1 to 9 to increase the loft of the ball.
15.	Miniature (min-ee-uh-cher) golf:	Miniature golf is a fun American game that uses a very small or greatly reduced golf course to simulate a game. Some courses are a full eighteen holes, others only nine.
16.	Mulligan (muhl-i-guhn):	A mulligan is a do over, or replay of a shot without a penalty, not in professional play but used in casual games.
17.	Par:	The par is the number of strokes a professional player is expected to use for each specific hole.
18.	Putt (puht):	A putt a gentle hitting of the ball across the green hopefully into the hole.
19.	Putter (puht-er):	The putter is the club used to strike the ball into the hole from the green.
20.	Rough (ruhf):	The rough is an irregular or pitched surface.
21.	Sand trap (sand-trap):	A sand trap is a bunker made of sand.
22.	Shank (shangk):	A shank is when a ball is hit with the heel of a golf club.
23.	Slice (slahys):	A slice is a curving shot to the right or the left.
24.	Tee (tee):	The tee is a small wooden stake that holds the ball in place for the swing.
25.	Wedge (wej):	The wedge is a golf club with a high loft and a short shaft. There are four main kinds of wedges used in golf, the pitching wedge, the gap wedge, the lob wedge, and the sand wedge, not sandwich.
26.	Wood (wood):	The wood is a massive wooden club used to drive the ball down the course.

9.17 Gymnastics, Track & Field

The modern version of gymnastics involves skills on pommel horses, rings, parallel bars, uneven bars, balance beam and floor exercises. A standard track has a length of 400m or 1312 feet.

Exercise 1: Repeat the list of terms and definitions aloud.
1. Arabesque (ar-uh-besk): An Arabesque is a standing floor exercise on one leg and the other leg raised about 45 degrees.
2. Back-to-back tumbling: Back-to-back tumbling is a floor exercise across the mat, then rebounds and then across again without stopping.
3. Balance beam: The balance beam is a 4-inch-wide wooden leathered covered beam apparatus (ap-uh-rat-uhs) upon which gymnasts perform tumbling and dance skills.
4. Bib: A gymnast's number worn on the front or back of the shirt.
5. Cartwheel(kahrt-hweel): A Cartwheel is a routine done on the floor, beam, or vault (vawlt) where the body turns over sideways with the legs and arms spread out.
6. Chalk (chawk): Chalk, also known as carbonate of magnesia, is used to protect the hands, make the surface of the equipment(ih-kwip-muhnt) less slippery and mark boundaries on the floor.
7. Discus (dis-kuhs): The discus is a round circular object that weighs 4.4 pounds and is 8 inches in diameter used in throwing.
8. Dismount(dis-mount): A dismount which ends the routine is the final skill in a routine and includes the landing on the mat.
9. Front tuck: In gymnastics, the front tuck is a floor exercise by running, jumping, rotating in the air, and landing on your two feet, solidly.
10. Gainer(gey-ner): A move in which a gymnast performs a backward flip while moving forward.
11. Handstand(handstand): A handstand is a routine where all your weight is held by your hands.
12. Horizontal(hawr-uh-zon-tl) bar: The horizontal bar, also known as the high bar, is a 2.4m bar upon which gymnasts perform skills.
13. Hurdle (hur-dl): The hurdle is a race with obstacles called hurdles that were first popularized in 1830 in England.
14. Kip: The kip is a training skill in trampolining (tram-puh-leen-ng).
15. Leotard (lee-uh-tahrd): The leotard is a piece of stretch clothing worn everywhere and used by gymnasts (jim-nasts) during workouts and competitions.
16. Long jump: The running jump is a long leap into an area of earth.
17. Parallel bars: The Parallel bars are a gymnastics apparatus used by men consisting of two 3.5m bars.
18. Pike: A pike is a posture in which your legs are straight out in front of you.
19. Pole vaulting: Modern pole vaults are made from fiberglass or carbon fiber, an Olympic event since 1896.
20. Pommel horse: An apparatus, the Pommel horse consists of a rectangular body and two pommels (handles) used by men.

21. Relay (ree-ley):	A series of races in which one competitor continues the competition for another member of the same team.
22. Ribbon(rib-uhn):	The ribbon is a long piece of material attached to a stick used in rhythmic(rith-mik) gymnastics. It is quite amazing to watch, once in Julie's Acting class a student who had been training for the Olympics gave the class a demonstration, all were mesmerized.
23. Shot put:	The weight of the ball was standardized to 16 pounds in 1906.
24. Somersault(suhm-er-sawlt):	A gymnastics maneuver in which a person flips, moving the feet over the head.
25. Sprint:	A fast run over short distances.
26. Steeplechase (stee-puhl-cheys):	A steeplechase is a race over a turf course with artificial ditches and hedges.
27. Tumbling:	Tumbling is a group of continuous postures that involve airtime such as a back tuck, a back handspring, or a round-off.

9.18 Ping Pong

Table tennis, ping pong (pawng) is a game played with one or two players on either side of a flat table with a short net in the center. Players use a small racket with a flat blade.

Most single games are played with 11 points winning a game. Each player is given 2 serves, and then they switch servers. At a tie score of 10-10 the serving is alternated between players.

Exercise 1: Repeat the phrases and definitions aloud.

1.	A player must have a two-point margin to win. The ball is served in an open palm position, white or orange colored. The ball is 40 mm. in diameter (1.6 inches).
2.	The table's playing surface (2.7m long x 1.5m wide), 76 cm above the floor.
3.	A rally is a ball in play. The player must allow a ball played toward them to bounce one time on their side of the table and must send it back so that it bounces on the opposite side of the table at least once.
4.	A point is a missed ball or a ball that strikes the wrong side of the table on the return.
5.	The server strikes the ball.
6.	The return, the ball having been hit, must go over the net assembly (uh-sem-blee).
7.	A match consists of an odd number of games.

9.19 Pool: Eight ball

The movie the Hustler is about pool sharks or hustlers. The following is a brief review of playing pool.

Exercise 1: Repeat the phrases and definitions aloud.

1.	Eightball(eyt-bawl) also known as solids and stripes and is played with a cue(kyoo) stick and sixteen balls. There are seven striped balls, seven solid-colored balls, a black eight ball, and a white cue (kyoo) ball.
2.	The balls are set on the table with a triangle, the black eight ball in the center, and the two bottom balls being either stripes(strahyps) or solids. A player breaks and the balls are scattered(skat-erd) on the table; some are pocketed (pok-it-id).
3.	Each player is assigned either stripes or solids based upon who gets the first ball in. The game is to get the rest of the shots into the holes, and then finally, after calling the pocket, the eight ball is legally pocketed.
4.	There are many rules around eight ball; if you get the eight ball in before the end of the game, you lose.
5.	Equipment(ih-kwip-muhnt): The table's playing surface is approximately nine by 4.5 feet.
6.	Cue stick specifications(spes-uh-fi-key-shuhns): No shorter than fifty three inches (53") and no longer than sixty three inches (63") no lighter than fifteen(15) ounces(ouns-ez) and no more massive than twenty-five(25) ounces, balance point at least thirty-three inches (33") from the tip of the cue, a leather (leth-er) cue tip.
7.	The break. After the triangle(trahy-ang-guhl) is removed, the player who won(wuhn) the toss gets the break or can pass it.
8.	Scratching(skrach-ng) the cue ball: There are many ways to scratch, especially if the cue ball goes into the pocket.
9.	The shooter: The shooter is the player whose turn it is to hit the cue ball.
10.	Apex (ey-peks) ball: The first ball in the triangle.

9.20 Sailing and Nautical terms

Nautical (naw-ti-kuhl) refers to sailors, ships, or any equipment(ih-kwip-muhnt) used in water.

Even if you do not enjoy sailing, the terms can be fun. May the wind fill your sails.
Exercise 1: Repeat the phrases and definitions aloud.

1.	Aft: Also called stern, the back of the boat.
2.	Boom: The boom is the horizontal pole that extends from the bottom of the mast that captures the wind.
3.	Bow (bou): The front of the ship.
4.	Cockpit(kok-pit): The cockpit is an open well in the deck of the boat.
5.	Deck: The deck is the horizontal primary working surface of the boat that covers the hull.

6.	Helm (helm): The wheel of the rudder.
7.	Hull(huhl): The hull is the watertight body, which is the bottom half of the boat.
8.	Jibbing: Jibbing is the opposite of tacking. The bow of the boat goes through the wind.
9.	Keel: A flat blade that sticks downward. The keel also holds ballast, which keeps the boat right side up.
10.	Leeward (lee-werd): Leeward is the opposite direction to where the wind is blowing.
11.	Mainsail(meyn-seyl): The mainsail is the large centered triangular sail that provides the driving force of the boat.
12.	Mast (mahst): The mast is the tall center spar that is vertical from the center of the boat.
13.	Port: The port is the left-hand side while facing the front or bow of the boat.
14.	Rigging(rig-ing): Rigging are the materials and equipment(ih-kwip-muhnt) that's used to propel the ship forward.
15.	Rudder (ruhd-er): The rudder is located beneath the boat.
16.	Spinmaker: A type of sail, also known as a spinnaker, is used to catch the wind in the front of the mast.
17.	Starboard (stahr-berd): The starboard is the right-hand side of the boat.
18.	Stern (sturn): The stern is the back of the boat opposite the bow.
19.	Tiller (til-er): A tiller is a lever attached to a rudder post.
20.	Yacht (yot): A yacht is a sailboat equipped for racing.

9.21 Surfing

Surfs up Dude… let's hit the waves.

Exercise 1: Repeat the phrases and definitions aloud.
Exercise 2: Drive to Malibu and talk to a surfer.
Exercise 3: Go surfing.

1.	Air/Aerial: Getting air and going aerial is when you and the board are flying into the air above the wave and then land back and continue the wave.
2.	Bail(beyl): To avoid a wipeout, you bail on the ride.
3.	Blank(blangk): The blank is the block from which a surfboard is created.
4.	Blown out: When the wind ruins the waves, it is called a blown out.
5.	Bomb(bom): A bomb is an enormous wave.
6.	Bottom turn: When you're at the bottom of the wave and make a sharp move.
7.	Carve(kahrv): When you carve, you are turning from one side to the other.
8.	Caught inside: Caught inside is when you are stuck inside the breaking surf.
9.	Choppy(chop-ee): Choppy is when the wind blows off the wave.
10.	Cross step: A cross-step is when one foot goes over the other as you move to the front of the board.

11.	Cutback(kuht-bak): A cutback is a surfing maneuver turning back to the breaking part of a wave.
12.	Deck: The deck is the top part of the surfboard.
13.	Ding: A ding is an indentation or bruise in the surface (sur-fis) of a surfboard.
14.	Drop-in: Dropping in is when you stand on the board.
15.	Duck dive: A duck dive is when you and the board go underwater to avoid an oncoming wave.
16.	Fin or Fins: Fins are on the bottom of the board to help in steering.
17.	Flat: No waves.

9.22 Swimming

An Olympic size swimming pool is 164 feet in length, 82 feet wide, and 6 feet deep. The volume of the pool is approximately 660,000(six hundred sixty thousand gallons of water), which weighs nearly 5.5 million pounds or about 2700 tons.

Everybody must learn how to swim, it's not hard, and it might save your life and/or someone else's.

Exercise 1: Practice saying each word aloud and the sentence that follows.
Exercise 2: Find a pool and practice each stroke on your own.
Exercise 3: Research when each stroke originated in the Olympics.

1.	Backstroke(bak-strohk): The backstroke is swimming on your back, one arm over the other. When swimming backstroke a 155-pound person burns 298(two hundred ninety-eight) calories in 30 minutes of swimming around in the pool.
2.	Breaststroke(brest-strohk): The breaststroke is swimming like a frog(frawg) with the breast on the water level and the two arms moving inward and the legs kicking together and fully extended. A 155-pound person burns 372(three hundred seventy-two) calories in 30-minutes of breaststroke.
3.	Butterfly(buht-er-flahy): The butterfly is like the breaststroke with the arms moving in tandem(tan-duhm) only this time it's above water. The most difficult of all strokes with the shoulders being thrust out of the water. A 185-pound person burns 488(four hundred eighty-eight) calories in 30 minutes of butterfly.
4.	Cap: The cap is worn on the head to reduce drag and protect in the water.
5.	Cycle(sahy-kuhl) count: The number of strokes divided by time.
6.	Freestyle(free-stahyl): The freestyle is the most common regular stroke with one arm over the other arm and head-turning to breathe from side to side as the legs kick.
7.	Goggles(gog-uhlz): Goggles protect the eyes and enable swimmers to see underwater more clearly.
8.	Heat(heet): One race or round of several in a competition.
9.	Riptide(rip-tahyd): The riptide is the bottom current on the beach from the water flowing back out to sea, very powerful and dangerous it claims many lives every year.

10.	Rubber(ruhb-er) shoes: Rubber shoes are non-slip shoes that can save your life while walking on a rocky coast with dangerous waves and slippery rocks.
11.	Stroke rate: Distance per stroke and number of strokes. The swimming tempo.
12.	Swimming time: The underwater time plus the overwater time plus the stroke rate times the cycle count. A 125-pound swimmer burns 180 calories per 30 minutes.
13.	Turn time: The time from touching the wall to start, to time the feet push off the wall.
14.	Underwater time: Underwater Time plus Turn Time.

9.23   Yoga Postures

This is Hollywood. Let's do some Yoga. It benefits the body, mind, and spirit. Whether the sun salutation or the plow, it all helps.

Exercise 1: Practice reciting the posture directions aloud.
Exercise 2: Write a description of your experience in doing the postures.
Exercise 3: Add additional postures.

Easy pose: This is the first posture; just sit in easy position with legs crossed.
Dog: The dog is the posture of the spine, which is your stomach low, and your hands and feet on the floor.
Cat: The cat is the posture of the spine, which is your stomach highly arched (ahrcht) with your hands and feet on the floor.
Mountain (moun-tn): The Mountain is a posture with the arms stretched upward as tall as a mountain. Stretch and take a deep breath (breth).
Forward(fawr-werd) bend: Please have a forward bend in the waist and relax. Take a deep breath.
The Triangle(trahy-ang-guhl): Hold those arms straight across and then touch one hand after another, forming a triangle on the floor going as far as possible.
Warrior(wawr-ee-er): The Warrior 2 is a posture with one leg stretched behind you diagonally and one at a ninety-degree angle.
Cobra(koh-bruh): The Cobra is a posture with the stomach on the ground and arms stretched by your side, just like a snake.
Downward (doun-werd) facing dog: This posture is like a downward-facing dog with your arms outstretched.
Head to Knee: For this posture, bring the head to your knee and take a deep breath.
Half Shoulder Stand: What is more fun than a half shoulder stand seeing everything upside down?
The Bridge(brij): For the bridge, posture lie on your back and lift like a draw bridge.
The Corpse (kawrps): For the corpse posture, just lie flat on your back, arms outstretched and relax everything.
The Plough (plou): For the plough posture, just sit on the mat and then swing legs overhead touching the mat with your toes. Take a few deep breaths.

> The Wheel(weel): For the wheel posture, just start in a knelling pose and then place the hands behind the hips on the floor, and then slowly bend backward. Take a deep breath.

9.24 Tennis

Tennis is one of the most popular sports in America. A good workout and in fresh air. A regulation tennis court is 36' x 78'. (thirty-six feet by seventy-eight feet)

Exercise 1: Repeat the terms aloud.
Exercise 2: Lookup each term and describe its use

1. Ace(eys)	31. Junk ball(juhngk bawl)
2. Ad court(kawrt)	32. Kick serve(surv)
3. Advantage(ad-van-tij)	33. Let(let)
4. Alley(al-ee)	34. Line judge(juhj)
5. Asphalt(as-fawlt)	35. Linesman(lahynz-muhn)
6. Backcourt(bak-kawrt)	36. Lob(lob)
7. Backspin(bak-spin)	37. Love(luhv)
8. Backswing(bak-swing)	38. Lucky loser
9. Ballboy(bawl-boy)	39. Match(mach)
10. Baseline(beys-lahyn)	40. Net(net)
11. Block(blok)	41. Net court judge(juhj)
12. Break point(breyk-point)	42. Over grip(grip)
13. Center mark(sen-ter mahrk)	43. Qualification(kwol-uh-fi-key-shuhn)
14. Challenge(chal-inj)	44. Racket(rak-it)
15. Chip(chip)	45. Racquet(rak-it)
16. Chop(chop)	46. Rally(ral-ee)
17. Davis cup(dey-vis kuhp)	47. Referee(ref-uh-ree)
18. Dead net(ded net)	48. Round robin(rob-in)
19. Default(dih-fawlt)	49. Serve(surv)
20. Deuce(dyoos)	50. Service line(lahyn)
21. Dink(dingk)	51. Shank (shangk)
22. Double bagel(duhb-uhl bey-guhl)	52. Sidespin(sahyd-spin)
23. Drop shot(drop shot)	53. Smash(smash)
24. Elbow(el-boh)	54. Tennis ball(ten-is bawl)
25. Fault(fawlt)	55. Topspin(top-spin)
26. First serve (furst surv)	56. Trajectory(truh-jek-tuh-ree)
27. Forehand(fawr-hand)	57. Tramlines(tram-lahynz)
28. Ground- stroke(strohk)	58. Umpire(uhm-pahyuhr)
29. Half volley(haf vol-ee)	59. Underspin(uhn-der-spin)
30. Hawkeye(hawk-ahy)	

9.25 Chess

One night while at dinner with Maureen, Heather, Phil and Benjamin, I asked if anyone could think of a subject or topic missed in American English. I waited a moment and had a piece of Apple pie and coffee, just then Benjamin spoke up. Do you have a section on Chess? Excellent, I responded, You're right, not yet, and I immediately started to add Chess, a game enjoyed by 25-30(twenty-five to thirty) million people worldwide.

Exercise 1: Read aloud the following description of the game of Chess.
Exercise 2: Play a game.

The earliest first game of chess was called Chaturanga and is from the sixth century in India(in-dee-uh). The first world championship(cham-pee-uhn-ship) of chess was held in 1886. Wilhelm Steinitz(stahy-nits) is considered the father of chess; he wrote The Modern (mod-ern) Chess instructor, which was published (puhb-lishd) in 1889.
Chess is a game played on a chessboard(ches-bawrd) by two people that play 16 pieces each according to specific directions for the motion of the pieces (King(king), Queen(kween), Bishop(bish-uhp), Knight(nahyt), Rook(rook), Pawn(pawn)), the object is to bring your opponent's King to checkmate.
The checkered(chek-erd) board has 64 squares. Horizontal(hawr-uh-zon-tl) rows of spaces are known as ranks and are numbered 1-8. Vertical(vur-ti-kuhl) columns are labeled A-H.
To name a move, use the abbreviation(uh-bree-vee-ey-shuhn), then the letter and number on the board, i.e. N= Knight; (Nc3) means Knight to square c3. For example, the lower-left corner is a1, and the upper-right corner is h8. Two important characters in chess notation are [+]to indicate check and [#] to indicate checkmate. For pawns, just the position is identified. The following diagram is the initial setup.

a8[Rook]	Knight	Bishop	Queen	King	Bishop	Knight	Rook h8
pawn	pawn	pawn	pawn	pawn	pawn	pawn	pawn h7
							h6
							h5
a4	b4	c4	d4		f3		h4
a3	b3	c3	d3				h3
a2[pawn]	pawn	pawn	pawn	pawn	pawn	pawn	pawn h2
a1 Rook	b1 Knight	c1 Bishop	d1 Queen	e1 King	f1 Bishop	g1 Knight	h1 Rook

1.	In the corner is the Rook, next to the Rook is the Knight, and then the Bishop with the Queen seated on her color and then the King. It then repeats on the other side, the last row.
2.	Eight Pawns, the pawn can move one or two spaces on the first position, after which only one space forward except when to take a piece when it moves in a diagonal.
3.	When a Pawn reaches the opposing end of the board, you may turn it into any piece other than a king. The Queen is the most powerful piece. A Pawn can promote into a Bishop, Knight, Rook, or Queen. A Queen typically is the choice when a Pawn promotes, but another piece may be more valuable, such as a Knight to gain an advantage with a fork(positional strategy) depending on the board position. You may also get more than one Queen.
4.	The King(K). The most important piece. When the King is attacked and can't move to safety, it is called a checkmate; the game is over. The King can travel only one square in any direction.
5.	Two Bishops(bish-uhp)(B), minor pieces, one on the white square, the other on black. The Bishop may move unlimited squares diagonally over any unoccupied spaces. The Bishop controls 13 squares from the center, and since it must stay on the same color, it only has access to half the board.
6.	Two Knights(nahyts), (N) minor pieces, is the only piece that can jump over other pieces. The Knight moves in a [L] shape. Two moves one direction and then a move to the right or left. Two moves horizontal or vertical and then a move at a right angle. From the middle of the board, it can dangerously attack many squares and is well-suited for a tactic known as a fork.
7.	Two Rooks(R), major pieces, they are able to travel an unlimited number of unoccupied squares in any straight direction. The Rook controls 14(fourteen) squares from the center.
8.	The Queen(Q) is a major piece and always started on her color. Black Queen on a black square. White Queen on a white square. The Queen is the most important piece; it can move in any singular direction diagonal(dahy-ag-uh-nl), horizontal(hawr-uh-zon-tl), or vertical(vur-ti-kuhl). The Queen can control 27 squares from the center. You may gain another queen when the opposing pawn reaches the last row.
9.	For the setup, the King, all the major, and minor pieces occupy the back row; the pawns(pawnz) are on the second line.
10.	A Fork: A fork(fawrk) is when one piece makes 2 or more attacks simultaneously. The attacking piece is the forker, the defending piece is being forked.
11.	To start a game, white or black moves first. The Pawns can traverse(trav-ers) or two squares. The Knight may also jump over other pieces.
12.	For example, one method of a simple trap known as the Scholar's(skol-erz) mate can be demonstrated: e4 e5 2. Qh5 Nc6 3. Bc4 Nf6 4. Qxf7#
13.	Draw: Games do not always end with a win or a loss. They may also end in a draw (a tie), which is the result of neither player winning.
14.	The four best chess opening moves for White are 1.e4, 1.d4, 1.c4 and 1.Nf3.

15.	A player should learn the King's Gambit(gam-bit), Queen's Gambit, Ruy Lopez and the English also learn the Sicilian Defense, French Defense, Scandinavian(skan-duh-ney-vee-uhn), and the Slav.
16.	During a game, you and your opponent take turns making moves. An important rule to know is the touch rule, which states that a player must move a piece when touched if the piece is a legal move. The best way experts agree to get better is to play the game.

Lesson 10

BLM: American Heroes, Anatomy, Astrology

10.1 Pronunciation Key 14

This is a fun list, go across the row, then down the column. No phonetics here.
Practice until they are easy. Go slow.

Exercise 1: Repeat the words aloud. These are all the sounds of the English language using different words.
Exercise 2: Create your own sentence for each.

Sound	Word
A	mass, tan, pal.
A	rake, gate, late.
A	train, gain, aid.
A	play, pray, tray.
A	tall, wall, halt.
Au	cause, because, clause.
Aw	law, paw, straw, jaw.
B	baby, tube, probe.
Ch	chap, chime, cheat, chase.
Ch	itch, pitch, etch, fetch.
Ch	each, reach, speech.
D	duck, dike, dear, date.
D	bid, bed, led, had.
D	hide, made, wade.
E	peck, bet, pet, mess.
E	dead, head, dread.
E	Pete, Eve, these.
E	peek, peep, seed, meet.
E	reap, meal, team, leaf.
F	feel, fine, fear, fan, fail.
F	staff, gaff, stiff, whiff.
F	chafe, life, knife.
F	leaf, loaf, beef, chief, thief.
G	got, gale, gain, goal, grow, glee, glow.
G	rig, dig, beg, keg, bag.
G	rogue, league, vogue.
I	bit, pit, miss, tin, pill.
I	ripe, mile, time, life.
I	try, my, cry, pry.
I	lie, die, tie.
J	Jim, Jill, jet, jerk, Jack.
J	giant, ginger, giraffe.
J	bridge, ridge, wedge.
J	rage, age, cage, huge.
K	king, kill, kit, kid.
K	cat, cut, cot, car, cool,
K	sick, pick, neck, deck,
K	pike, hike, like, mike, bake,

K	peak, seek, sneak, break,	O	fog, bog, dog, frog.	S	case, chase, erase.
L	leg, lamb, lot, lunch,	Oi	boil, toil, spoil, join.	S	rice, price, twice.
L	pill, mill, bell, tell, dull,	Oo	book, hook, look, cook.	S	caps, tops, cats.
L	file, mile, smile, gale	Oo	bull, full, bush.	Sh	ship, shack, shall.
L	feel, heal, mail, pool,	Ou	cough, trough, bought,	Sh	wish, dish, mesh.
M	man, mud, mock, mine,	Ou	house, mouse, found.	T	tin, ten, tack, top.
M	dim, them, stem, ham,	Ow	clown, crown, down, drown, frown, gown, town, howl, scowl, prowl.	T	knit, rat, flat.
M	time, rhyme, same,			T	write, kite, Pete.
M	limb, lamb, dumb, thumb,	Oy	boy, coy, joy, toy.	U	luck, cluck, nut, putt, rub.
N	nip, neck, nod, nudge,	P	pug, pop, peach.	U	son, some, won.
N	knit, knot, knuckle,	P	nip, rap, flap.	U	rule, duke, brute.
N	win, pin, men, den,	P	pipe, ripe, shape.	U	moon, croon, room.
N	mine, fine, dine,	R	rip, rid, red, rest, rat, rough.	U	new, dew, blew.
O	lock, clock, not, pot.	R	wrath, wrap, wry.	U	blue, true, sue, cue.
O	rope, cope, wrote.	R	fire, wire, here.	V	vibe, vine, veer.
O	soap, goat, boat, oak.	R	stir, her, fur, car.	V	give, live, love.
O	low, grow, snow, flow.	S	sip, send, set, sack.	X	fix, mix, six, tax.
O	hoe, toe, woe, foe, Joe.	S	circle, circus, cent.	Z	zinc, zigzag, zero.
O	long, song, strong.	S	kiss, miss, dress.	Z	sneeze, freeze, breeze.
				Z	ease, please, tease.

10.2   Black Lives Matter: American Heroes

The definition of a hero is a person with achievements and noble qualities, someone who is known for feats of courage. I'd like to believe that we all have these. The following list is of those with resilience that braved difficulties and made their mark in history with contributions in dance, music, art, politics, business, science, and countless other areas.

Exercise 1: Review the following list aloud.
Exercise 2: Expand and create a biography for a hero.
Exercise 3: Add your favorite hero to the list.

1. Alvin Ailey (ey-lee) (1931 – 1989). Alvin Ailey is a dancer and choreographer (kawr-ee-og-ruh-fer) who helped to establish modern dance as an American art form by incorporating ballet, jazz, and Afro-Caribbean idioms into the choreography. Ailey performed for the first time in 1958 at New York's 92nd Street YM-YWHA(Young Men's and Young Women's Hebrew(hee-broo) Association) setting the stage for his artistic insight. He was born in Texas and created the Alvin Ailey American Dance Theater which is made of 32(thirty-two) dancers. The dance theatre was born (bawrn) out of the Civil (siv-uhl) Rights Movement, a struggle (struhg-uhl) that called for black people to be seen as human (hyoo-muhn) and asked those who believed in equal (ee-kwuhl) rights for all to use what they had to push the cause forward (fawr-werd), peacefully.

2. Aretha Franklin (frangk-lin) (1942 – 2018). Known as the Queen of Soul, Ms. Franklin has won (wuhn) eighteen Grammys and has sold more than seventy-five million albums. In 1987, she was added to the Rock and Roll Hall of Fame. She was inducted into the UK Music Hall of Fame in 2005 and into the Gospel Music Hall of Fame in 2012. The Pulitzer Prize jury in 2019 awarded Franklin a posthumous special citation.

3. August Wilson (wil-suhn) (1945 – 2005). August Wilson was an American playwright who confronted racism in his theatrical work. Wilson's plays include Fences (which won (wuhn) a Pulitzer Prize and a Tony Award), The Piano Lesson (a Pulitzer (pool-it-ser) Prize and the New York Drama Critics' Circle Award), Jitney (jit-nee), Ma Rainey's Black Bottom, Gem of the Ocean, Joe Turner's Come and Gone, Two trains Running, Seven Guitars, Radio Golf, King Hedley ll, and How I learned What I learned.

4. Barack Obama (oh-bah-muh) (1961).President Obama is a Democrat and was the first African American to be elected to the presidency. He was the 44TH president of the United States and was re-elected in 2012 for a second term. In 2009, Barack Obama was awarded the Nobel Peace Prize. President Obama graduated from Harvard Law School. His two books Dreams from My father (fah-ther) and The Audacity (aw-das-i-tee) of Hope have combined sold more than 7 million copies.

5. Benjamin O. Davis Sr. (dey-vis) (seen-yer) (1880 – 1970). Mr. Davis Sr. was the first African American to rise to the rank of Brigadier (brig-uh-deer) General. He is a Graduate (graj-oo-it) of Howard University. He was awarded the Distinguished (dih-sting-gwisht) Service Medal, Bronze Star Medal, World War I Victory Medal, American Campaign Medal, American Defense Service Medal, Army of Occupation Medal, Mexican Border Service Medal, Philippine Campaign Medal, and the Spanish War Service Medal.

6. Big Six: Dr. Martin Luther King Jr., James Farmer (fahr-mer), John Lewis (loo-is), A. Philip Randolph (ran-dolf), Roy Wilkins (wil-kinz) and Whitney Young (yuhng) were the leaders of six prominent (prom-uh-nuhnt) civil rights organizations who were pivotal in the creation of the March on Washington for Jobs and Freedom in 1963, at the apex (ey-peks) of the Civil Rights Movement in the United States.

7. Billie Holiday (hol-i-dey) (1915 –1959). Billie Holiday's singing style, inspired by instrumental jazz, created a new way of changing sound and tempo. Ms. Holiday is considered one of the best, if not, the best American vocalist, always selling out shows in the 50s, including two sold-out shows at Carnegie Hall. Ms. Holiday has four Grammy Awards and is inducted into the Grammy Hall of Fame, Rock and Roll Hall of Fame, the ASCAP Jazz Wall, and the Ertegun Jazz Hall of Fame.

8. Booker T. Washington (wosh-ing-tuhn) (1856 – 1915). Educator, Civil rights activist, in 1901 Washington published a best-selling autobiography, Up from Slavery, which had a significant effect on the African American community. Mr. Washington had a crucial role in developing the Tuskegee University, which has a faculty of nearly 200 and an endowment of approximately $2 million. He published five books: The Story of my Life and work, Up from Slavery, The Story of the Negro, My Larger Education, and The Man Farthest Down.

9. Chadwick Aaron Boseman(bohs-muhn) (1976-2020) an American actor and producer. He played several historical figures, including Jackie Robinson in 42 (2013), James Brown in Get on Up (2014), and Thurgood Marshall in Marshall (2017). His role as the superhero Black Panther awarded him an NAACP Image Award in 2019, Two Screen Actors Guild Awards, and an MTV Movie award. Mr. Boseman is a graduate of Howard University (BFA) and the British American Drama Academy and has appeared in more than two dozen films, and television shows.

10. Denzel Washington (wosh-ing-tuhn) (1954). American actor. His many movies include Glory (1989), Malcolm X (1992), Philadelphia (1993), The Preacher's Wife (1996), The Hurricane (1999), The Manchurian Candidate (2004). He's won (wuhn) two Academy Awards, three Golden Globe Awards, a Screen Actors Guild Award, and a Tony Award.

11. Dr. Charles Drew (droo) (1904 – 1950). Medical Doctor. After becoming the first African American to receive a Ph. D. from Columbia University, he developed new blood transfusions and storage theories, creating the first blood banks.

12. Duke Ellington (el-ing-tuhn) (1899 – 1974). American jazz pianist was the most celebrated jazz composer and bandleader of his time. Ellington earned 14 Grammys. Mr. Ellington wrote over 900 compositions, including Mood Indigo (1930). Mr. Ellington won(wuhn) a Presidential Medal of Freedom, 14 Grammy Awards, a Pulitzer Prize, and a French Legion of Honor.

13. Ella Baker (bey-ker) (1903 – 1986). Civil rights activist. Baker was given the nickname Fundi, which is Swahili (swah-hee-lee), for a person who teaches a craft to the next generation. Ella attended Shaw University in Raleigh (raw-lee), North Carolina, and graduated with valedictorian (val-i-dik-tawr-ee-uhn) honors. Ms. Baker is one of the most influential American leaders of the twentieth (twen-tee-ith) century and perhaps (per-haps) the most prominent (in-floo-en-shuhl) woman in the civil rights movement.

14. Frederick Douglass (duhg-luhs) (1818 – 1895). Abolitionist, Writer. Douglass escaped from slavery in Maryland and became a leader of the Abolitionists in New York and Massachusetts. Douglass wrote several autobiographies, describing his experiences as a slave. His books include in Narrative of the Life of Frederick Douglass, an American Slave, My Bondage (bon-dij) and My Freedom (1855), and Life and Times of Frederick Douglass (1881). Douglas devoted most of his time, immense talent, and boundless energy to ending slavery and gaining equal rights for African Americans.

15. Gordon Parks (pahrks) (1912 – 2006). Photographer, Director. Mr. Parks is remembered for his iconic photos of poor Americans during the 1940s (taken for a federal government project), and for his photographic essays for Life magazine. Gordon Parks is also known for directing the 1971 hit film Shaft. He has published two books, Camera Portraits: 1948; and Flash Photography, 1947. Life hired Parks as a photographer after publishing a fantastic photo essay about a young leader of a gang in Harlem. For two decades, Parks worked on subjects like poverty, racism, segregation, Broadway, sports, and fashion. He also took portraits of Muhammad Ali, Stokely Carmichael, and Malcolm X.

16. Harriet Tubman (tuhb-muhn) (1820 – 1913). Abolitionist. Ms. Tubman used the 90-mile Underground Railroad to make the trip from Maryland to Philadelphia in 1849. The Underground Railroad was a network of safe locations. She returned to Maryland to make some thirteen missions to rescue approximately 70 enslaved people. The first woman to lead an armed expedition (ek-spi-dish-uhn) in the war, she guided the raid at Combahee Ferry (fer-ee).

17. Henrietta Lacks (laks) (1920 – 1951). Henrietta Lacks is famous as the originator of specialized HeLa cells used in research. Lacks was unaware she was the source of these cells from a tumor biopsied during treatment in Baltimore, Maryland in 1951. The cells rapidly reproduce and stay alive long enough to undergo multiple tests. These immortalized human cell lines are one of the most important in medical research. There are almost 11,000 registered patents with HeLa cells.

18. Ida B. Wells (welz) (1862 – 1931). Journalist, Civil Rights activist who raised civil rights issues in the pages of her Memphis Free Speech, the newspaper she co-owned. Ms. Wells reported racial incidents and inequality and was one of the founders of the NAACP. In 2020, Wells was honored with a Pulitzer Prize special citation for reporting on violence against African Americans during the era of lynching.

19. Jackie Robinson (rob-in-suhn) (1919 – 1972). Baseball player, activist. Robinson broke segregation when he played first base for the Brooklyn Dodgers on April 15, 1947. Robinson was added to the Baseball Hall of Fame in 1962. During his 10-year MLB career, Robinson won (wuhn) the inaugural (in-aw-gyer-uhl), Rookie of the Year Award in 1947, was an All-Star for six consecutive seasons from 1949 through 1954. In 1949—the first black player so honored. Robinson played in six World Series and contributed to the Dodgers' 1955 World Series championship. In 1972, Robinson was posthumously awarded the Congressional Gold Medal and Presidential Medal of Freedom in recognition of his work.

20. James Baldwin (bawld-win) (1924 – 1987). Novelist, Playwright. One of the 20th century's most celebrated writers, Baldwin broke new literary ground with his essay on the Black experience in America. James Baldwin published the 1953 novel Go Tell It on the Mountain, receiving acclaim for his insights on race, spirituality, and humanity. While working odd jobs, Baldwin wrote short stories, essays, and book reviews, some of them later collected in the volume Notes of a Native Son (1955). He befriended actor Marlon Brando in 1944, and the two were roommates for a time. They remained friends for over twenty years.

21. Jay Z (zee) (1969). Musician, Entrepreneur. His thirteen Billboard No. 1 albums are the most by any solo artist in music history. Jay-Z is one of the world's highest-selling musical artists, with over fifty million albums and seventy-five million singles worldwide. He has won (wuhn) a total of twenty-two Grammy Awards, the most by a rapper, and holds the top number for the most number one albums by a solo artist on the Billboard 200, with fourteen.

22. Jean-Michel Basquiat (bas-key-ay) (1960 – 1988). Artist. Because without Basquiat, there'd be no graffiti (gruh-fee-tee). Basquiat's work revolves around single heroic figures, icons, athletes, prophets, warriors, cops, musicians, kings, and phrases. His first show was in 1980. Mr. Basquiat soon connected with stars

Andy Warhol and Keith Haring in New York's Lower East Side. I lived in the lower east village in 1986, and I recall a metal highway divider with SAMO written on it and a slick poster with Basquiat and Warhol wearing boxing gloves being given out at the Mary Boone Gallery.

23. Jesse Jackson (jak-suhn) (1941). Civil Rights Activist, Politician. Reverend Jackson ran for president in 1984. After contributing with Martin Luther King, Jr., in the civil rights movement, Reverend Jackson ran but failed to win the Democratic Party's 1984 and 1988 presidential (prez-i-den-shuhl) nominations. His son, Jesse Jackson, Jr., a Democrat from Illinois, was a member of the US House of Representatives from 1995 to 2012.

24. Jesse Owens (oh-uh nz) (1913 – 1980). Track and Field Athlete. Owens already had earned several world records and was recognized as the fastest man alive. In 1935, he equaled or broke six world records in forty-five minutes, and in 1936, he won four gold medals at the Olympic Games in Berlin.

25. Jimi Hendrix (hen-driks) (1942 – 1970). Musician, Singer US rock musician. Remembered for the flamboyance and originality of his improvisations, he significantly widened the scope of the electric guitar. His real career lasted only four years, but he is still regarded as one of the most influential guitarists in history. Hendrix's performance of the US national anthem, The Star-Spangled Banner, was the most electrifying (ih-lek-truh-fahy-ing) moment of Woodstock (wood-stok), and it was probably the single most significant moment of the sixties.

26. Jody Vanessa Watley(wot-lee)(1959) is an American songwriter, singer, who got discovered on Soul Train at the age of fourteen. With an impressive thirty-two Top Ten Singles and thirteen No. 1 Singles. Ms. Watley is the first African American woman to portray Betty Rizzo in the Broadway revival of Grease (grees). Her first solo studio album, titled Jody Watley, was released in March 1987. The album peaked at number ten on the US Billboard two hundred, number one on the Top R&B/Hip-Hop Albums chart and sold two million copies in the United States. In 1987, she was honored with a Grammy Award, and in 2008, she was the recipient (ri-sip-ee-uhnt) of a Lifetime Achievement Award from Billboard magazine.
In 1986, prior to her Grammy, I answered a call from Ms. Watley, who was at a company managing focus groups in midtown Manhattan. I eventually ended up working there. In the office with Ms. Watley was really a memorable experience. In a quiet moment, she would turn the music way up on the small boom box and dance for just a second. She said she would get a Grammy someday, and sure enough she received a Best New Artist Grammy less than a year later.

27. Rep. John Lewis(loo-is) (1940–2020) was an American politician and revered (ri-veerd) civil rights icon who served in the United States House of Representatives

for Georgia's Fifth congressional district (dis-trikt) from 1987 until his passing in 2020. Rep. Lewis has been awarded more than 50 honorary (on-uh-rer-ee) degrees from universities around the world. In 1965, Rep. Lewis led the Selma to Montgomery marches across the Edmund Pettus Bridge (brij). He fulfilled many key roles in the civil rights movement including its actions to end legalized racial (rey-shuhl) segregation (seg-ri-gey-shuhn) in the United States. Lewis is also well known for the March books which are an autobiographical black and white graphic (graf-ik) novel trilogy (tril-uh-jee) about the Civil (siv-uhl) Rights Movement, told through the perspective of Congressman Lewis. The series is written by Rep. Lewis and Andrew Aydin and illustrated, lettered by Nate Powell.

28. Kamala (kom-uh-luh) Harris (har-is) (1964-). Kamala Harris is America's first female, first Black and first South Asian vice president-elect. She is a politician and lawyer who has served as a United States senator from California since 2017. Harris is a graduate of Howard University and the University of California, Hastings (hey-stingz) College of the Law. Harris launched her presidential campaign forty-seven years to the day after Chisholm's presidential campaign. Harris previously was District (dis-trikt) Attorney of San Francisco, Attorney General of California, and Senator from California.

29. Kobe Bryant (brahy-uhnt) (1978 –2020). Widely regarded (ri-gahrd-id) as one of the greatest players of all time, Bryant won many accolades (ak-uh-leyds) as an American professional basketball player, including five NBA championships. At the 2008 and 2012 Summer Olympics, Kobe won two gold medals as a member of the US national team. Bryant entered the (NBA) directly from high school. In 2018, he received the Academy Award for Best Animated Short Film for his 2017 film Dear Basketball. In January 2020, at age 41, Kobe died tragically in a helicopter accident in Calabasas, California, with his thirteen-year-old daughter Gianna and seven others.

30. Katherine Johnson (jon-suhn) (1918—2020). Mathematician(math-uh-muh-tish-uhn), Physicist(fiz-uh-sist), In 2015, then-President Barack Obama awarded Johnson the Presidential Medal of Freedom(free-duhm)for her work at NASA and her historical(hi-stawr-i-kuhl)role as one of the 1st African-American women to work as a NASA scientist. In 2016, she won the Silver Snoopy Award and a NASA Group Achievement (uh-cheev-muhnt) Award. Taraji P. Henson represented her as a lead character (kar-ik-ter) in the 2016 film Hidden Figures. In 2019, Johnson was awarded the Congressional (kuh n-gresh-uh-nl), Gold Medal.

31. Louis Armstrong (ahrm-strawng) (1901 –1971). Louis Armstrong was an American trumpeter (truhm-pi-ter), composer, vocalist (voh-kuh-list), and actor who was among the most influential (in-floo-en-shuhl) figures in jazz. His career (kuh-reer) spanned five decades, from the 1920s to the 1960s. In 2017, Mr. Armstrong was inducted into the Rhythm (rith-uhm) & Blues Hall of Fame.

Throughout his riverboat experience, Armstrong's musicianship began to mature and expand. At twenty, he could read music. Armstrong had nineteen "Top 10" records, including Stardust, What a Wonderful World, When The Saints(seynts) Go Marching In, Dream(dreem) a Little Dream of Me, Ain't Misbehavin, You Rascal You, and Stompin' at the Savoy, Grammy Award for 1964 Male Vocal Performance Hello, Dolly!, Armstrong(ahrm-strawng) was posthumously awarded the Grammy (gram-ee)Lifetime Achievement Award in 1972.

32. Madam C.J. Walker (waw-ker) (1867 – 1919). American entrepreneur (ahn-truh-pruh-nur), philanthropist (fi-lan-thruh-pist), and political and social activist. Walker made her fortune (fawr-chuhn) by developing and marketing a line of cosmetics (koz-met-iks) and hair care products (prod-uhkts) for black women through the business she founded, Madam C. J. Walker Manufacturing (man-yuh-fak-cher-ing) Company. At the time of her death (deth), she was considered the wealthiest (wel-thee-iest) self-made black woman in America. Walker (waw-ker) was inducted into the National Women's Hall of Fame (feym) in Seneca (sen-i-kuh) fall, New York, in 1993. In 1998, the U.S. Postal (pohs-tl) Service issued a Madam (mad-uhm) Walker commemorative (kuh-mem-uh-rey-tiv) stamp as part of its Black Heritage (her-i-tij) Series.

33. Malcolm X (eks) (1925 – 1965). Civil Rights activist, Minister, Malcolm X's legacy was cemented posthumously (pos-chuh-muhs-lee), with The Autobiography of Malcolm X, written with Alex Haley. Malcolm X was a US political activist (ak-tuh-vist), born Malcolm Little. He joined the Nation of Islam (is-lahm) in 1946 and became a vigorous (vig-er-uhs) campaigner for black rights, initially focusing on the use of violence. In 1964, he converted to orthodox (awr-thuh-doks) Islam and moderated his views on black separatism; he was assassinated the following year. He was honored with Malcolm X Day, where he is commemorated in various cities across the United States.

34. Dr. Martin Luther King Jr. (joon-yer) (1929 – 1968). Leader of the Civil rights movement, Baptist minister, delivered the I Have a Dream Speech. Co-founder of the Southern Christian (kris-chuhn) Leadership Conference, a key figure in the March on Washington for Jobs and Freedom in 1963, the Montgomery bus boycott, the Selma to Montgomery March in 1965, and a recipient of the Nobel Peace Prize in 1964. Martin Luther King, Jr. Day was established as a holiday in cities and states throughout the United States beginning in 1971.

35. Mary McLeod Bethune (buh-thyoon) (1875 – 1955). Civil rights activist, Educator. Appointed by President Harry S. Truman (troo-muhn), Bethune was the only woman of color at the founding conference of the United Nations (ney-shuhns) in 1945. In 1935, Bethune became a special advisor on minority affairs to President Roosevelt An early member(mem-ber) of the National Association for the Advancement of Colored People; she helped represent(rep-ri-zent) along

with W.E.B. DuBois the group at the 1945 conference on the founding of the United Nations.

36. Maya Angelou (an-juh-loo) (1928 – 2014). US novelist and poet; She was active in the Civil Rights Movement and worked with Martin Luther King Jr. and Malcolm X. Ms. Angelou earned a myriad of accolades(ak-uh-leydz) including three Grammy awards, the Presidential Medal of Freedom, The first volume of her autobiography, I Know Why the Caged Bird Sings, which recounts her harrowing(har-oh-ing) experiences as a black child in the US South, was followed by six more: Gather(gath-er) Together in My Name, Singin' and Swingin' and Gettin' Merry Like Christmas, The Heart of a Woman, All God's Children Need Traveling Shoes, A Song Flung(fluhng) Up to Heaven, and Mom & Me & Mom.

37. Michael Jordan (jawr-dn) (1963). Athlete, Basketball player, Owner of the Charlotte Hornets. Turned Air Jordan into a billion-dollar brand. Jordan led the Chicago (shi-kah-goh) Bulls to six National Basketball Association championships and earned the NBA's Most Valuable (val-yoo-uh-buhl) Player Award five times. With five regular-season MVPs and three All-Star MVPs, Jordan became the most decorated (dek-uh-rey-tid) player in the NBA.

38. Michelle Obama (oh-bah-muh). Michelle Obama is an American attorney and is married to the 44th president of the United States, Barack Obama. She is the first African American first lady and has worked for the Harvard Legal Aid Bureau, assisting low-income tenants with housing cases. Michelle Obama has authored two books; Becoming is the memoir published in 2018, selling more copies than any other book published in the United States in 2018, breaking the record in just 15 days. The first lady's first book, American Grown, was published in 2012, promoting healthy eating and the White House Kitchen Garden through the seasons. From the South Side of Chicago, Illinois, the first lady is a graduate of Princeton University and Harvard Law School. In her early legal career, she worked at the law firm Sidley Austin where she met Barack Obama. Former First Lady Michelle Obama is a frequent speaker for the Democratic Party and recently addressed the Democratic National Convention.

39. Miles Davis (dey-vis) (1926–1991). American jazz trumpeter, composer, and bandleader. Miles Davis is said to be one of the most original, leading, and revered figures in music history. Miles Davis has won eight Grammy Awards. Miles Davis had Sickle Cell Anemia, which caused joint pain and led to other issues. But In 1986, Miles was given a Doctor of Music, honoris causa, from New England Conservatory. His album Kind of Blue (1959) created modal jazz. I saw Miles play twice. Once in Boston at Kix club on June 27, 1981, when he just started to return after five years off and once at The Hollywood Bowl on August 25, 1991, with my friends Rudolph, Jacey, and the Sixth Street Royal Family. Many critics have regarded the recording Kind of Blue as the most celebrated

jazz record; in 2019, it was certified Quintuple Platinum (plat-n-uh m) by the (RIAA) for shipments of over five million copies.

40. Morgan Freeman (free-muhn) (1937). Morgan Freeman is one of the most famous American actors and film narrator (nar-ey-ter). Freeman was given an Academy Award in 2005 for Best Supporting Actor with Million (mil-yuhn) Dollar Baby. In 1980, he won two Obie (oh-bee) Awards, for his portrayal of Shakespearean anti-hero Coriolanus (kawr-ee-uh-ley-nuhs) at the New York Shakespeare Festival. I happened to be in NYC in the summer of 1980, and I went to the Delacorte Theatre and saw Coriolanus. That night was full of surprises as a thunderstorm passed through in the middle of the show. Morgan stayed in character through the lightning and rain, receiving that Obie award. Other awards include Cecil B. DeMille Award, Golden Globe Award, 2 Black Reel Awards, 7 NAACP Image Awards, SAG award, SAG Life Achievement Award, 8 Film critic awards, and others.

41. Muhammad Ali (ah-lee) (1942–2016). Boxer, Activist, born Cassius Marcellus Clay. He won the world heavyweight champion three times. At 18, he won a gold medal in the light heavyweight division at the 1960 Summer Olympics. After converting (kuh n-vurt-ing) to Islam and changing his name, he was stripped of his title for refusing army service on conscientious (kon-shee-en-shuhs) objector (ob-jikt-ter) grounds. This decision was overthrown by the US Supreme (suh-preem) Court in 1976, and his title was reinstated. Some of Ali's awards include NAACP Image Award, Sports Illustrated Sportsperson of the Year, Arthur Ashe Courage Award, BBC Sports Personality World Sport Star of the Year, Associated Press Male Athlete of the Year, Bambi – Millennium (mi-len-ee-uhm) Award, Milliyet Sports Award for World Athlete of the Year, BET Humanitarian (hyoo-man-i-tair-ee-uhn) Award and Audie Award for Autobiography/Memoir, The Greatest: My Own Story.

42. Oprah Winfrey (win-free) (1954). Media mogul, host, philanthropist, first African American female billionaire and now the richest woman on earth. Ms. Winfrey has won many accolades (ak-uh-leydz) throughout her career. Including an Academy award, 18 daytime Emmy awards, a People's Choice Award, a Golden Globe, an NAACP Image Award, two primetime Emmys. In 2013, Winfrey (win-free) was awarded the Presidential Medal of Freedom by President Obama and honorary doctorate degrees from Duke and Harvard. Her show the Oprah Winfrey Show, aired for 25 seasons, from 1986 to 2011. Oprah eventually became the leader in daytime talk shows. Oprah later created her own studio, OWN. In 1986 as an actor studying Moliere in New York I happened upon an ad in the Village Voice for a story on dating. What started as an article eventually ended up as a feature on AM Chicago. They flew me to Chicago, and I spent fifteen minutes discussing relationships with Oprah. I was so young, and Oprah was asking me serious questions. That was the summer of 1986, oh and I used my French pseudonym on the show, Pierre Gustav.

43. Quincy Jones (kwin-zee) (johnz) (1933). Musician, Producer, Songwriter, Activist. Winner of twenty-seven Grammy awards, including a Grammy Legend Award in 1992.

Honorary Doctor of Music from Berklee College of Music (1983), Golden Plate Award of the American Academy of Achievement in 1984, Humanitarian Award at the BET Awards in 2008, John F. Kennedy(ken-i-dee) Center Honors(on-erz) in 2001. National Medal (med-l) of Arts from President Barack Obama on March 2, 2011. Mr. Jones received an honorary doctorate (dok-ter-it) from the Royal (roi-uhl) Academy of Music, London (luhn-duhn), in 2015. In 2013. Ahmet Ertegun Award (uh-wawrd), Rock and Roll Hall of Fame in The Jean Hersholt Humanitarian Award, and others.

44. Richard Allen (al-uhn) (1760 – 1831). U.S. clergyman, Preacher, Former Slave. Educator. Allen is the leader and founder of the (AME) African Methodist Episcopal Church in America. That church now has 6,000 churches, with a membership of two and a half million people, it was the country's first independent black denomination.

45. Richard Pryor (prahy-er) (1940 – 2005). Comedian, actor, writer. Pryor is listed as number one on Comedy Central's list of comics. Rolling Stone put him first on its list of the best stand-up comics. The recipient of an Emmy and five Grammys, including the Grammy Lifetime Achievement Award. Mr. Pryor also won two American Academy of Humor awards and the Writers Guild of America Award. The first-ever Kennedy Center Mark Twain Prize for American Humor was presented to him in 1998. Some of his films include: Lady Sings the Blues, The Mack, Uptown Saturday Night, Silver Streak, Car Wash, Bingo Long Traveling All-Stars & Motor Kings, Which Way Is Up? Greased Lightning, Blue Collar, and the Muppet Movie. In Pryor's book, 1995, Pryor convictions, and other life sentences, Richard Pryor talks about the full story of his life from six broken marriages to multiple sclerosis.

46. Robert Abbott (ab-uht) (1870 – 1940). Abbott founded The Chicago Defender in 1905, which grew to have the highest circulation of any black-owned newspaper. Mr. Abbott was an American lawyer, newspaper publisher, and editor. He attended Hampton University and Kent College of Law. Mr. Abbott is the Founder and publisher of the Chicago Defender. He was the Founder and publisher of The Chicago Defender newspaper and the Bud Billiken Parade and Picnic. Its success resulted in Abbott becoming one of the first self-made millionaires of African American descent.

47. Sammy Davis Jr. (Sam-ee) (dey-vis)(joon-yer) (1925-1990). Sammy Davis Jr. was a highly popular performer and civil rights, activist. Mr. Davis helped change racial barriers in show business in the 50s and 60s, especially in Las Vegas, where he often performed as part of the Rat pack with Frank Sinatra and Dean Martin. Mr. Davis was awarded the Kennedy Center Honors in 1987, and in 2001 he was posthumously awarded a Grammy Lifetime Achievement award. When Sammy Davis, Jr. published his autobiography in 1965, Yes, I Can, it was an immediate long-running bestseller. He won a Spingarn Medal by the NAACP in 1968, and Mr. Davis has Eight Billboard Top 20 Pop hits.

48. Serena Williams (wil-yuh mz) (1981). Williams was homeschooled by her father and with her sister. She is a two-time Olympic gold medal Tennis player. She has won 23 Grand Slam titles (the record), four Olympic gold medals, six US Opens, seven Wimbledon titles, seven Australian Opens, three French Opens, 23 doubles titles, and a career Golden Slam. She has 792 Career matches and has won $90,643,816 in career prize money.

49. Shirley Chisholm (chiz-uhm) (1924 – 2005). Politician. Shirley Chisholm (chiz-uhm) became the first black woman elected to the US Congress, representing the 12th District of New York for seven terms from 1969 to 1983. She graduated from Brooklyn College (BA) and Columbia University (MA). Chisholm was posthumously (pos-chuh-muhs) awarded the Presidential Medal of Freedom in 2015.

50. Sidney Poitier (pwah-tyey) (1927). Actor, Director. Sidney Poitier has won many awards including an Academy Award for best actor in Lilies of the Field, a Golden Globe Cecil B. DeMille Award, an Academy Honorary Award, AFI Lifetime Achievement Award, Golden Globe Award for Best Actor, Kennedy Center Honors, SAG Lifetime Achievement Award, Presidential Medal of Freedom, Grammy, BAFTA, NAACP Image Award and a Coretta Scott King Award. Notable movies: Guess Who's Coming to Dinner, In the Heat of the Night, and To Sir with Love, I met Sidney Poitier in the lobby of the DGA at an event, I said nervously, "you look good for your age." He laughed and said, so do you—fast comeback. Great actor.

51. Sojourner Truth (soh-jur-ner) (trooth) (1797 – 1883). American Abolitionist(movement to end slavery) and women's rights activist. Her memoirs, The Narrative of Sojourner Truth: A Northern Slave, was published in 1850. Born into slavery, she escaped with her daughter to freedom in 1826 and was released in 1827. She became an enthusiastic evangelist and preached in favor of black rights and women's suffrage (suhf-rij). In 1864, she visited the White (hwahyt) House by President Lincoln (ling-kuhn). Sojourner was the only woman to have a national platform before the Civil war, and she was the first African (af-ri-kuh n American woman to win a lawsuit in the United States. Sojourner was Homeschooled, Dutch was her primary language.

52 Stevie Wonder (wuhn-der) (1950). Singer, Musician, Songwriter, Producer. Stevie Wonder was blinded as a result of a hospital incubator accident as an infant. Mr. Wonder was known as a child prodigy with a number one hit song called Fingertips in 1963. This Billboard Hot 100 hit single was recorded live by "Little" 13-year-old Stevie Wonder for Motown's then Tamla label. Wonder has won 25 Grammy Awards, as well as a Grammy Lifetime Achievement Award. He has sold over 100 million records. Leon, a coworker, and I rode the elevator up 15 flights with Stevie Wonder once. I worked for RTV(Radio TV Reports) at that time, and we were in the same building as Motown. After complimenting him on his great work, we

suggested that he sweat the suits for more money at Motown. He laughed and asked, who are you cats?

53. Thurgood Marshall (mahr-shuhl) (1908 – 1993). Supreme Court Judge for 24 years. He is arguably the most pivotal figure in the destruction of Jim Crow and the most consequential lawyer of the 20th century. Mr. Marshall graduated from Lincoln University and Howard University School of Law. Founded the NAACP Legal (lee-guhl) Defense and Educational Fund.

54. Toni Morrison (mawr-uh-suhn) (1931 – 2019). Novelist, Playwright. Nobel Prize for Literature (1993). Ms. Morrison's novels depict the black American experience and heritage, often focusing on rural life in the South. Her notable works include in The Bluest Eye, Beloved (made into a film), Sula, Tar Baby, and Paradise. Attended Howard University (BA) and Cornell University (MA). Winner Presidential Medal of Freedom, Nobel Prize in Literature, Pulitzer Prize, and a National Humanities Medal.

55. Willie Howard Mays Jr. (1931). Willie (wil-ee) Mays is called one of the best baseball players of all time and was elected (ih-lek-tid) to the Baseball (beys-bawl) Hall of Fame in 1979. In November 2015, Mr. Mays was awarded (uh-wawrd-id) the Presidential Medal of Freedom by President Barack Obama at the White House. His many books include: Say Hey: The Autobiography(aw-tuh-bahy-og-ruh-fee) of Willie Mays, 24, Born to Play Ball, Willie Mays My Life in and Out of Baseball As Told to Charles Einstein, Willie Mays, Play ball, Grand Slam.

56. W. E. B. Du Bois (doo-bois) (1868 – 1963). Sociologist, Writer, Activist leader of the Niagara Movement, a group of African American activists whose mission was for equal rights. Wrote the seminal work, Souls of Black Folk, published in 1903, and in 1895 he becomes the first African American to earn (urn) a Ph.D. from Harvard University. Then in 1935, he wrote his magnum opus, Black Reconstruction in America. His 1940 autobiography Dusk of Dawn is considered the first scientific treatise in the field of American sociology.

57. Zora Neale Hurston (hur-stuhn) (1891 – 1960). Part of the Harlem Renaissance. She was a Novelist, and writer her works include Jonah's Gourd Vine, Their Eyes Were Watching God, Dust Tracks on a Road, and Seraph on the Suwanee (1948). Her novels explore folklore, especially that of the Deep South.

10.3 Human Anatomy

Learning the names of body parts and anatomy can be lifesaving in cases of emergency. This list contains Human Anatomy (u-nat- uh-mee), Physiology (fiz-ee-ol-uh-jee) & Hygiene (hahy-jeen) terms.

This list is difficult, but worthwhile. For a first pass, you can just read the terms, then for the second pass try definitions and sentences. Over the years I've tutored many students, for example one emergency room doctor had trouble with saying the word, blood.

Take the time to learn all of your body parts. This list goes beyond basic information.
Exercise 1: Repeat the word aloud and then the sentence.
Exercise 2: Draw a human body and label the parts listed below.

Abrasions (uh-brey-zhuhnz): E.g., Gloves (gluhvs) and long pants will help reduce abrasions and lacerations in case of a fall on a motorcycle. Def. Scrapes or cuts into the skin.	
Ankle (ang-kuhl):	The ankle is the joint between the foot and the leg.
Antiseptic (an-tuh-sep-tik):	Antiseptic is being cleaned of germs and other organisms.
Aorta (ey-awr-tuh):	The aorta is the main blood vessel out of the heart.
Artery (ahr-tuh-ree):	The artery is the tubular branching blood vessels that carry blood from the heart through the body.
Auditory nerve (aw-di-tawr-ee):	The auditory nerve is in the inner ear.
Bandages (ban-dij): A piece of material used to bind or band an injury of the skin. Would you like a bandage for that laceration (las-uh-rey-shuhn)?	
Bicep (bahy-sep): The bicep which connects the forearm to the upper arm is used for lifting and pulling movements and is the favorite of bodybuilders.	
Breast (brest):	The front part of the body. The infant nursed on her mother's breast.
Calf (kaf):	The calf is the back part of the leg below the knee (nee).
Capillary (kap-uh-ler-lee):	The capillary is the smallest of blood vessels.
Cardiovascular (kahr-dee-oh-vas-kyuh-ler) disease: Cardiovascular disease are illnesses that affect the heart.	
Cartilage (kahr-tl-ij): Unlike other connective tissues, cartilage does not contain blood vessels; therefore, it grows and repairs more slowly.	
Cheek (cheek):	The cheek is below the eye and between your mouth and ear.
Chest: The chest is the front surface (sur-fis) of a person's or animal's body between their neck and the abdomen. E.g., He did bench presses trying to make his chest more muscular (muhs-kyuh-ler).	
Clippers (klip-ers):	I need to clip my nails. Where are the toenail clippers?
Cough (kawf) He coughs a lot because he is sick.	
Cuticle (kyoo-ti-kuhl):	Be careful of that cuticle at the base of your fingernail.
Dermatology (dur-muh-tol-uh-jee): Dermatology is a branch of medicine focusing on the hair, nails, and skin and its related diseases.	
Dimples (dim-puhlz): Dimples are muscular indents on the face and in the cheeks.	

Double vision: You should see an ophthalmologist (op-thuh-l-mol-uh-jist) immediately about that double or blurred vision.
Drooping: As we age, much of our body begins to droop, muscles sag, cheeks sink in, and neck hangs like a chicken. You'll see.
Ear (eer): The ear is the organ of hearing and equilibrium in vertebrates (vur-tuh-breyts). The ear contains the following: outer ear canal, eardrum, hammer, anvil (an-vil), stirrup (stir-uhp), cochlea (kok-lee-uh), Eustachian (yoo-sta-shan) tube, semicircle canals, and nerves).
Elbow (el-boh): The joint in the human arm that connects the upper arm to the forearm. is called the elbow. In plumbing there is an elbow joint pipe. There is also elbow macaroni which is often used in one of America's favorite foods, macaroni and cheese. .
Endocrinology (en-doh-kruh-nol-uh-jee): The endocrine system uses glands that secrete hormones into the body.
Esophagus (ih-sof-uh-guh-s): The mouth is connected to the esophagus, a muscular pathway, the esophagus is connected to the stomach.
Esthetician (es-thi-tish-uhn): Your epidermis looks beautiful, did Tina, the Esthetician do a dermabrasion?
Eye (ahy): The eye is the organ of sight. The eye is composed of the following parts: the white portion called the sclera (skleer-uh). In the center of that is the iris (ahy-ris), which is then covered by a clear curvilinear(kur-vuh-lin-ee-er) membrane called the cornea (kawr-nee-uh), in the center of that is the pupil (pyoo-puhl) which light passes through to the retina (ret-n-uh). Also included are the eyebrow, the upper eyelid, eyelashes, lower eyelid, tear duct, lens, and the optic nerve.
Eye drops: Eye drops contain a saline solution used to moisten the eyes.
Eyebrow (ahy-brou): The eyebrow is a region of hair above the eye that follows the shape of the brow ridges. The eyebrows are also crucial in facial expressions.
Farsighted (fahr-sahy-tid): He was farsighted and could see objects at a distance much better than up-close.
Finger (fing-ger): Each of five slender jointed parts attached to the hand. E.g., the piano player has long, beautiful fingers.
Foot: The award-winning actor put his foot in the wet cement. Parts of his foot include ankle, heel, sole, arch, ball of foot, big toe, instep, and toenails.
Forehead: The front of your head. E.g., be careful you don't hit your forehead on the trunk door as Schocket did.
Gastroenterology (gas-troh-en-tuh-rol-uh-jee): Gastroenterology is the study of the digestive system.
Gene (jeen): The basic unit of hereditary (huh-red-i-ter-ee).
Hair: Your hair smells like freshly laundered linen (lawn-derd lin-uhn), said William Holden in the film, Sunset Blvd.
Hand: The hand is the end part of the human arm below the wrist used for grasping and gripping. There are five fingers: the thumb, the index finger, the middle finger, the ring finger, and the pinky.
Heart (hahrt): The heart is the organ that receives blood through the veins and pumps it through the arteries. The heart contains the following: right atrium, left atrium,

myocardium, right ventricle, inferior vena cava, pulmonary veins, pulmonary artery, superior vena cava, aorta, pulmonary artery, pulmonary veins, left ventricle.	
Hepatology (hep-uh-toh ol-uh-jee): The study of the liver, pancreas, biliary tree, gallbladder as well as their disorders.	
Hypothermia (hahy-puh-thur-mee-uh): The mountain climber (klahy-mer) got stuck on top of the mountain all night and suffered from hypothermia.	
Joints: We move the limbs at the joints.	
Kidney: Kidneys separate the water and waste products from our blood, so drink plenty of cranberry juice to help yours.	
Knee (nee): The knee is the joint of your leg.	
Larynx (lar-ingks): The larynx is the upper part of the trachea (trey-kee-uh) that contains the vocal cords.	
Ligament (lig-uh-muhnt): The fibrous tissue of a ligament is used in holding organs in place and bones together.	
Lips: Lips are the least protected part of the skin against the sun on the body. Lips are the most sensitive to touch, cold and heat. Lips only have three to four layers compared to fifteen layers on other parts of the skin.	
Liver (liv-er): The liver secretes (si-kreets) bile (bahyl) and is essential for metabolism and the production of red blood cells.	
Lung (luhng): A pair of organs located in the rib cage. Drink plenty of fluids to help your lungs.	
Menopause (men-uh-pawz): Menopause is the period that marks the end of your menstrual cycles. Average age in the United States is fifty-one. The television commercial asks, are you suffering from hot flashes during menopause?	
Metabolism (muh-tab-uh-liz-uh m): The combination of production, maintenance, and destruction within the organism.	
Mouth: The mouth is an orifice through which food and air enters the body. The Dentist says, open your mouth wider.	
Muscle (muhs-uhl): Muscle is tissue composed of cells or fibers; do you have the muscle to lift that?	
Nails (neylz): Nails are horn-like covers or claws on the tips of the fingers or at the ends of toes.	
Nail polish: Nail polish is a type of lacquer that can be applied to human fingernails or toenails.	
Nearsighted (neer-sahy-tid): Myopic (mahy-op-ik), nearsighted people can only see objects up close.	
Neck: The neck is the part of the body that connects the head to the torso.	
Nose (nohz): The nose is the body's primary organ of smell. The nose is a protuberance (proh-too-ber-uhns) in vertebrates that contains the nostrils and is part of the respiratory system.	
Nostrils (nos-truhl): Can you flare or widen your nostrils?	
Ointment (oint-muhnt): An oily (oi-lee) preparation for the skin.	

Organic (awr-gan-ik):	A farming method without the use of manufactured fertilizers, or pesticides. Is that produce 100 %(one hundred per-cent) organic?
Physique (fi-zeek):	Circuit (sur-kit) training is excellent for physique. The form, size and development of the body.
Razor (rey-zer):	Where will I find razors for shaving?
Ridge (rij):	The gum ridge located at the top of your mouth is vital in making proper sounds.
Scissors (siz-erz):	People used to say, "Pair of scissors" now they say, "scissors."
Skin:	Bruce, a legacy celebrity Director of Hair and Makeup mentioned Estee Lauder (law-der), Lancôme and MAC and added that makeup artists use the following: a concealer, to disguise (dis-gahyz) discoloration, a matt finish to reduce shine, and a luminous (loo-muh-nuhs) or a silky finish for dispersing the reflection of light on the skin.
Skull (skuhl):	The skull contains the brain and keeps the face in one place. The bones that comprise the skull are the following: parietal (puh-rahy-i-tl), occipital (ok-sip-i-tl), temporal (tem-per-uhl), auditory canal (aw-di-tawr-ee kuh-nal), zygomata (zahy-goh-muh-tuh), mastoid(mas-toid), mandible(man-duh-buhl), maxilla(mak-sil-uh) nasal, sphenoid(sfee-noid) and frontal(fruhn-tl).
Soap:	Soap is a substance used with water for washing and cleaning, available in scented or unscented forms.
Stethoscope (steth-uh-skohp):	The stethoscope is a Doctor's instrument worn around the neck and eventually placed in the ears for examining a patient's heart, lungs, and liver by listening through the devices channeling membrane (mem-breyn) and amplifying abilities.
Stomach (stuhm-uhk):	The stomach is the organ (awr-guhn) where food passes through in the initial stages of digestion.
Stroke (strohk):	Some of the signs of a stroke are numbness in arm, leg or face, sudden difficulty in speaking, blurred or double vision, loss of balance, extreme headache. Also known as F.A.S.T. (face drooping, arm weakness, speech difficulty, and time to call 911). Also see S.T.R. (smile, talk, raise) Examine the tongue, if it is crooked or goes to one side, seek immediate medical attention.
Teeth:	Teeth are used to masticate (or chew) food and are the hardest substance of the body. Types of teeth are premolars, incisors, and canine molars. The parts of a tooth are enamel, dentine, crown, neck, root canal gum tissue, cement, nerve, blood vessels, and bone. Humans have from 28 to 32 teeth. White sharks have 3,000 triangular teeth.
Tendon (ten-duhn):	A tendon is a tough band of fibrous (fahy-bruhs) connective tissue that can withstand tension while holding bones and muscles together.
Throat (throht):	The throat (throht) is the front of the neck below the chin and above the collarbone.
Thumb (thuhm):	The thumb is the short, first digit of the hand, set lower and separated from the other fingers.
Toes (tohz):	Toes are the digits of the foot.
Tongue (tuhng):	The tongue is a versatile (vur-suh-tl) organ in vertebrates attached to the floor of the mouth and used for ingestion of food, the sense of taste and is the instrument of speech.

Travel (trav-uhl) kit:	The travel kit contains: Shampoo (sham-poo), crème rinse (kreem rins), soap (sohp), shaving (shey-ving) crème, nail polish (neyl pol-ish), nail polish remover (ri-moo-ver), band-aids(band-eyds), needle(need-l) and thread(thred), and a full sewing(soh-ing) kit with buttons(buht-nz) and scissors(siz-erz).
Tympanic nerve (tim-pan-ik nurv):	The tympanic nerve (nurv) is connected to the inner ear and transfers nerve impulses to the brain.
Vein (veyn):	The veins are any of the blood vessels that carry blood from the capillaries to the heart.
Vertebra (ver-tuh-bruh):	The vertebra encloses the spinal (spahyn-l) cord.
Waist (weyst):	Your waistline is decreasing; Jeff, have you been working out between writing scripts, raising Gypsy, and selling coins?
Wrist (rist):	The wrist is the joint between the hand and the arm.

10.4 Difficult words and sentences 2

From the many difficult and confusing American English words.

Exercise 1: Repeat the word and then the sentence aloud.
Exercise 2: Create a new complete sentence for each word.

1.	Acoustic (uh-koo-stik): Those acoustic tiles are great; I can hardly hear anything.
2.	Allegiance (uh-lee-juhns): Currently there are 43 states that require reciting the Pledge of Allegiance in public schools.
3.	Ambulance (am-byuh-luhns): The ambulance had a deafening siren so that all would hear and move aside.
4.	Appointment (uh-point-muhnt): She arrived on time for her appointment.
5.	Approve (uh-proov): Please read and then approve the assignment.
6.	Asthma (az-muh): Be aware of the trigger mechanisms for asthma such as dust, pollen, hair, mold, cold, moisture, fur, and food allergies.
7.	Attaché (a-ta-shey): The attaché case needs to go through the security checkpoint.
8.	Attention (uh-ten-shuhn): Please pay attention to the details; sometimes, they are the most important part.
9.	Bacon (bey-kuhn): I ordered a bacon, lettuce, and tomato sandwich, otherwise known as a BLT.
10.	Beachwood (beech-wood): Beachwood canyon leads to a magnificent view of the Hollywood Sign.
11.	Boat (boht): Have you ever been on a boat? A boat is a small craft propelled (pruh-peld) on water designed with buoyancy (boi-uhn-see) to float.
12.	Britain (Brit-n): Have you been to Britain?
13.	Charade (shuh-reyd): Have you seen the debonair (deb-uh-nair) Cary Grant and Walter Matthau in Stanley Donen's film entitled Charade (shuh-reyd)?
14.	Choke (chohk): Open the choke first, to let the fuel go into the carburetor and then start the car.
15.	Combustion (kuhm-buhs-chuhn): Do you know the combustion ratio of your engine?

16.	Concert: The Led Zeppelin concert at Madison Square Garden in 1974 was sold out, but if you look carefully in the film of the tour, you can see me in the audience, second row, second seat, next to my sister, Randee.
17.	Cosmology (koz-mol-uh-jee): In the study of Cosmology, there are still many unanswered questions regarding the fate of the universe.
18.	Courageous(kuh-rey-juhs): Be courageous, and mighty forces will come to your aid, says Frances McDormand in the Rock n' Roll film, Almost Famous, a quote from the writer, Goethe(gur-tuh).
19.	Curly (kur-lee): Is her hair that curly?
20.	Debut (dey-byoo): The product will make its debut this spring.
21.	Decision (dih-sizh-uhn): I haven't made my decision yet about running for Governor.
22.	Definitely (def-uh-nit-lee): I definitely will be at bowling practice, don't worry.
23.	Dehumanize (dee-hyoo-muh-nahyz): Don't allow them to dehumanize the people.
24.	Democratic (dem-uh-krat-ik): That was very democratic of you.
25.	Dishes: Let me get the dishes.
26.	Education (ej-oo-key-shuhn): Education is the cornerstone of growth.
27.	Entrepreneur (ahn-truh-pruh-nur): He was a great entrepreneur and started many different businesses.
28.	Epicures (ep-i-kyoo-ree-uh-niz-uhm): Of course, the epicure's meeting was held inside the gourmet restaurant.
29.	Fabulous (fab-yuh-luhs): That's a fabulous ice-skating routine.
30.	Financial (fi-nan-shuhl): Can we see your financial statement for the business.
31.	Forms: Did they use the correct forms?
32.	Fox (foks): The quick brown fox jumped over the lazy dog.
33.	Gamble (gam-buhl): She likes to gamble at the casinos in Las Vegas.
34.	Gorgeous (gawr-juhs): That Ferrari looks gorgeous, said the student from Italy.
35.	Government (guhv-ern-muhnt): It's July 4th, most government offices are closed today.
36.	Halloween (hal-uh-ween): What's your costume for Halloween?
37.	Harmony (hahr-muh-nee): Astronomy is often referred to as the harmony of the spheres (sfeers).
38.	Height (hahyt): In case you were wondering, the height of the Golden Gate Bridge is 746' (seven-hundred forty-six feet).
39.	Heinous (hey-nuhs): The color of that car was a heinous lime green.
40.	Heirloom (air-loom): Did you want the heirloom tomatoes in your salad?
41.	Idea (ahy-dee-uh): What was that idea you had about a perpetual motion machine?
42.	Illinois (il-uh-noi): Have you been to Chicago, Illinois? It's a great American city full of old restaurants and Jazz clubs.
43.	Internship (in-turn-ship): Is it too early to apply for the internship?
44.	Invent (in-vent): Well, did you invent anything practical this time?
45.	Kettle (ket-l): Please put a kettle on the stove for Tea.
46.	Law: Have you ever thought of going to Law School?

47.	Lemon (lem-uhn): Would you like a lime or lemon with your iced tea?
48.	Lighten (lahyt-n): Toss the ballast (bal-uhst) to lighten (lahyt-n) the load.
49.	Lipton (lip-tuhn): In the movie Rosemary's Baby, Ruth Gordon says to Mia Farrow; it's just Lipton's.
50.	Low: Drive slowly over the potholes, your car has low clearance.
51.	Mach (mahk): A fighter jet is flying supersonic, aka Mach 1, when it travels above the speed of sound.
52.	Miners (mahy-ners): The miners wore masks to help them breathe underground.
53.	Minors (mahy-ners): Are you an underage minor?
54.	Morbid (mawr-bid): She had a morbid fascination and was always walking through the cemetery (sem-i-ter-ee).
55.	Mountain (moun-tn): Would you like to climb that mountain?
56.	Often (aw-fuhn): Sam B. would often bring Linus the Yorkshire (yawrk-sheer) Terrier (ter-ee-er) in for a visit to the café.
57.	Outsourcing (out-sawrs-ing): Sorry, I hear they will be outsourcing your job.
58.	Oysters (oi-sters): There are many different varieties of oysters.
59.	Parenthesis (puh-ren-thuh-sis): Please write the years served in office in parenthesis.
60.	Penitentiary (pen-i-ten-shuh-ree): They got locked up at the penitentiary for robbery, assault, and battery.
61.	Phonograph(foh-nuh-graf): Is that phonograph in working order?
62.	Plenitude (plen-i-tood): There was a plenitude of volunteers at the zoo.
63.	Quantum (kwon-tuhm): Can you explain quantum mechanics again?
64.	Raven (rey-vuhn): The Raven by Edgar Allan Poe is one, if not the best, American Poem ever written.
65.	Reckless (rek-lis): Sol said, don't be reckless with that new credit card.
66.	Record(ri-kawrd): Let's record that record(rek-erd).
67.	Ricochet (rik-uh-shey): Careful that bullet might ricochet off the marble walls.
68.	Sanctuary (sangk-choo-er-ee): In the film, Logan's Run, they are looking for sanctuary, a place where the sun shines, and the rivers flow with fresh water.
69.	Schizophrenia (skit-suh-free-nee-uh): She suffered badly from schizophrenia and needed help.
70.	Douglas(duhg-luhs): Ask Douglas, for his legal opinion; he went to Harvard(hahr-verd).
71.	Species: The structure of the animal kingdom uses the following classification system: Phylum/division/class/order/family/genus/species.
72.	Strategy (strat-i-jee): Chess is most certainly a game of strategy.
73.	Succeed: You will succeed at this job if you come early, work hard, and stay late, said the Manager.
74.	Suggestion (suh-g-jes-chuhn): A suggestion is an idea, plan, or concept to try. May I suggest?
75.	Taught (tawt): He taught at the University.
76.	Taunt (tawnt): Don't taunt the tigers, if you want to live.

77.	Taut (tawt): Make that line taut.
78.	Terrarium (tuh-rair-ee-uhm): Did you see the lizards amongst (uh-muhngst) the cacti (kak-tahy) in the terrarium at the school?
79.	Thermometer(ther-mom-i-ter): If the thermometer reads more than 98.6 degrees, you have a fever.
80.	Toiled: They toiled in the field all day.
81.	Trestle (tres-uhl): The train went over the trestle.
82.	Vandalism (van-dl-iz-uhm): The vandalism at that store was thorough and costly.
83.	Washes: Who washes their car in winter?
84.	Worm (wurm): In the film, Office Space, Milton's T-shirt says, I ate the worm.
85.	Worse (wurs): Did the storm get worse?
86.	Zinc (zingk): Iron (ahy-ern) is coated with Zinc for added protection.

10.5 Tongue Twisters 5

For Tongue Twisters, the best strategy is to look carefully at each and every word. Keep your eye on the word.

Also, students do much better when they know what all the words mean, so please look up new words or phrases.

Exercise 1: Repeat the following tongue twisters aloud. Practice until they flow easily. Go slow at first, then faster and faster and faster…remember to have fun. Laugh.

Exercise 2: Create your own tongue twister.

For maximum benefits, try to repeat each tongue twister three times. (3x)
1. Betty Botter bought some butter(buht-er),
But, she said, the butter's bitter;
If I put it in my batter,
It will make my batter bitter.
But, a bit of better butter,
Will make my batter better.
So, she bought a bit of butter,
Better than her bitter butter,
And she put it in her batter,
And the batter was not bitter.
So, it was better Betty Botter,
Bought a bit of better butter.
2. I am not the pheasant plucker (fez-uhnt pluhkr),

I'm the pheasant plucker's mate.
I am only plucking pheasants,
Cause the pheasant plucker's running late.
Say each 3x... (Three times)
3. Three free throws.
4. Shy Shelly says she shall sew sheets.
5. Knapsack (nap-sak) straps.
6. Which wristwatches are Swiss (swis) wristwatches?
7. Red leather (leth-er), yellow leather (leth-er).
8. The rain in Spain stays mainly in the plain.
9. In Hartford, Hereford, and Hampshire (hamp-sheer), hurricanes hardly ever happen.
10. Madame Minnie made a mound of many melons.
11. Rubber Baby Buggy Bumpers.
12. She sells seashells at the seashore. Are the seashells she sells seashells for sure?
13. How much wood would a woodchuck chuck if a woodchuck could chuck wood? A woodchuck would chuck all the wood he could if a woodchuck could chuck wood.
14. Clean clams crammed in clean cans.

10.6 Synonyms 7

Words with the same or similar meanings. Try to research the differences between these words and their uses. Deep learning or shallow.

Exercise 1: Practice saying the following synonyms aloud. Go across the row.
Exercise 2: Create a sentence for each word.

Word	Synonym	Synonym
1. Adequate(ad-i-kwit)	sufficient(suh-fish-uhnt)	enough(ih-nuhf)
2. Almost(awl-mohst)	nearly(neer-lee)	hardly(hahrd-lee)
3. Alone(uh-lohn)	solitary(sol-i-ter-ee)	single(sing-guhl)
4. Approximate(uh-prok-suh-mit)	about(uh-bout)	rough(ruhf)
5. Ask(ahsk)	inquire(in-kwahyuhr)	question(kwes-chuhn)
6. Bring(bring)	take(teyk)	fetch(fech)
7. Buy(bahy)	get(get)	purchase(pur-chuhs)
8. Can(kan)	may(mey)	could(kood)
9. Chance(chahns)	opportunity(op-er-too-ni-tee)	occasion(uh-key-zhuhn)
10. Cheap(cheep)	inexpensive(in-ik-spen-siv)	bargain(bahr-guhn)
11. Damp(damp)	moist(moist)	humid(hyoo-mid)

12. Habit(hab-it)	custom(kuhs-tuhm)	tradition(truh-dish-uhn)
13. Infrequent(in-free-kwuhnt)	rare(rair)	scarce(skairs)
14. Join(join)	enroll(en-rohl)	enlist(en-list)
15. Just(juhst)	already(awl-red-ee)	yet(yet)
16. Meditate(med-i-teyt)	ponder(pon-der)	think(thingk)
17. Memorial(muh-mawr-ee-uhl)	commemoration(kuh-mem-uh-rey-shuhn)	monument(mon-yuh-muhnt)
18. Mention(men-shuhn)	allude(uh-lood)	refer(ri-fur)
19. Merge(murj)	blend(blend)	fuse(fyooz)
20. Narrow(nar-oh)	confined(kuhn-fahynd)	restricted(ri-strik-tid)
21. Nature(ney-cher)	aspect(as-pekt)	character(kar-ik-ter)
22. necessary (nes-uh-ser-ee)	mandatory(man-duh-tawr-ee)	requisite(rek-wuh-zit)
23. negate(ni-geyt)	contradict(kon-truh-dikt)	refute(ri-fyoot)
24. negligent (neg-lij-uhnt)	careless(kair-lis)	remiss(ri-mis)
25. negotiate(ni-goh-shee-yet)	bargain(bahr-guhn)	deal(deel)
26. nervous(nur-vuhs)	uneasy(uhn-ee-zee)	anxious(angk-shuhs)
27. nice(nahys)	affable(af-uh-buhl)	benign(bih-nahyn)
28. noble(noh-buhl)	aristocratic (uh-ris-tuh-krat-ik)	distinguished (dih-sting-gwisht)
29. noise(noiz)	sound(sound)	racket(rak-it)
30. novice(nov-is)	beginner(bih-gin-er)	nonprofessional(non-pruh-fesh-uh-nl)
31. nuisance(noo-suhns)	annoyance(uh-noi-uhns)	offense(uh-fens)
32. obedient(oh-bee-dee-uhnt)	faithful(feyth-fuhl)	loyal(loi-uhl)
33. objection(uhb-jek-shuhn)	disapproval(dis-uh-proo-vuhl)	protest(proh-test)
34. obligatory(uh-blig-uh-tawr-ee)	compulsory(kuhm-puhl-suh-ree)	required(ri-kwahy-uhrd)
35. pay(pey)	salary(sal-uh-ree)	wages(wages)
36. place(pleys)	location(loh-key-shuhn)	spot(spot)
37. propose(pruh-pohz)	intend(in-tend)	suggest(suhg-jest)
38. reason(ree-zuhn)	explanation(ek-spluh-ney-shuhn)	excuse(ik-skyooz)
39. refuse(ri-fyooz)	reject(ri-jekt)	decline(dih-klahyn)
40. rubbish(ruhb-ish)	garbage(gahr-bij)	trash(trash)
41. slim(slim)	lean(leen)	skinny(skin-ee)
42. speak(speek)	talk(tawk)	discuss(dih-skuhs)
43. start(stahrt)	begin(bih-gin)	commence(kuh-mens)

44. steal(steel)	take(teyk)	rob(rob)
45. still(stil)	already(already)	yet(yet)
46. taste(teyst)	try(trahy)	sample(sam-puhl)
47. thin(thin)	slim(slim)	slender(slen-der)
48. thus(thuhs)	therefore(thair-fawr)	consequently(kon-si-kwent-lee)
49. travel(trav-uhl)	journey(jur-nee)	voyage(voi-ij)
50. trouble (truhb-uhl)	worry (wur-ee)	bother (both-er)
51. under (uhn-der)	below (bih-loh)	beneath (bih-neeth)
52. wide (wahyd)	big (big)	large(lahrj)
53. win (win)	beat(beet)	triumph (trahy-uhmf)
54. world (wurld	earth(urth)	land(land)

10.7 Compare and Contrast 4

There are many words in English that sound so similar. Here is a list of often confused words. Practice the following pairs of words aloud. To be sure they are pronounced differently, check the phonetics of the word.

Exercise 1: Review aloud the different sounds and the sentences that follow.
Exercise 2: Create another sentence for each word.

Pair (pair)
Fair (fair)
Do you have a matching pair of wine glasses?
That's a fair question to ask.
Also (awl-soh)
Although (awl-th-oh)
It also started to thunder.
Although I ate earlier, I'm still hungry.
Angry (angry)
Hungry (huhng-gree)
Don't be angry there's still food left.
How can you still be hungry?
Art (ahrt)
Heart (hahrt)
There is a real art to parallel parking.
She sent him a card with a heart on it for Valentine's Day.

Ate (eyt)
Hate (heyt)
I ate before I got here.
I hate being late to a movie.
Back (bak)
Bag (bag)
Let's get back to basics, where do you think you parked?
The bag is in the trunk.
Bass (beys)
Bash (bash)
The standup bass is a large woodwind instrument.
Jump with Joey played many musical bashes at the King King when it was on 6th and La Brea.
Batch (bach)
Badge (baj)
What batches of classes are you taking this semester?
We don't need any badges, is a famous line from the film The Treasure of Sierra(see-er-uh) Madre(mah-drey).
Stir (stur)
Star (stahr)
Did you stir the soup?
A receding star produces a redshift.
Decibels (des-uh-belz)
Decimals (des-uh-muhlz)
Keep the decibels down, said the parent.
More digits to the left of the decimal said the musician.
Straight (streyt)
Street (street)
Don't dawdle come straight home.
Which street do you live on?
Taxes (taks)
Texas (tek-suhs)
Taxes are collected at the time of purchase.

Texas gals are the best.
Tech (tek)
Take (teyk)
The new office is very tech oriented.
Let's take a break.
Ten (ten)
Tale (teyl)
Take all the time you want; you have ten minutes.
It was a tall tale he told.
Test (test)
Taste (teyst)
Let's test the second stage before the launch.
This parfait (pahr-fey) tastes delicious.
Tone (tohn)
Torn (tawrn)
I hope you are not off-key and tone-deaf like the last sound engineer.
She was torn between her career and raising a family.
Wash (wosh)
Watch (woch)
Please wash the red metallic Aston Martin by hand.
Watch out for cars running red lights.
Jet (jet)
Yet (yet)
I'm late let's jet.
Did they announce the winners yet?
Way (wey)
We (wee)
Which way do we go?
We are not going anywhere.
Well (wel)
Whale (hweyl)
Well, that is the end of my paycheck, for sure.

The Blue whale can make sounds as loud as 180 decibels, the loudest sound of any animal on earth.
West (west)
Waste (weyst)
Go west, young man.
Don't waste your time; get busy.
Wish (wish)
Witch (wich)
I'd like to wish for three more wishes.
How many witches are in the play, Wicked?
Woke (wohk)
Walk (walk)
He woke early for the exam.
Let's take a walk in the forest.
Spanish (span-ish)
Spinach (spin-ich)
Is it time for Spanish class?
I'd like the sautéed spinach with garlic.
Rule (rool)
Role (rohl)
Roll (rohl)
Better to rule on the road, then serve donuts in the office.
Can I audition for that role?
Did you see the car rollover?
Really (ree-uh-lahy)
Weary (weer-ee)
Do you really want the last piece of Apple pie?
Everyone was weary after the 20-mile marathon.

10.8 Prefixes, Suffixes and Roots 2

The following pages contain a list of prefixes and suffixes along with definitions and example sentences. Notice how the words are constructed with these new beginnings and endings.

Prefixes can be used to form negatives also by adding (un, in, im, il, ir, dis, de, non).

Exercise 1: Recite aloud the following words, definitions, and example sentences.

Example word: Prefix/Definition	Example Sentence	Prefix	Meaning
Abnormal (ab-nawr-muhl): Deviating from the usual.	That reading is abnormal.	Ab-	From
Antemeridian (an-tee-muh-rid-ee-ehn): In the morning.	We traveled across the antemeridian.	Ante-	Before
Antiseptic (an-tuh-sep-tik): Scrupulously (skroo-pyuh-luhs) clean or pure.	Antiseptics is the answer to killing germs and microorganisms.	Anti-	Against
Antifreeze (an-ti-freez): is an addictive that not only lowers the freezing point of water-based solutions but also raises their boiling point. Used mostly in radiators.	The antifreeze protects the engine fluids from freezing.	Anti-	Against
Antihero (an-tee-heer-oh): is a central figure in a story that lacks the standard characteristics of a hero.	The antihero wasn't a conventional hero, he lacked the qualities of courage, sacrifice, and commitment.	Anti-	Against
Antisocial(an-tee-soh-shuhl): Having difficulty behaving in a normal or friendly manner.	He was very antisocial and didn't seek the company of others.	Anti-	Against
Antivirus: is software designed to prevent, detect, and remove malware from the computer.	He bought the antivirus software to protect his laptop.	Anti-	Against
Autocracy (aw-tok-ruh-see): An autocracy is a form of government in which supreme power (social and political) is in the hands of one person.	That country is clearly an autocracy.	Auto-	Self
Cocreate: To bring different parties together in order to produce an outcome.	To create (something) by working with one or more others.	Co-	Together/with

Coexist(koh-ig-zist): To exist at the same time and or the same place.	Neanderthals are an extinct subspecies from the genus Homo who coexisted in Eurasia about 400,000 years ago.	Co-	Together/with
Cooperate(koh-op-uh-reyt): To work together towards a mutually beneficial ending.	When stopped by police, it is mandatory that they cooperate with their demands.	Co-	Together/with
Cosign(koh-sahyn): To sign for a loan or lease with another party to guarantee payment.	They required a cosigner for the car loan.	Co-	Together/with
Contradiction (kon-truh-dik-shuhn): An assertion of the contrary or opposite.	That's a contradiction in terms.	Contra-	Against
Discount (dis-kount): To deduct a certain amount from a bill or purchase.	Everything at the store has a 10% discount.	Dis-	Not
Disappear (dis-uh-peer): To no longer be visible.	Where did she disappear to?	Dis-	Not
Disbelief(dis-bi-leef): Refusal to accept (ak-sept) something is real or true.	Moses shook his head in a state of disbelief.	Dis-	Not
Disconnect(dis-kuh-nekt): To break a connection or agreement with two or more parties.	Sorry, but we got disconnected on that phone call.	Dis-	Not
Disinfect(dis-in-fekt): Using a chemical to destroy bacteria and clean the area.	First, they need to disinfect the wound.	Dis-	Not
Extragalactic (ek-struh-guh-lak-tik) Coming from outside the Milky Way Galaxy.	The extragalactic visitor landed his UFO at the airport.	Extra-	More
Foreclose (fawr-klohz): To take possession of a mortgaged property.	Did they foreclose on that house yet?	Fore-	Before
Foreground (fawr-ground): The part of the picture that is nearest to the photographer.	The alien was in the foreground of the photo.	Fore-	Before
Foresee (fawr-see): To be aware of something before it happens.	Can he foresee any problems we might have?	Fore-	Before
Foreword (fawr-wurd): A short introduction to a book,	Has he written the foreword yet?	Fore-	Before

usually written by a person other than the author.			
Hypercritical: (hahy-per-krit-i-kuhl) Someone who is excessively and unreasonably critical especially of small faults.	Please don't be hypercritical with the intern.	Hyper-	More
Illegible (ih-lej-uh-buhl): Something that is not clear enough to be read.	That note is illegible, what does it say?	Il-	Not
Impartial (im-pahr-shuhl): Treating all rival members of the group equally and fairly.	But can the jury be impartial?	Im-	Not
Inactivity (in-ak-tiv-i-tee): a state of lack of activity, laziness.	After five minutes of inactivity, the computer turns itself off.	In-	Not
Inappropriate (in-uh-proh-pree-it): Unbefitting.	That comment is inappropriate.	In-	Not
Incorrect (in-kuh-rekt): Wrong.	Happily, they were incorrect.	In-	Not
Injustice (in-juhs-tis): A lack of justice.	The injustice was over a recent pay cut.	In-	Not
Involuntary (in-vol-uhn-ter-ee): Done without will, or control.	That's an involuntary reaction.	In-	Not
Interchangeable: (in-ter-cheyn-juh-buhl, Objects that can be substituted for each other without any effect.	The lenses are interchangeable, said the photographer.	Inter-	Between
Interact (in-ter-akt): The connection and mixing of two or more objects or subjects for a desired result.	At the petting zoo, children can interact with small animals.	Inter-	Between
Interlock (in-ter-lok): When two or more objects connect or fit together.	The building is secure with many interlocking mechanisms.	Inter-	Between
Intermingle (in-ter-ming-guhl): To mix or mingle together.	Did the guests intermingle at the party?	Inter-	Between
Interstellar (in-ter-stel-er): To travel between stars.	That's clearly an interstellar spacecraft.	Inter-	Between
Intramural (in-truh-myoor-uhl): Using only students at the same school or college:	Is football an intramural sport?	Intra-	inside
Irrational (ih-rash-uh-nl): Not logical or reasonable.	Is that number an irrational number also?	Ir-	Not

Magnification (mag-nuh-fi-key-shuhn): The process of magnifying something usually visually as with a magnifying glass.	What is the strongest magnification on that microscope?	Magni-	Great
Misfire (mis-fiuhr): To fail to fire or to discharge improperly.	That motor misfired and needs a tune-up.	Mis-	Not
Misbehave (mis-bi-heyv): To act badly or improperly to a specific situation.	Every character in a script needs a few misbehaviors.	Mis-	Not
Misinform (mis-in-fawrm): To release false or incorrect information for a desired effect.	The students were misinformed about the upcoming tornado.	Mis-	Not
Mislead (mis-leed): To guide astray or in the wrong direction for a desired purpose.	During the interrogation he misled the team.	Mis-	Not
Misspell (mis-spel): To spell something incorrectly or against the standard.	Watch out for misspellings on the paper.	Mis-	Not
Monochromatic: (mon-uh-kroh-mat-ik) Pertaining to the light of one color or a narrow range of wavelengths.	I used the monochromatic filter.	Mono-	One
Multivitamin (muhl-ti-vahy-tuh-min) A pill that contains a combination of vitamins.	My brain needs a multivitamin.	Multi-	many
Nonviolent (non-vahy-uh-luhnt): Using peaceful means to bring about political or social change.	I thought the demonstration was supposed to be nonviolent, why are they burning that car?	Non-	Not
Nonlinear (non-lin-ee-er): Something that is not in a straight line.	Let's solve that non-linear equation.	Non-	Not
Nonsense (non-sens): Spoken or written words that are confusing or irrational.	What a bunch of nonsense.	Non-	Not
Omnivorous (om-niv-er-uhs): The eating of both animal and plant foods.	That ostrich is omnivorous.	Omni-	All
Overdone (oh-ver-duhn): When something is cooked too long or an exaggeration	That chicken is overdone.	Over	Too much

of a bad situation or romance.			
Overflow (oh-ver-floh): To run over a level previously set.	The water in the cup was overflowing.	Over	Too much
Overpower (oh-ver-pou-er): To overtake a situation through the use of force.	The mob overpowered the security team.	Over	Too much
Polyglot (pol-ee-glot): The ability to speak or write several different languages.	How many languages does Belle, the polyglot from Germany know?	Poly-	Many
Postmortem (pohst-mawr-tuhm): After the death.	They're going to perform a postmortem.	Post-	After
Premeditated (pri-med-i-tey-tid). An idea or thought about an event or action before the occurrence.	Was that a premeditated murder?	Pre-	Before
Precaution (pri-kaw-shuhn): A measure taken before an event to secure positive results.	I had to remind the cat lady to put the harness on the Persian cat as a precaution.	Pre-	Before
Predetermine (pree-di-tur-min): A precaution taken to prevent a negative outcome of an event or situation.	Is the universe predetermined?	Pre-	Before
Premature (pree-muh-choor): Mature or ready before the chosen time.	That Oscar acceptance speech is a bit premature; don't you think?	Pre-	Before
Preview (pree-vyoo): An earlier or an advance viewing.	Will they preview that new film?	Pre-	Before
Reissue (ree-ish-oo): Anything that is issued or rereleased.	They reissued the vinyl.	Re-	Back/again
Reassign (re-uh-sahyn): To change or alter an assignment or situation.	After that negative comment, he was reassigned to Siberia.	Re-	Back/again
Regain (ree-geyn): To gain or get what was once gone.	Regain your confidence and be fierce.	Re-	Back/again
Resend (ree-send): To send or ship something an additional time.	Can you resend that email?	Re-	Back/again
Reuse (re-yooz): To use again an object or material that had previously been used.	We can easily reuse that glass container.	Re-	Back/again

Retrospective (re-truh-spek-tiv): Is looking at a previously shown exhibit or performance.	I'm going to the retrospective at the museum.	Retro-	Back
Semisweet (sem-ee-sweet): A slightly sweet substance or material for consumption.	Do they have those semisweet dark chocolate cookies?	Semi-	Half
Submarine (suhb-muh-reen): A sealed boat used to go underwater.	The submarine can stay underwater for long periods of time.	Sub-	Under
Subconscious (suhb-kon-shuhs): Concerning the part of the mind that one is not even aware of but that influences one's actions and emotions.	Hypnotism works on the subconscious.	Sub-	Under
Subfloor (suhb-flawr): The subfloor runs under that floor.	The cable systems run through the subfloor.	Sub-	Under
Subtitle (suhb-tahyt-l): Captions that appear displayed on the screen that either transcribes or translates the original dialogue.	The subtitle revealed additional details about the research study.	Sub-	Under
Supertanker (soo-per tang-ker): A very large container ship usually associated with the transport of oil or gas.	The supertanker had an oil spill.	Super-	More
Transmitter (trans-mit-er): A device used to communicate between different parties.	Can the transmitter go under water?	Trans-	Across
Ultramodern (uhl-truh-mod-ern): A situation or condition that is beyond the standard usually directed towards the future.	I like the ultramodern kitchen.	Ultra-	More
Unreliable (uhn-ri-lahy-uh-buhl): A person, thing or device that is not always available or working properly.	That driver is unreliable.	Un-	Not
Universe (yoo-nuh-vurs): That which contains all and everything.	How large is the Universe?	Uni-	One

10.9 Noun suffixes

Exercise: Recite aloud the following examples and their sentences. Review suffixes and meanings.

Word example	Example Sentences	Suffix	Meaning
Participation (pahr-tis-uh-pey-shuhn): Taking part in some action or event.	Class participation is very important.	-tion	Act of
Motherhood (muhth-er-hood): The state of being a mother or sharing a goodness.	She's enjoying her motherhood.	-hood	State of
Happiness (hap-ee-nis): The state of having good fortune, pleasure and the resulting joy which is produced.	Your happiness is intertwined (in-ter-twahynd) with your outlook on life.	-ness	State of
Makeshift (meyk-shift): A temporary substitute for an item or situation.	We can use your makeshift invention until the standard part arrives.	-ship	State of
Multitude (muhl-ti-tood): A variety of choices or options.	There are a multitude of choices.	-tude	State of
Kingdom (king-duhm): A state, country or government having a king or queen at top.	The kingdom has a dragon at the entrance.	-dom	State of
Volunteer (vol-uhn-teer): A person who offers his or her services for free or to complete a program or degree.	Let's volunteer at the zoo.	-eer	A doer of

Verb suffixes

Exercise: Recite aloud the following examples and their sentences. Review suffixes and meanings.

Example	Example Sentences	Suffix	Meaning
Substantiate (suh b-stan-shee-yet): To establish either by proof or evidence.	That contract helps to substantiate his claim.	-ate	To make
Liquefy (lik-wuh-fahy): To create a liquid or make something become liquid.	They need to liquify that aluminum to make a model of the ant colony nest.	-ify	To make
Harmonize (hahr-muh-nahyz): To bring something either musical or an action into agreement.	We need to harmonize the singers.	-ize	To make
Harden (hahr-dn): To make something harder than it already is, or to make someone more difficult to reach.	The high heat was used to harden the metal.	-en	To cause to be

Adjectival suffixes

Exercise: Recite aloud the following examples and their sentences. Review suffixes and meanings.

Example	Example Sentences	Suffix	Meaning
Reliable (ri-lahy-uh-buhl): Something or someone that is dependable and can be trusted and counted on.	This car is very reliable and started right up.	-able	Able to be
Contemptible (kuhn-temp-tuh-buhl): Someone or something that is despicable or mean.	Your attitude towards this court is contemptible.	-ible	Able to be
Compensate (kom-puhn-seyt): To provide for or be an equivalent, recompense, to remunerate.	Can we review the compensation plan?	-ate	Full of
Plentiful (plen-ti-fuhl): In abundance, existing in great quantity.	The oranges are plentiful this year.	-ful	Full of
Humorous (hyoo-mer-uhs): Something or someone that is funny and/or comical.	That's a very humorous film.	-ous	Full of
Rarely (rair-lee): An occurrence that happens infrequently.	It rarely rains in Los Angeles.	-y	Full of
Ageless (eyj-lis): A person who is not aging or not appearing to grow old.	Her beauty is ageless, but you should see the painting.	-less	Without
Snakelike (sneyk-lahyk): A treacherous person.	She's always so snakelike at the casino (kuh-see-noh).	-like	Characteristic of
Happily (hap-uh-lee): A person or situation having a happy time.	I will happily drive you to the airport.	-ly	Characteristic of

10.10 Common Root Words

Exercise 1: Recite aloud the following roots, definitions, and sentences.

Sentence	Root	Meaning
1. Did you activate the card?	act	to do
2. Have you seen the film, Aquaman?	aqua	water
3. Meet me in the auditorium (aw-di-tawr-ee-uhm).	audi	hear
4. Tesla has auto drive.	auto	self
5. The bibliography (bib-lee-og-ruh-fee) is at the end of the book.	biblio	book
6. Have you read Gauguin's autobiography Noa, Noa?	bio	life
7. Can I see your marine chronometer (kruh-nom-i-ter)?	chrono	time
8. Let them circle around.	circ	round
9. Have you ever ridden (rid-n) a unicycle (yoo-nuh-sahy-kuhl)?	cycl	circle
10. Did you find the document?	doc	teach
11. Are you a geologist?	geo	earth

10.11 Onomatopoeias

Onomatopoeias (on-uh-mat-uh-pee-uhs) Words that suggest the source of the sound.

Exercise 1: Repeat aloud the following onomatopoeias (on-uh-mat-uh-pee-uhs) and their sentences.

Exercise 2: Create your own sentence after listening to the sound.

1. Bang (bang): The gun let out a loud bang sound.	
2. Bling (bling-bling): She wore so much jewelry, all I could hear was bling every time she moved.	
3. Boom (boom): The jet gave off a sonic boom as it passed Mach 1.	
4. Bow-wow (bow-wow): The dog made a bow-wow sound.	
5. Buzz (buhz): The bumble bees buzzed as they flew from flower to flower.	
6. Chirp (churp): The cell phone's ringer made a chirping sound; it sounded just like a small bird.	
7. Clang (klang): The monk hit the bell, which caused a clanging sound.	
8. Clink (klingk): They clinked their glasses together at the end of the toast.	
9. Coo (koo): Did you hear the pigeons coo?	
10. Crackle (krak-uhl): The fire made a crackle sound as it burned.	

10.12 Astrology

Discussing astrology is always a fun topic and it's international.

Months of the year, Constellations, Birthstones, and Birth flowers.

Exercise: Repeat the sign, the dates covered, the Constellation description, birthstone, and flower aloud.

Aquarius (uh-kwair-ee-uhs): January (jan-yoo-er-ee) 20th- February (feb-roo-er-ee) 18th: The Water Bearer (bair-er), Amethyst (am-uh-thist), Violet (vahy-uh-lit).
Pisces (pahy-seez): February (feb-roo-er-ee) 19Th - March (mahrch) 20th: The Fishes, Aquamarine (ak-wuh-muh-reen), Jonquil.
Aries (air-eez): March 21st - April (ey-pruhl) 18Th: The Ram, Diamond (dahy-muhnd), Sweet pea.
Taurus (taur-uhs): April 20th - May (mey) 20th: The Bull, Emerald (em-er-uhld, Lily of the Valley.
Gemini (jem-uh-nahy): May 21st - June (joon) 20Th: The Twins, Pearls, Rose.
Cancer (kan-ser): June 21st - July (joo-lahy) 22nd: The Crab, Ruby, And Larkspur (lahrk-spur).
Leo (lee-oh): July 23rd - August (aw-guhst) 22nd: The Lion, Peridot(per-i-doh), and Poppy.
Virgo (vur-goh): August 23rd - September (sep-tem-ber) 22nd: The Virgin, Sapphire (saf-ahyuhr), and Astor.
Libra (lee-bruh): September 23rd - October (ok-toh-ber) 22nd: The Balance, Opal, Calendula (kuh-len-juh-luh).
Scorpio (skawr-pee-oh): October 23rd - November (noh-vem-ber) 21st: The Scorpion, Topaz (toh-paz, and Chrysanthemum (kri-san-thuh-muhm).
Sagittarius (saj-i-tair-ee-uhs): November 22nd - December (dih-sem-ber) 21st: The Archer, Turquoise (tur-koiz), Narcissus (nahr-sis-uhs).
Capricorn (kap-ri-kawrn): December 22nd - January 19Th: The Goat (goth), Carnation, and Garnet (gahr-nit).
In Astrology, Monday is ruled by the Moon.
Tuesday is ruled by Mars (mahrz), the best day of the week, to deal with challenges.
Wednesday is ruled by Mercury (mur-kyuh-ree); the brain is receptive (ri-sep-tiv) to study.
Thursday is ruled by Jupiter (joo-pi-ter) and is considered a lucky day.
Friday is ruled by Venus (vee-nuhs), the best day for romance and love.
Saturday is ruled by Saturn (sat-ern), a good day to create important documents.
Sunday is ruled by the Sun and is the start of the week.

Lesson 11

Antonyms, Mortgages, Business English

11.1 Pronunciation Key 15 with sentences

Exercise 1: Repeat the words and the sentences aloud.
Exercise 2: Create a new sentence for each word, repeat aloud.

Word spelling (phonetic spelling)	Sentence	Phonetic sound key: short (sound) with (letters). The [x] sound using [y]
Word example	Sentence example	Sound produced
1. glass(glas)	Did she break the glass?	short [a]
2. lady(ley-dee)	Ladies and gentlemen, may I introduce Three Dog Night.	long [a]
3. elephant (el-uh-funt)	Why is there an elephant in the kitchen?	short [e]
4. cheese(cheez)	Order the cheese plate.	long [e]
5. picnic(pik-nik)	Can we have a picnic today?	short [i]
6. tiger (tahy-ger)	Tigers are strong enough to swim upriver.	long [i]
7. dog (dawg)	Rachel Hunter's black Pomeranian is named Relic.	short [o]
8. toad(tohd)	Toads live on land; frogs live in water.	long [o]
9. butterfly (buht-er-flahy)	Did she see that butterfly?	short [u]
10. cube (kyoob)	The cube has six sides.	long [u]
11. gym (jim)	I'm on my way to the gym.	[y] short [i] sound
12. dry(drahy)	Let the paint dry.	[y] long [i] sound
13. party(pahr-tee)	What time does the party start?	[y] long [e] sound
14. note(noht)	Let me give him the note.	silent [e] creates long vowel sound

15. they(they)	They should have returned by now.	long [a] sound digraphs (ai, ay, ea, ei, ey)
16. saw(saw)	Does he have a saw?	long[aw]
17. haul(hawl)	We need to haul all that stuff to the new location.	long[au]
18. bee (bee)	Betsy liked to be called Bee.	long[e] sound with [ee]
19. seal(seel)	Orcas like to eat seals.	long[e] sound with [ea]
20. bread(bred)	Can I have a slice of rye bread?	short[e] sound with [ea]
21. build(bild)	Let's build the house by the beach.	short[i] sound with[ui]
22. thief(theef)	The thief escaped through the window.	long[e] sound with [ie]
23. mind(mahynd)	Do you mind if I sit here?	long[i] sound with [uy], [ind], [ight]
24. snow(snoh)	Segolene avoided the snow in Montreal.	long[o] sound with [ow],
25. road(rohd)	Always take the long road.	long[o] sound with [oa]
26. point(point)	Elephants can understand pointing.	long[o] sound with [oi]
27. royal(roi-uhl)	Here comes the Royal procession.	long[o] sound with [oy]
28. book(book)	Finish the book.	long [u] sound with [oo]
29. blew(bloo)	She blew that calculus exam.	long [u] sound with [ew]
30. blue(bloo)	Can we wear blue jeans?	long [u] sound with [ue]
31. view(vyoo)	Does that apartment have a view of the park?	long [u] sound with [iew]
32. bath(bahth)	That dog needs a bath.	the [b] sound
33. circle(sur-kuhl)	There are 360 degrees in a circle.	Soft [c]
34. cookie(kook-ee)	Make sure she bakes a chocolate chip cookie.	Hard [c]
35. cheese(cheez)	Can I order a grilled cheese sandwich?	the[ch] sound
36. lock(lok)	Don't forget to lock the car at night.	the [ck] sound
37. dog(dawg)	Is that a dog on my couch?	the [D] sound
38. flower(flou-er)	California has many beautiful wildflowers.	the [f] sound
39. gift(gft)	Please accept this gift.	hard[g]sound
40. gentle(jen-tl)	Gentle Giant was a classic rock band.	soft [g] sound

41. trough(trawf)	Icebergs carve out troughs on the seafloor.	[gh] sound [f]
42. weight(weyt)	What is the weight of that fish?	[gh] silent
43. house(hous)	He lived in the house on the top of that hill.	[h] sound
44. jog(jog)	Did they go on a jog this morning?	[j] sound
45. kitten(kit-n)	A kitten is a baby cat.	[k] sound
46. knock(nok)	Remember to knock first.	the [kn] sound [n]
47. ladybug (ley-dee-buhg)	Is that a ladybug on your arm?	the [L] sound
48. mirror (mir-er)	Did you break the mirror?	the [m] sound
49. nest(nest)	Have you tried the birds' nest soup?	the [n] sound
50. panda(pan-duh)	The Panda exhibit is always popular.	the [p] sound
51. phone(fohn)	My phone is dead.	the [ph] sound [f]
52. quarter(kwawr-ter)	Do you have a quarter for the meter?	the [kw] sound with [qu]
53. rainbow(reyn-boh)	Did you see the rainbow?	the [r] sound
54. soap(sohp)	That soap smells like lilac.	the [s] sound
55. scene(seen)	Let's rehearse the scene.	the [sc] sound with [s]
56. escape(ih-skeyp)	The snake escaped from the cage.	the [sk] sound with [sc]
57. shoe(shoo)	Nice shoes.	the [sh] sound [sh]
58. train(treyn)	I'll take the train.	the [t] sound
59. thimble (thim-buhl)	Use a thimble on your finger(fing-ger) to prevent cuts.	the [th soft sound]
60. they(they)	They went to the Hollywood Bowl to see a concert under the stars.	the [th hard sound]
61. switch (swich)	Can we switch times?	the [tch] sound [ch]
62. verb(vurb)	Verbs are the engines of the sentence.	the [v] sound
63. water(waw-ter)	Water levels are rising.	the [w] sound
64. wheel(weel)	Who invented the wheel?	the [wh] sound [w]
65. whole(hohl)	Can we order a whole pizza?	the [wh] sound [h]
66. exam(ig-zam)	What time is that exam?	the [x] sound [x]
67. xylophone (zahy-luh-fohn)	Have you ever seen a xylophone?	the [x] sound [z]

The Hollywood Tutor's AMERICAN ENGLISH © 2020 Mitch Rubman. All rights reserved. No part of this publication may be reproduced or distributed in any form or by any means without the written permission of the copyright owner

68. yolk(yohk)	No egg yolks, please, just the white part.	the [y] sound [y]
69. buzz(buhz)	The bee is buzzing around.	the [z] sound [z]
70. rise(rahyz)	Do you know when sunrise occurs?	the [z] sound with [s]

11.1 Pronunciation Key 16

Exercise 1: Repeat the words and sentences aloud. Read across the rows and then down to the next sound.

Exercise 2: Create a sentence for each word.

Letter sound symbols	Sample words
1. A	aberration (ab-uh-rey-shuhn), abhor, abrasive, abstract, abundant.
2. B	brick, bank, globe(glohb), bribe, tribe.
3. Ch	choke(chohk), chalk, chat, chip, check.
4. D	dab, dude(dood), daisy, did, den, dash, rid, bride.
5. E	echo, eon(ee-uhn), earth, egg.
6. F	feet, coffee, carafe(kuh-raf), staff, gaff, safe, deaf.
7. G	gag, log, finger(fing-ger), give, get, gap, gun, gear.
8. H	horse(hawrs), happy, hungry, hamster.
9. I	pick(pik), pike, pipe, pie.
10. J	Jennifer, Judy, just (juhst), Jim, Jill.
11. K	kite, kit, keep, king, kiss, kick(kik), meek.
12. L	lip, leg, fill, sell, lull(luhl), foul.
13. M	mouse(mous), mice, moss, miss, met, him.
14. N	nap, nope, north(nawrth), nip, neck, near, noon.
15. Ng	long, finger(fing-ger), sang.
16. O	Oscar, only, old.
17. P	put, pit, hiccup (hik-uhp), pin, pen, pack, pile.
18. Q	quick, quote, question, query.
19. R	Roger, Randee, real, rare.
20. S	soup, psychology(sahy-kol-uh-jee), sack, sun, sock, seem.
21. Sh	shy, glacial (gley-shuhl), sure, ship, shape, shed, rush.
22. T	tan, tab, tin, tug(tuhg), top, tack.
23. Th	tooth, thought(thawt), that, booth.
24. U	uncle, universe, use, umbrella.
25. V	vice, vape (veyp), voice, vine, veer, vile.
26. Wh	who, whole (hohl), wheel, well.
27. X	xylophone, xerox, xenon, xenophobic
28. Y	Yetta(yet-uh), yellow, year, yet.
29. Z	zipper, Xerox, resign(ri-zahyn), zinc, zip, zero, zodiac.

11.2 Dialogue: Mortgage Refinance

Life, liberty, and the pursuit of property are key elements in creating America, go get yourself a piece of the good earth. Here is a short dialogue about the mortgage refinance process based on working at a law firm.

Exercise 1: Repeat aloud the following dialogue.

Legal aid:	Are you interested in getting help?
Homeowner:	Yes.

Legal aid:	Are you still having trouble making mortgage payments?
Homeowner:	Yes.

Legal aid:	Have you missed payments?
Homeowner:	Yes.

Legal aid:	How many have you missed?
Homeowner:	Nine.

Legal aid:	Are you getting any help?
Homeowner:	No.

Legal aid:	Do you have any other sources of income?
Homeowner:	No.

Legal aid:	Who is your current lender?
Homeowner:	B of B.

Legal aid:	Are you in foreclosure (fawr-khoh-zher)?
Homeowner:	Yes.

Legal aid:	Is there a sale date?
Homeowner:	Yes.

Legal aid:	What is your current loan balance?
Homeowner:	$253,454 (two-hundred fifty-three thousand, four hundred fifty-four dollars).

Legal aid:	Do you know what the Fair Market value is?
Homeowner:	Yes, $203,000 (two-hundred and three thousand dollars). I'm underwater.

Legal aid:	Have you applied for a trial modification before?
Homeowner:	Yes.
Legal aid:	What happened?
Homeowner:	I was rejected.
Legal aid:	Did you make any payments towards a modification?
Homeowner:	No, not really.
Legal aid:	Did they say they would review your trial?
Homeowner:	I don't think so.
Legal aid:	How much is your current mortgage payment?
Homeowner:	$1625(sixteen hundred twenty-five dollars) per month.
Legal aid:	Is there someone else contributing to your monthly income?
Homeowner:	I'm also getting a pension.
Legal aid:	What would you like to accomplish? A lower payment?
Homeowner:	Yes, that sounds great. I'd like to lower the principal.
Legal aid:	What is the total amount of credit card debt?
Homeowner:	A hundred and eighteen thousand dollars.
Legal aid:	I will need all your receipts(ri-sets) for the last three years, including tax statements, utility bills, medical bills, insurance(in-shoor-uhns) costs, and legal fees, as well as any additional income like rent, stocks, sales, etc. You will also need to sign this form for third-party authorization.
Homeowner:	Very well. When will I find out?
Legal aid:	Let us run the numbers, and I'll get back to you.
Homeowner:	Thanks.

11.3   Antonyms 4

Antonyms are words that are opposite in meaning to another.

Exercise 1: Practice saying the following antonyms aloud going across the rows.
Exercise 2: Create a sentence for each word.

1. frank(frangk)	2. secretive(see-kri-tiv)
3. full(fool)	4. empty(emp-tee)
5. generous(jen-er-uhs)	6. mean(meen)
7. gentle(jen-tl)	8. rough(ruhf)
9. gather(gath-er)	10. distribute(dih-strib-yoot)
11. glad(glad)	12. sorry(sor-ee)
13. gloomy(gloo-mee)	14. cheerful(cheer-fuhl)
15. giant(jahy-uhnt)	16. tiny(tahy-nee)
17. granted(grant-id)	18. refused(ri-fyoozd)
19. great(greyt)	20. small(smawl)
21. guardian(gahr-dee-uhn)	22. ward(wawrd)
23. guest(gest)	24. host(hohst)
25. guilty(gil-tee)	26. innocent(in-uh-suhnt)
27. happy(hap-ee)	28. sad(sad)
29. hard(hahrd)	30. soft(sawft)
31. harmful(hahrm-fuhl)	32. harmless(hahrm-lis)
33. hasten(hey-suhn)	34. dawdle(dawd-l)
35. hate(heyt)	36. love(luhv)
37. healthy(hel-thee)	38. ill(il)
39. here(heer)	40. there(thair)
41. heavy(hev-ee)	42. light(lahyt)

The Hollywood Tutor's AMERICAN ENGLISH © 2020 Mitch Rubman. All rights reserved. No part of this publication may be reproduced or distributed in any form or by any means without the written permission of the copyright owner

43. height(hahyt)	44. depth(depth)
45. hero(heer-oh)	46. coward(kou-erd)
47. hill(hil)	48. valley(val-ee)
49. horizontal(hawr-uh-zon-tl)	50. vertical(val-ee)
51. hinder(hin-der)	52. aid(eyd)
53. honest(on-ist)	54. dishonest(dis-on-ist)
55. humble(huhm-buhl)	56. proud(proud)
57. hunger(huhng-ger)	58. thirst(thurst)
59. imitation(im-i-tey-shuhn)	60. genuine(jen-yoo-in)
61. immense(ih-mens)	62. tiny(tahy-nee)
63. imprison(im-priz-uhn)	64. free(free)
65. include(in-klood)	66. exclude(ik-sklood)

11.4 William Shakespeare

William Shakespeare (1564–1616), English playwright.

Exercise 1: Practice the following dialogue.
Exercise 2: Read one of Shakespeare's plays listed below.

Student: How many words do I need to learn?
Teacher: Here are some basic facts. At age two most children have a vocabulary of 300 words. In all his work Shakespeare used 31,534 different words and created 1700 words.
Student: How many words does an adult know?
Teacher: Currently, an average adult American native speaker of English has a vocabulary of between 10,000 to 35,000 words. Speakers of English in non-English-speaking countries might have an average of about 4,500 words
Student: How about a professor? How many words would they need to know?
Teacher: A professor may know as many as 80-100,000 words. The average dictionary has between 500,000-1,000,000 words. There are approximately 60-100,000 verbs in the English language. My friend Mucci, his favorite book Ulysses written by James Joyce, has about 30,000 different words.

Student: How can I learn more vocabulary?
Teacher: Have you ever read Shakespeare?
Student: No, what plays did he write?
Teacher: The following is a list of all of Shakespeare's plays. All's Well That Ends Well, Antony and Cleopatra, As You Like It, A Comedy of Errors, Coriolanus(kawr-ee-uh-ley-nuhs), Cymbeline(sim-buh-leen), Hamlet, Henry IV Part 1, Henry IV Part 2, Henry V, Henry VI Part 3, Julius Caesar, King John, King Lear, Love's Labor's Lost, Measure for Measure, The Merchant of Venice, The Merry Wives of Winsor, A Midsummer Night's Dream, Much Ado About Nothing, Othello, Richard ll, Richard lll, Romeo and Juliet, Rape of Lucrece(loo-kree-shuh), The Tempest, Timon of Athens, Titus(tahy-tuhs) Andronicus, Troilus and Cressida, Twelfth Night, Two Gentlemen of Verona, Two Noble Kinsmen, A Winter's Tale.
Student: Thank you.
Teacher: Which one will you read first?
Student: Perhaps Julius Caesar
Teacher: That will be a play you will never forget. Remember "Beware the Ides of March."
Student: I don't understand.
Teacher: You will.

11.5 Difficult words and sentences 3

Some of these words are more complicated than the last list, go slow, and review new words.

Exercise 1: Practice reciting aloud the following words and sentences.
Exercise 2: Create a sentence for each word.

1. Adolescence (ad-l-es-uhns):   He was going through adolescence when his voice cracked.
2. Advocate (ad-vuh-keyt):   She was an advocate for senior citizens.
3. Amber (am-ber):   The dinosaur DNA (Deoxyribonucleic acid) for the film Jurassic Park was found in amber, which is fossilized (fos-uh-lahyzd) tree sap.
4. Antibiotic (an-ti-bahy-ot-ik):   The antibiotics, penicillin (pen-uh-sil-in) and erythromycin (ih-rith-ruh-muhy-sin) are hard on the stomach and should be taken with food.
5. Ball (bawl):   Did you catch the fly ball?
6. Bowl (bohl):   That teak bowl is beautiful.
7. Carousel (kar-uh-sel):   Did you go for a ride on the carousel?
8. Chauvinistic (shoh-vuh-nist-ichk): Don't be so chauvinistic, vote for a female President.
9. Chronic (kron-ik):   Do you suffer from chronic back pain?

10.	Club (kluhb):	He was hiding at the clubhouse, west.
11.	Coconut (saf-ahyuhr):	Coconut water is great and refreshing.
12.	Conceit (kuhn-seet):	What was the conceit or main idea of the movie?
13.	Conceited (kuhn-see-tid):	The conceited couple thought they would never lose the dance competition.
14.	Confidence (kon-fi-duhns):	With that level of confidence, you can succeed at anything you try.
15.	Convent (convent):	The Convent got a new roof.
16.	Crouching (krouch-ng):	Have you seen the film, Crouching Tiger, Hidden Dragon?
17.	Cryogenic (krahy-uh-jen-ik):	It's less expensive to just cryogenically freeze the head and not the whole body.
18.	Dash:	The new Senator has great stamina, dash, and fortitude.
19.	Demographic (dem-uh-graf-ik):	Did they take a demographic survey of your neighborhood?
20.	Economic (ek-uh-nom-ik):	Is the train more economical than the bus?
21.	Ergonomic (ur-guh-nom-ik):	Those human-engineered chairs are very ergonomic and are easy to sit in for extended periods comfortably (kuhmf-tuh-buhl-lee).
22.	Exam (ig-zam):	Study hard so you won't fail your exam.
23.	Fever (fee-ver):	Nino, the filmmaker, suffered from Hay fever.
24.	Flair:	She had a flair for simplicity.
25.	Frequency (free-kwuhn-see):	Frequency is measured in cycles per second.
26.	Frequent (free-kwuhnt):	He was a frequent visitor to the planetarium (plan-i-tair-ee-uhm) once a month.
27.	Frequently (free-kwuhnt-lee):	It frequently rains on weekends downwind from the city due to the release of heat absorbed by concrete during the week.
28.	Geographic (jee-uh-graf-ik):	The geographic map showed all the terrain and elevations.
29.	Geometry (jee-om-i-tree):	How did you do on the proofs for the Geometry exam?
30.	Graduate (graj-oo-it):	She was a graduate of Harvard and could find a job anywhere.
31.	Grain (greyn):	Some diets are grain-free, just protein and vegetables.
32.	Grass (gras):	Will you replace the grass?
33.	Gusto (guhs-toh):	They ate the spaghetti with gusto.
34.	Hindsight (hahynd-sahyt):	In hindsight, that umbrella (uhm-brel-uh) was a clever idea.
35.	Hollow (hol-oh):	Hollow out the pumpkin to make a Jack-o-lantern for Halloween (hal-uh-ween).
36.	Hypothetical (hahy-puh-thet-i-kuhl):	Here's a hypothetical problem for you to analyze (an-l-ahyz).
37.	Iconic (ahy-kon-ik):	Marilyn Monroe is truly an iconic figure, especially in Hollywood.

38.	Iguana (ih-gwah-nuh):	Have you seen the 1964 film Night of the Iguana with Richard Burton and Ava Gardner based on the play by the American author Tennessee Williams?
39.	Immediately (ih-mee-dee-it-lee):	I immediately reported the fire before it spread.
40.	Infestation (in-fe-stey-shuhn):	The infestation of caterpillars threatens the food supply.
41.	Joyce (jois):	Mucci asked, have you ever read Ulysses (yoo-lis-eez) by James Joyce?
42.	Latin (lat-n):	Latin is the official language of the Roman Empire spoken from the second or first century BC.
43.	Mandibles (man-duh-buhl):	The Tarantula has huge mandibles to hold and eat its prey, don't you think?
44.	Nightingale (nahyt-n-geyl):	Can you hear the nightingale bird sing? See the film, Eyes Wide Shut.
45.	Odometer (oh-dom-i-ter):	The odometer says 100,000 miles on it.
46.	Omnivore (om-nuh-vawr):	Yes, I'm an omnivore. I eat vegetables and animals.
47.	Operating (op-uh-rey-ting):	Rob, the Surgeon, was operating all night and couldn't be reached for surgery (sur-juh-ree).
48.	Orthodontic (awr-thuh-don-tiks):	He needed a lot of orthodontic work to correct that bite.
49.	Particularly (per-tik-yuh-ler-lee):	I hear that Multivariate Calculus (kal-kyuh-luhs) is particularly hard.
50.	Patriotism (pey-tree-uh-tiz-uhm):	They waved their flags as a sign of patriotism.
51.	Pronounce (pruh-nouns):	How do you pronounce the King's name?
52.	Puberty (pyoo-ber-tee):	Congratulations, you have reached puberty.
53.	Retention (ri-ten-shuhn):	Customer retention is critical, as customer acquisition is expensive.
54.	Ridiculous (ri-dik-yuh-luhs):	What a ridiculous idea, I like it.
55.	Self-Assurance (uh-shoor-uhns):	Use that self-assurance to nurture your dreams.
56.	Senility (si-nil-i-tee):	Do a crossword puzzle every day to avoid senility.
57.	Sister (sis-ter):	The sister prayed for world peace.
58.	Sparkle (spahr-kuhl):	There is still some sparkle in those eyes.
59.	Status quo:	Let's keep it status quo or the existing state of affairs.
60.	Strawberry (straw-ber-ee):	Which flavor jam do you prefer strawberry, blueberry, blackberry, raspberry, orange marmalade (mahr-muh-leyd), or grape?
61.	Symbiosis (simbee-oh-sis):	Inside the termite (tur-mahyt), a protozoan (proh-tuh-zoh-uhn) digests the wood in one of the earliest known symbiotic relationships dating back to the Cretaceous (kri-tey-shuhs) period, the age of the Dinosaurs.
62.	Tax (taks):	Let's take care of the tax first.
63.	Telephonic (tel-uh-fon-ik):	Did the telephonic equipment (ih-kwip-muhnt) arrive on time?
64.	Tortoise (tawr-tuhs):	That Indian star tortoise is well over a hundred years old and lives on land.

65.	Tourist (toor-ist):	That tourist is well over a hundred years old.
66.	Turtle (tur-tl):	The turtle lives in water.
67.	Vigor (vig-er):	Repeat the sentences aloud with vigor.
68.	Vivacity (vi-vas-i-tee):	Some Nursing Home residents had a vivacity for living way into their 90s.
69.	Xenophobic (zen-uh-foh-bik):	She was very xenophobic and never left the apartment.
70.	Zest:	The soccer team had a zest for winning.

11.6 Clichés, Idiomatic expressions and Proverbs 3[G-M]

Enjoy the vast array of smart and clever wit as best expressed in the written word.
Exercise 1: Practice aloud the following proverbs and then the sentences that follow.
Exercise 2: Create your own sentence and repeat aloud.

1.	Green with envy: He turned green with envy when he saw his friend's Ferrari.
2.	Grinning from ear to ear: During the acceptance speech, she was grinning from ear to ear.
3.	Hail, Mary: Is a prayer asking for help from the Blessed Virgin Mary, the mother of Jesus.
4.	Hand in hand: As they walked hand in hand down the aisle, he cried; it was his first daughter.
5.	Have a big mouth: A big mouth, to have a habit of speaking too much and making inappropriate comments. See the classic Honeymooners TV show for an example.
6.	Have a sweet tooth: My sweet tooth makes me crave sweet foods, like cake or candy.
7.	Have an axe to grind: The fired worker has a real axe to grind, look out, he has a gun.
8.	Have ants in your pants: He can't sit still and keeps jumping around it's like he's got ants in his pants or ADD.
9.	Have the world by the tail: To have the world by the tail is when you have great influence and opportunity.
10.	Hay is for horses: Please use my name and remember, hay is for horses.
11.	Head over heels: The first time. I fell head over heels in love and was mesmerized (mez-muh-rahyzd).
12.	Heads up: Heads up, the food is here, tell them to come inside.
13.	Heart on his sleeve: You can tell it was a bad breakup, he's wearing his heart on his sleeve.
14.	Heart skipped a beat: My heart skipped a beat when I realized I had just won the Powerball lottery.
15.	The heir apparent: Did you see the next Royal in line for succession, he's the heir (air) apparent to the throne.
16.	Hold your horses: The foods coming, just hold your horses.
17.	Homie: A homey is a close, good friend. What's up homey?

18.	Hunkey dory: I checked the guest list, it's all hunkey dory, please send out the invitations.
19.	I am getting the hang of it: I flew the drone right under the bridge and didn't hit anything I am getting the hang of it.
20.	All's fair in love and war. I confronted her new lover and caused quite a commotion because all's fair in love and war.
21.	Inspiration is where you find it. I had given up all hope, but now I see how important my job is, I'm excited about the construction. After all, inspiration is where you find it.
22.	You made your bed, now lie in it. I hope you studied for the exam, in any case, you've made your bed, now lie in it.
23.	Shake on it. I look forward to working together; let's shake on it.
24.	Strike while the iron is hot. I'll stay at this job awhile since it's always good to strike while the iron is hot.
25.	I'll scratch your back if you scratch mine: To help someone in exchange for something in return.
26.	I don't quote me: I'm not the spokesperson, so please don't quote me on that.
27.	If I were you: If I were you, I'd get out of here, now, the bus leaves in ten minutes.
28.	If it were me: If it were me, I'd just pay the fee.
29.	If you can't beat them, join them. This means sometimes it's better to switch sides if you are going to lose and want to win.
30.	If you can't stand the heat, get out of the fire: To make someone leave or stop complaining about a current situation which is the heat.
31.	If you wish something done right, do it yourself. As everybody knows, for the best results, do it yourself.
32.	In a jiffy: I'll get to the dishes in a jiffy, right away.
33.	In life, you only get one chance to make a first impression, so do it right the first time and make a good first impression.
34.	In one ear and out the other: It went in one ear and out the other without any change, said Jama.
35.	In the blink of an eye: In the blink of an eye, the hawk appeared.
36.	In the nick of time: They changed that tire in the nick of time as there was a crack in the wall of the tire.
37.	In the same boat: From the look of things, it appears that we are in the same boat.
38.	In this day and age: In this day and age, most cars are becoming electric.
39.	Incomplete actions: Rats dream about incomplete actions; in case you were wondering.
40.	Inside and out: I checked the car, inside and out, it looks good to me.
41.	Inspiration is where you find it. Meaning you can be inspired by many things.
42.	It's always something: If it's not the rent, it's the location, but it's always something.
43.	It's in the bag: The director told me, it's in the bag.
44.	It's not rocket science: Can't you put that IKEA dresser together, it's not rocket science, said MJ.

45.	It's not that bad: Don't worry, it's not that bad, they will have a second seating.
46.	It's not the end of the world: It's only a flat tire, not the end of the world.
47.	It's time to settle down because you know, a rolling stone gathers no moss.
48.	Jumping the shark: Fonzie from Happy Days jumped the shark while water skiing.
49.	Keep your chin up: Remember to keep your chin up even when times are tough.
50.	Keep your eyes peeled: We can surf here but keep your eyes peeled for sharks.
51.	Keep your fingers crossed: I bought some Powerball tickets, so please keep your fingers crossed.
52.	Keep your mouth shut and your ears open. It's your first staff meeting, so please keep your mouth shut and ears open, don't say anything.
53.	Kit and caboodle: How much for the whole kit and caboodle? I want everything.
54.	Knock your socks off: That new show is great and will knock your socks off.
55.	Kudos: Kudos, and congratulations on your graduation.
56.	Lay off: Hey lay off her, I'll take your order; she's had a grueling day.
57.	Let me think about it: I can't decide between the Ford and Ferrari, let me think about it.
58.	Let the dust settle: Let the dust settle and we see how things work, before we buy any more equipment.
59.	Let's do the hard work first, because… you should never put off till tomorrow what you can do today. Procrastination (proh-kras-tuh-ney-shuhn) is the disease of tomorrow.
60.	Live and learn: As time goes on, you will live and learn that what you put out, you get back.
61.	Live and let live: That's ok. Live and let live, said the bear as the fox got away.
62.	Look before you leap: Before making that big decision, remember to look before you leap. Eyes open.
63.	Loose cannon: That Director was a loose cannon and screamed at the assistant.
64.	Lose your marbles: Don't lose your marbles over that ticket.
65.	Love makes the world go around: Don't be so mean, remember its love that makes the world go around.
66.	Make a beeline for. Lookout, the starving students, are going to make a beeline for the food.
67.	Make ends meet: It's not a lot of money, but it will help make ends meet.
68.	Make hay while the sun shines: Always remember to make hay while the sun shines since it might rain tomorrow.
69.	Make no bones about something: To have no hesitation in dealing with something.

11.7   Compare and Contrast 5

Some of these words sound identical and are true homonyms others sound slightly different and are near homonyms. They all have different meanings and uses. Review the phonetics carefully to catch the subtle differences.

Exercise 1: Practice reciting each sentence aloud.
Exercise 2: Create your own sentences.

Allowed (uh-loud): He wasn't allowed outside during the storm.
Aloud (uh-loud): Say the sentences aloud, instead of just repeating the sentence in your head.
Break (breyk): I need a coffee break.
Brake (breyk): The brake light is on.
Chord (kawrd): The terms of a circle are the circumference, diameter, chord, radius, and arc.
Cord (kawrd): Please plug the cord into the socket.
Flea (flee): That dog needs a flea bath.
Flee (flee): Don't flee the scene of an accident.
Know (noh): I know the right answer; I just can't remember it.
No (noh): The answer is no.
Lessen (les-uhn): That tranquilizer will lessen the pain.
Lesson (les-uhn): She arrived early for her lesson.
Not (not): I'm still not jumping off that diving board.
Knot (not): That accident tied my stomach into knots.
Patience (pey-shuhns): It's going to take patience, persistence, and a lot of work to make that project happen.
Patient (pey-shuhnt): Patients are advised to take a number and sit in the waiting room.
Pray (prey): Pray for world peace.
Prey (prey): That fish was prey to the bear.
Soar (sawr): The Bald Eagle, our National emblem, soared high into the sky.
Sore (sawr): The horseback riding made my butt sore.
Steak (steyk): How would you like your steak?

Stake (steyk): The tent has nine stakes in case of strong wind.
Who's (hooz): Who's responsible for this mess?
Whose (hooz): Whose milk is in the refrigerator?
Ate (eyt): Thanks, but I already ate.
Eight (eyt): Please set the table for eight.
Capital (kap-i-tl): Would you like to invest some capital?
Capitol (kap-i-tl): The Capitol of the United States is in Washington, DC.
Coarse (kawrs): The hair on my beard is very coarse.
Course (kawrs): Did you take that Math course?
Foul (foul): He committed a bad foul and got thrown out of the game.
Fowl (foul): The zoo has a beautiful, special waterfowl section.
Lead (leed): The lead shielding should protect you from the radiation.
Led (led): The father led the bride down the aisle.
Made (meyd): Is this watch made in Switzerland?
Maid (meyd): The Maid of the Mist is an amazing boat ride around Niagara Falls.
One (wuhn): This game is one for the books.
Won (wuhn): This is the first game we won this year.
Peace (pees): I voted for world peace.
Piece (pees): You want a piece of me?
Rain (reyn): Prince(prins) will always be remembered for his hit album, Purple rain, which sold more than 22 million copies.
Rein (reyn): Pull on the reins to slow down the horse.
Reign (reyn): His reign lasted until he was deposed (dih-pohzd).
Sew (soh): Let me sew that button on for you.
So (soh): So, what?
Some (suhm): Some mornings, I have iced coffee instead of hot coffee.
Sum (suhm): Please calculate the sum of all the parts.

Tail (teyl): That dog was chasing its tail.	
Tale (teyl): Rudolf Porter, that's a tall tale.	
Your (yawr): Is that your final answer?	
You're (yer): You're under arrest.	

11.8   Business English

Exercise 1: Practice saying the following terms aloud.
Exercise 2: Create a sentence for each word.

1. Abandon (uh-ban-duh-n)	27. BAA - Budget Adjustment Act
2. Accessory (ak-ses-uh-ree)	28. Bailiff (bey-lif)
3. Accountability (uh-koun-tuh-bil-i-tee)	29. Balance Sheet
	30. Balanced Budget
4. Accounting Period	31. Bankrupt (bangk-ruhpt)
5. Accounts Payable	32. BDA – Blanket Delegation of Authority
6. Accounts Receivable	
7. Accrual Accounting	33. BDS – Budget Development System
8. Accrual Basis	
9. Accumulated Depreciation (dih-pree-shee-ey-shuhn)	34. BGS – Buildings and General Services
10. Acknowledgment (ak-nol-ij-muhnt)	35. Bigamy (big-uh-mee)
11. Adjudicate (uh-joo-di-keyt)	36. BISCHA – Banking, Insurance, Securities and Healthcare Administration
12. Affidavit (af-i-dey-vit)	
13. Agency Funds	
14. Alibi (al-uh-bahy)	37. Boilerplate (boi-ler-pleyt)
15. Alimony (al-uh-moh-nee)	38. Bonafide (boh-nuh-fahyd)
16. Allocation (al-uh-key-shuhn)	39. Bond
17. Amortization (am-er-tuh-zey-shuhn)	40. Book Value
	41. Bookkeeping (book-kee-ping)
18. Annul (uh-nuhl)	42. Budget (buhj-it)
19. Appropriation (uh-proh-pree-ey-shuhn)	43. Budget Year
	44. Budgeting (buhj-it-ng)
20. Arraign (uh-reyn)	45. Burglary (bur-gluh-ree)
21. Asset (as-et)	46. CAFR - Comprehensive Annual Financial Report.
22. Assets (Fixed and Current)	
23. Audit (aw-dit)	47. Capital Asset
24. Audit Trail	48. Capital Lease
25. Auditor (aw-di-ter)	49. Capital Outlay
26. Automated Clearing House (ACH)	50. Capital Surplus

51. Capitalization Policy
52. Capitalized Expense(ik-spens)
53. Carry-Forward
54. Cash Basis(bey-sis)
55. Cash Disbursements
56. Cash Discount
57. Cash Flow
58. Cash Receipts (ri-seetz)
59. Cash-Basis Accounting
60. Certified Public Accountant(uh-koun-tnt)
61. Chart of Accounts
62. Clearance Pattern(pat-ern)
63. Clearing Account
64. Closing the Books/Year End Closing
65. Coercion (koh-ur-shuhn)
66. COLA – Cost of Living Allowance
67. Collateral (kuh-lat-er-uhl)
68. Communication and Information
69. Component (kuhm-poh-nuhnt)
70. Comprehensive Annual Financial Report (CAFR)
71. Consensus Revenue Estimates
72. Construction in Progress (CIP)
73. Consumer Price Index (CPI)
74. Contingent Liability(lahy-uh-bil-i-tee)
75. Control Activities
76. Control Environment
77. Control Objectives
78. Cost Accounting
79. Cost of Goods Sold
80. Counselor (koun-suh-ler)
81. Coupon(koo-pon)
82. Current Year - The fiscal year in progress (prog-res).
83. Debit (deb-it)
84. Defendant (dih-fen-duhnt)
85. Deficit Financing
86. Departmental Accounting
87. Depreciation (dih-pree-shee-ey-shuhn)
88. Detective Control
89. DHR - Department of Human Resources
90. DII – Department of Information and Innovation
91. Disbursement (dis-burs-muhnt)
92. Dividends (div-i-dend)
93. DOE - Department of Education
94. DOL - Department of Labor
95. Donated Asset(as-et)
96. Double-Entry Bookkeeping
97. DPS – Department of Public Safety
98. Drawdown(draw-doun)
99. Dunning (duhn-ng)
100. EAP – Employee Assistance Program
101. Effectiveness (ih-fek-tiv-nes)
102. Efficiency(ih-fish-uhn-see)
103. Electronic Benefit Transfer (EBT)
104. Embezzle (em-bez-uhl)
105. Encumbrance (en-kuhm-bruhns)
106. Enterprise Funds
107. Entrepreneur (ahn-truh-pruh-nur)
108. Equity (ek-wi-tee)
109. Executive(ig-zek-yuh-tiv) Budget
110. Executive Order
111. Expenditures(ik-spen-di-chers)
112. Expenses(ik-spensz
113. Financial Accounting
114. Financial Statement
115. Fiscal Period Fiscal Year (FY)
116. Fixed Asset
117. Fixed Charges
118. Franchise(fran-chahyz)

119.	Fugitive (fyoo-ji-tiv)
120.	Full-time Equated (FTE) Position
121.	Fund
122.	Fund Balance
123.	FY - Fiscal Year
124.	GAAP – Generally Accepted Accounting Principles
125.	GASB – Governmental Accounting Standards Board
126.	General Fund (GF)
127.	General Ledger
128.	Goal(gohl)
129.	Goodwill
130.	Grant(grahnt)
131.	HCM - Human Capital Management
132.	Income Statement
133.	Indictment (in-dahyt-muhnt)
134.	Internal Control System
135.	Internal Service Fund (ISF) Invoice
136.	Inventory Valuation
137.	Invoice(in-vois)
138.	IT – Information Technology
139.	JFO – Joint Fiscal Office
140.	Job Costing
141.	Ledger (lej-er)
142.	Liabilities(lahy-uh-bil-i-teez)
143.	Line Item
144.	Liquid Asset
145.	Liquidate (lik-wi-deyt)
146.	Loan(lohn)
147.	Management Intervention
148.	Management Override
149.	Master Account
150.	Merchandise(mur-chuhn-dahyz)
151.	Mission(mish-uhn)
152.	Monitoring(mon-i-ter-ng)
153.	Negotiable(ni-goh-shee-uh-buh)
154.	Net Income
155.	Non-Cash Expense
156.	Non-Depreciable Capital Assets
157.	Non-operating Income
158.	Obligation(ob-li-gey-shuhn)
159.	Operating Budget
160.	Operating Expenditure(ik-spen-di-cher)
161.	Operating Expense (opex)
162.	Operating Income
163.	Organization
164.	Outlays
165.	Owner's Equity(ek-wi-tee)
166.	Payroll(pey-rohl)
167.	Periodic Inventory
168.	Perpetual Inventory
169.	Personal Services
170.	Personnel(pur-suh-nel)
171.	Petty Cash
172.	PO – Purchase Order
173.	Policy(pol-uh-see)
174.	Posting(poh-sting)
175.	Present Value
176.	Preventative Control
177.	Prior Year (PY)
178.	Procedure(pruh-see-jer)
179.	Process(pros-es)
180.	Profit and Loss Statement
181.	Program(proh-gram)
182.	Promissory (prom-uh-sawr-ee)
183.	Proprietary Funds
184.	Reasonable Assurance
185.	Reconciliation (rek-uh-sil-ee-ey-shuhn)

186.	Reliable (ri-lahy-uh-buhl)	206.	Statute (stach-oot)
187.	Restricted Funds	207.	Subpoena (suh-pee-nuh)
188.	Retained Earnings	208.	Sub-recipient
189.	Retained Payable	209.	Subsidiary (suh-b-sid-ee-er-ee) Accounts
190.	ROI- Return on Investment	210.	Supplemental Appropriations
191.	Revenue (rev-uhn-yoo)	211.	Supplies
192.	RFP – Request for Proposal	212.	Surplus (sur-pluhs)
193.	RFQ- Request for Quote	213.	SWCAP – Statewide Cost Allocation Plan
194.	RFR –Request for Review	214.	Syndicate (sin-di-kit)
195.	RIF – Reduction in Force	215.	Tariff (tar-if)
196.	Risk Appetite (ap-i-tahyt)	216.	Tax Credits
197.	Risk Assessment (uh-ses-muhnt)	217.	Taxes (taksz)
198.	SAO – State Auditor's Office	218.	Treasury Stock
199.	Separation of Duties	219.	Usury (yoo-zhuh-ree)
200.	Shareholder Equity	220.	Writ (rit)
201.	Single Audit	221.	Write-down
202.	Single-Entry Bookkeeping	222.	Write-off
203.	SOS – Secretary of State	223.	Year-End Closing
204.	Special Funds	224.	Zero-Base Budgeting
205.	Statement of Account		

11.9 Difficult words and sentences 4

These are slightly more difficult words, some include definitions, some with examples of usage.

Exercise 1: Practice reciting each word and sentences aloud.
Exercise 2: Create your own sentence.

1. Abject (ab-jekt): A situation or condition of the most despicable kind, extremely bad, unpleasant, and degrading. E.g. they suffered through abject poverty.
2. Aberration (ab-uh-rey-shuhn): A state or condition markedly different from the norm. E.g. this aberration will not last.
3. Abjure (ab-joo r): To reject or disavow a formerly held belief. E.g. they abjured the conspiracy theories.
4. Abnegation (ab-ni-gey-shuhn): The denial, rejection or relinquishing of a doctrine or belief. E.g. After the scandal, the senator's abnegation of his office was expected.
5. Abrogate (ab-ruh-geyt): To revoke formally. E.g. most cafes have abrogated the rights of smokers.
6. Abscond (ab-skond): To run away, often taking something or somebody along. E.g. Wes, the puppy absconded with the treats.

7. Abstruse (ab-stroos): Something or someone that is difficult to penetrate. E.g. why are you being so abstruse?

8. Accede (ak-seed): To yield to another's wish or opinion. E.g. Management would not accede to the striker's demands.

9. Accost (uh-kawst): To speak to someone. E.g. the paparazzi was accused of accosting the celebrity.

10. Accretion (uh-kree-shuhn): An increase by natural growth or addition. E.g. the accretion of plastics in the oceans is an enormous problem for marine mammals so most cafes have eliminated plastic straws.

11. Acumen (uh-kyoo-muhn) (ak-yuh): Shrewdness shown by keen insight. E.g. Bloomberg's business acumen is well known.

12. Adamant (ad-uh-muhnt): Being impervious to pleas, persuasion, and requests. E.g. He is adamant; he is not going to resign. In the movie Network, Duvall is asked about the decision to keep Howard on the air and he replies that the boss is adamant. See if you can find the moment with Ned Beatty.

13. Admonish (ad-mon-ish): To scold or reprimand to take to task. E.g. I was admonished for not wearing a tie to the wedding reception.

14. Adumbrate (a-duhm-breyt) to describe roughly or give the main points or summary. E.g. We'll need to adumbrate the story before writing the actual script.

15. Adverse (ad-vurs): In an opposing direction. E.g. the antidote created some adverse reactions.

16. Advocate (ad-vuh-keyt): A person who pleads for a person, cause, or idea. E.g. She was an advocate for the poor and downtrodden.

17. Affluent (af-loo-uhnt): Having an abundant supply of money or possessions of value. E.g. The Rockefeller's wealth and affluence are known worldwide.

18. Aggrandize (uh-gran-dahyz): Add details to. E.g. they had hoped to aggrandize the family name by their donation to the university.

19. Alacrity (uh-lak-ri-tee): Liveliness and eagerness. E.g. Orion drove his new Lamborghini SUV with obvious alacrity.

20. Alias (ey-lee-uhs): A name that has been assumed temporarily. E.g. Joe Klein's alias for Primary Colors was simply, Anonymous, which he mentioned while at dinner, at the Ritz Carlton for the change of the millennium.

21. Ambivalent (am-biv-uh-luhnt): Uncertain or unable to decide about what course to follow. E.g. As a freshman, I was ambivalent as to a major.

22. Amenable (uh-mee-nuh-buhl): Disposed or willing to comply. E.g. the administration was amenable to the changes the PTA suggested for the school.

23. Amorphous (uh-mawr-fuhs) having no definite form or distinct shape. E.g. The Solar System began as an amorphous cloud of dust and gas.

24. Anachronistic (uh-nak-ruh-nis-tik: Chronologically misplaced. E.g. having students at all levels in the same classroom is a bit anachronistic these days.

25. Anathema (uh-nath-uh-muh: A formal ecclesiastical (ih-klee-zee-as-ti-kuh l) curse, or someone or something that is intensely disliked or loathed. E.g. the drivers were anathema to the toll road proposal.

26.	Annex (uh-neks): To attach to, or as an attachment. E.g. fortunately, the Bill of Rights was annexed to the Constitution in the late 1700s.
27.	Antediluvian (an-tee-di-loo-vee-uh) n., of or relating to the period before the biblical flood, out of date, outdated. E.g. the warden's ideas were clearly antediluvian for this time period.
28.	Antiseptic (an-tuh-sep-tik): Thoroughly clean and free of disease-causing organisms. E.g. the operating room needs to be absolutely antiseptic to prevent complications from contamination.
29.	Apathetic (ap-uh-thet-ik): Showing little or no emotion or animation, uninterested, indifferent, and halfhearted. E.g. don't become apathetic, change is possible.
30.	Antithesis (an-tith-uh-sis): The exact opposite. E.g. Love is the antithesis of hate.
31.	Apocryphal (ah-pok-ruh-fuhl): Being of questionable authenticity, fictitious. E.g. Sea Serpents are apocryphal legends from the early days of exploration.
32.	Approbation (ap-ruh-bey-shuh): n., Official approval. E.g. the academy's approbation helped make the film a blockbuster.
33.	Arbitrary (ahr-bi-trer-ee): Based on or subject to individual discretion or preference; capricious, whimsical, random. E.g. many of the presidents' decisions appear to be quite arbitrary.
34.	Arboreal (ahr-bawr-ee-uhl): Of or relating to or formed by trees. E.g. the arboreal monkeys favored the tops of trees.
35.	Arcane (ahr-keyn): Mysterious, secret. E.g. That book has a lot of arcane material in it.
36.	Archetypal (ahr-ki-tahy-puhl): adj., of an original type after which other things are patterned. E.g. the characters in that film are quite archetypal, there was a King, Queen, and a Magician.
37.	Arrogate (ar-uh-geyt): Seize and take control without authority. E.g. they arrogated that portion of land for grazing.
38.	Ascetic (uh-set-ik): Someone who practices self-denial as a spiritual discipline, self-disciplined. E.g. The monks at the monastery were all ascetics.
39.	Aspersion (uh-spur-zhuh) n: A disparaging remark, belittle. E.g. that comment created a lot of aspersion around the politician.
40.	Assiduous (uh-sij-oo-uhs) adj., Marked by care and persistent effort. E.g. her assiduous effort paid off in the end when she made the Dean's list.
41.	Atrophy (a-truh-fee): v., a decrease in the size of organic life caused by disease or disuse. E.g. don't let the fruit atrophy on the tree.
42.	Bane (beyn): Something causing misery or death. E.g. Cigarettes were the bane of her existence and eventually killed her.
43.	Bashful (bash-fuhl): Self-consciously timid. E.g. some rescue dogs can be quite bashful at first.
44.	Beguile (bih-gahyl) v., Influence by slyness; charm. E.g. she beguiled him and then took his car.
45.	Bereft (bih-reft): v., adj., Sorrowful through loss or deprivation. E.g. the bereft mother cried all day.

46.	Blandishment (blan-dish-muhnt): n., Flattery intended to persuade. E.g. the blandishments of the sales departments are sometimes quite outrageous.
47.	Bilk (bilk): v., n., to cheat somebody out of what is due, especially money. Synonyms include defraud, cheat, trick, dupe, deceive, fool, hoax, hoodwink. E.g. they were bilked out of their initial investments.
48.	Bombastic (bom-bas-tik): adj., Lofty in style. E.g. the politician gave a mostly bombastic speech.
49.	Cajole (kuh-johl): v., Influence or urge by gentle urging, caressing, or flattering.
50.	Callous (kal-uhs): adj., v., emotionally hardened, heartless, unfeeling, and cold-hearted.
51.	Calumny (kal-uh m-nee): n., a false accusation of an offense.
52.	Camaraderie (kah-muh-rah-duh-ree): n., the quality of affording easy familiarity and sociability.
53.	Candor (kan-der): n., the quality of being honest and straightforward.
54.	Capitulate (kuh-pich-uh-leyt): v., to surrender under agreed conditions.
55.	Carouse (kuh-rouz): v., n., to engage in boisterous, drunken merrymaking.
56.	Carp (kahrp): v., n., any of various freshwater fish of the family Cyprinidae.
57.	Caucus (kaw-kuhs): n., v., to meet, to select a candidate or promote a policy.
58.	Cavort (kuh-vawrt): v., to play boisterously.
59.	Circumlocution (sur-kuhm-loh-kyoo-shuhn): An indirect way of expressing something.
60.	Circumscribe (sur-kuh m-skrahyb): v., to go around another figure. To restrict something.
61.	Circumvent (sur-kuh m-vent): Find a way around. E.g. Jeff Monroe complained that I tried to circumvent him, even though we worked for the same company.
62.	Clamor (klam-er): Utter or proclaim insistently and noisily.
63.	Cleave (kleev): Separate or cut with a tool, such as a sharp instrument.
64.	Cobbler (kob-ler): A person who makes or repairs shoes.
65.	Cogent (koh-juhnt): A powerfully persuasive argument.
66.	Cognizant (kog-nuh-zuhnt) adj., having or showing knowledge or understanding or realization.
67.	Commensurate (kuh-men-ser-it): Corresponding in size or degree or extent, proportionate; adequate.
68.	Complement (kom-pluh-muhnt) n., something added to embellish or make perfect.
69.	Compunction (kuh m-puhngk-shuhn) n., a feeling of deep regret, usually for some misdeed.
70.	Concomitant (kon-kom-i-tuhnt): adj., n., Following or going with as a consequence.
71.	Conduit (kon-dwit): A passage through which water or electric wires can pass.
72.	Conflagration (kon-fluh-grey-shuhn): A very intense and uncontrolled fire.
73.	Congruity (kuhn-groo-i-tee): The quality of agreeing; being suitable and proper.
74.	Connive (kuh-nahyv): v., to form intrigues in an underhand manner.
75.	Consign (kuh n-sahyn): To give over to another for care or safekeeping.

76.	Constituent (kuhn-stich-oo-uhnt): adj., one of the individual parts making up a composite entity.
77.	Construe (kuh n-stroo): To make sense of; assign a meaning to.
78.	Contusion (kuh n-too-zhuhn): An injury in which the skin is not broken.
79.	Contrite (kuh n-trahyt): Feeling or expressing pain or sorrow for sins or offenses.
80.	Contentious (kuh n-ten-shuhs): Showing an inclination to disagree.
81.	Contravene (kon-truh-veen): To go against, as of rules and laws.
82.	Convivial (kuh n-viv-ee-uhl): Fond of the pleasures of good company.
83.	Corpulence (kawr-pyuh-luhns): The property of excessive fatness. His corpulence was a continuing health problem.
84.	Covet (kuhv-it): To wish, long, or crave for.
85.	Cupidity (kyoo-pid-i-tee): Extreme greed for material wealth.
86.	Dearth (durth): An insufficient quantity or number.
87.	Debacle (dey-bah-kuhl): A sudden and violent collapse.
88.	Debauch (dih-bawch): v., a wild gathering involving excessive drinking.
89.	Debunk (dih-buhngk): v., to debunk advertising slogans, expose while ridiculing to expose a claim as being pretentious, false, or exaggerated.
90.	Defunct (dih-fuhngkt) adj., n., No longer in force or use; inactive.
91.	Demagogue (dem-uh-gog): A leader who seeks support by appealing to popular passions.
92.	Denigrate (den-i-greyt): v., to charge falsely or with malicious intent denigration.
93.	Derivative (dih-riv-uh-tiv): adj., n., a compound obtained from another compound.
94.	Despot (des-puht): v., a cruel and oppressive dictator.
95.	Diaphanous (dahy-af-uh-nuhs): adj., so thin as to transmit light, delicate, and translucent.
96.	Didactic (dahy-dak-tik): adj., Instructive, especially excessively.
97.	Dirge (dirge): A memorial to a dead person.
98.	Disaffected (dis-uh-fek-tid): adj., Discontented as toward authority.
99.	Discomfit (dis-kuhm-fit): v., to cause to lose one's composure.
100.	Disparate (dis-per-it): adj., fundamentally different or distinct in quality or kind.
101.	Dispel (dih-spel): v., to cause to separate and go in different directions.
102.	Disrepute (dis-ri-pyoot): n., the state of being held in low esteem.
103.	Divisive (dih-vahy-siv) adj. dissenting with the majority opinion.
104.	Dogmatic (dawg-mat-ik): adj., pertaining to a code of beliefs accepted as authoritative.
105.	Dour (douuh-r): adj., showing a brooding ill humor.
106.	Duplicity (doo-plis-i-tee): n., acting in bad faith.
107.	Practice (prak-tis) n. The actual application or use of an idea, belief, or method as opposed to theories about such application or use.
108.	Duress (doo-res): n., a compulsory force or threat.

11.10 Composers and Musicians

A composer is someone who writes music. A musician is someone who performs the music. This list as in others, is a compilation of other lists. If all these composers were listened to, that would be a pleasant event.

Exercise 1: Read aloud the following biographies of composers.
Exercise 2: Listen to each composer's work and write a description.

1.	Antonio Vivaldi (vi-vahl-dee) (1678-1741) was an Italian Baroque composer, violinist. His best-known work is a series of violin concertos entitled, the Four Seasons.
2.	Claude Debussy (deb-you-see) (1862-1918) is one of the most prominent figures of Impressionistic music. A French composer, he wrote Clair de lune, a favorite third movement from the Suite Bergamasque.
3.	Florence Price (prahys) (1887-1953) Florence Price was the first African(af-ri-kuhn) American woman to have her music performed by a major symphony orchestra in 1933.
4.	Francis Johnson (1792-1844) Francis Johnson was known as the first African American to have his works printed as sheet music, published in Philadelphia.
5.	Francis Scott Key (1779-1843) the national anthem, The Star-Spangle Banner, was based on his poem and used the music of John Stafford Smith's, To Anacreon in Heaven.
6.	Frederic Francois Chopin (chop-in) (1810-1849) Chopin was a Polish composer and virtuoso pianist who wrote primarily for the solo piano.
7.	George Bridgetower (1778-1860). George Bridgetower an Afro-European virtuoso violinist and composer. He visited Vienna in 1803, where he performed with Ludwig van Beethoven. Beethoven was impressed and dedicated his great Violin Sonata No. 9 in A major (Op.47) to Bridgetower.
8.	George Gershwin (gursh-win) (1898-1937) was an American composer and pianist (pee-an-ist). Mr. Gershwin's most famous works include Rhapsody in Blue (1924), an American in Paris (1928), and Porgy and Bess (1935). Woody Allen used Gershwin extensively in the film Manhattan.
9.	George Walker (1922-2018) Mr. George Walker is the first African American to win the Pulitzer Prize for music. He received the Pulitzer for Lilacs in 1996. His most famous and performed work remains Lyric for Strings (1946), a soothing composition for string orchestra.
10.	Gustav Mahler (mah-ler) (1860-1911) was born in Austria. Mahler was a late-Romantic composer and one of the leading conductors in his generation.
11.	Igor Stravinsky (struh-vin-skee) (1882-1971) was a Russian and later naturalized French and American composer, pianist, and conductor. One of the best and most influential (in-floo-en-shuhl) composers of the twentieth century.
12.	Itzhak Perlman (purl-muhn) (1945-) is an Israeli American violinist, conductor, and educator.
13.	Jakob Ludwig Felix Mendelssohn (men-dl-sahn) (1809-1847) was a German composer, pianist (pee-an-ist), organist, and conductor of the early Romantic period.

14.	Johann Sebastian Bach (bach) (1685-1750) Bach is one of the foremost composers of the Baroque period.
15.	Johannes Brahms (joh-han-eez brahmz) (1833-1897) Brahms was a German composer and pianist (pee-an-ist). He was a master of counterpoint and development composition.
16.	Joseph Bologne(1745 – 1799)The Chevalier de Saint-Georges is remembered as the first classical composer of African origins. Saint-Georges wrote string quartets (kwawr-tets), symphonies, and concertos in the late 18th century.
17.	Ludwig van Beethoven (bey-toh-vuhn) (1770-1827) Beethoven was a German composer and pianist (pee-an-ist). His best-known compositions include 32 piano sonatas (suh-nah-tuhs), 16 string quartets (kwawr-tets), five concertos for piano, and nine symphonies (sim-fuh-nees). The Philharmonic had a night concert of Beethoven's Third concerto (kuhn-cher-toh) …it sold out. It is known that. Towards the end of his life, Beethoven was almost deaf, yet he still created some of his best works.
18.	Maurice Ravel (rav-uhl) (1875-1937), along with Debussy, is one of the most prominent French figures associated with impressionistic music. He is known primarily for his melodies and masterful orchestration.
19.	Pyotr Ilyich Tchaikovsky (chahy-kawf-skee) (1840-1893) was the first Russian composer whose music made an impression internationally.
20.	Richard Georg Strauss (1864-1949) was a leading German composer of the late Romantic and early modern eras. Strauss was a prominent conductor throughout Germany and Austria.
21.	Samuel Coleridge-Taylor (1875 – 1912) Samuel Coleridge-Taylor fought against racial prejudice all his short life. He combined African American folk music with concert music, composing pieces like his African Suite, remembered for the three cantatas based on the epic poem, Song of Hiawatha (hahy-uh-woth-uh).
22.	Scott Joplin (jop-lin) (1868 – 1917) Known as the King of Ragtime(rag-tahym), was one of the most important and influential composers and pianists at the turn of the 20th century.
23.	Sergei Rachmaninoff (rahkh-mah-nuh-nawf) (1873-1943) was a Russian composer, pianist, and conductor. He was always considered one of the best piano players of his day.
24.	Wilhelm Richard Wagner (vahg-nuhr) (1813-1883) was a German composer, theatre director, and conductor who is primarily known for his operas. He is forever memorialized in the film Apocalypse (uh-pok-uh-lips) now (1979), which uses his opera, Ride of the Valkyries (val-keer-ees), in a riveting helicopter attack scene.
25.	William Grant Still (1895 – 1978). Still is the first African American to be a conductor for a major orchestra. And to have an opera produced by a major opera company, the New York City Opera, to have his First Symphony performed by a leading orchestra, and to have an opera performed on national TV.
26.	Wolfgang Amadeus Mozart (moth-sahrt) (1756-1791) starting composing music at the age of five. Throughout his life, he wrote more than 600(six hundred) works, many of which are considered the most beautiful ever created.

27. **Wynton Marsalis (born 1961) Trumpeter**(truhm-pi-ter). Wynton (win-tn) Marsalis(mahr-sal-is) is one of the biggest stars in jazz; in 1997, Marsalis became the first jazz musicians to win a Pulitzer(pool-it-ser) Prize for Music with his oratorio Blood on the Fields. Marsalis has won nine Grammys; he has also won the National Medal of Arts, the National Humanities Medal, and been named an NEA Jazz Master.

Lesson 12

The Internet, Computers, Jobs, Cover letter

12.1 Pronunciation Key 17 with sentences

These are all the sounds of the English language using different words and sentences. The student should practice these words until easy and familiar. Enjoy the shoe list.
Exercise: Repeat the words and sentences aloud.

Consonants	Word	Sentences
1. B	Bad(bad)	It's too bad they called the game because of the weather.
2. C	Cat(kat)	Did the student see my new cat, Trixie?
3. CH	Chain(cheyn)	In the must-see movie, Cool Hand Luke, Paul Newman is part of a chain gang.
4. D	Did(did)	Did she see the unicorn?
5. F	Fall(fawl)	Did he fall when they went skiing?
6. G	Get(get)	Get in the boat.
7. H	Hat(hat)	Has she seen my new hat?
8. J	Jam(jam)	Please pass the grape jam.
9. L	Leg(leg)	He doesn't have a leg to stand on, said the attorney (uh-tur-nee).
10. M	Motor(moh-ter)	Where's the motor?
11. N	Now(nou)	Now when we say action, he walks this way.
12. NG	Sing(sing)	Please sing the song as it's written.
13. P	Pen(pen)	Hand me a pen; I'm ready to sign.
14. R	Red(red)	That car is a bright red.
15. S	See(see)	Did she see the rainbow?
16. SH	Shoe(shoo)	The top shoe designers are: Jimmy(jim-ee) Choo, Manolo Blahnik(blaanihk), Prada, Gucci(goo-chee), Givenchy(jee-vawn-shee)Chanel(shuh-nel), Burberry(bur-buh-ree), Marc Jacobs (mahrk jey-kuhbz), Steve Madden(mad-n), Michael Kors(kawrz), Saint Laurent(san law-rahn), Christian Dior(kris-chuhnn dee-awr), Christian Louboutin, Fendi, Giuseppe Zanotti, Versace(ver-sat-je), Tory(tawr-ee) Burch, Louis Vuitton (loo-ee vuht-n), Dolce & Gabbana (dawl-che & gab-ban-uh),

			Bruno(broo-noh) Magli, Kate Spade (keyt speyd), DKNY, Kenneth Cole (ken-ith kohl), Stuart(stoo-ert) Weitzman, and Salvador Ferragamo.
	17. T	Tea(tee)	I'd like a cup of tea and a biscuit(bis-kit).
	18. TH	Thin(thin)	You are looking very thin today.
	19. V	Van(van)	That van can carry a lot of luggage (luhg-ij).
	20. W	Wet(wet)	It's wet outside, does she have an umbrella?
	21. Y	Yes(yes)	Yes, I'll grab an umbrella.
	22. Z	Zoo(zoo)	Let's go to the zoo and visit the animals.
Vowels			I saw the total lunar eclipse.
	23. A	Saw(saw)	I can't see the movie, that head is in the way.
	24. E	See(see)	Can he please sit down?
	25. I	Sit(sit)	So, would they like to join us for dinner?
	26. O	So(soh)	Please put the gun down.
	27. U	Put(poot)	Would he like a soy burger?
	28. Y	Soy(soi)	It's too bad they called the game because of the weather.

12.2   The Internet: Technology, Social Media, Computers

Exercise 1: Repeat the word and then the sentence aloud.
Exercise 2: Create a complete sentence for each word.

[Number Key (trillions000, billions000, millions000, thousands000, hundreds000)]

1.	Amber alert (am-ber uh-lert): An amber alert is a child abduction(ab-duhk-shuhn) public notification(noh-tuh-fi-key-shuhn) system run by the Department of Justice that lets the general population know about missing children and is transmitted to all cell phones, and other Wi-Fi devices and is on electronic billboards throughout the state and/or nationally.
2.	Amazon (am-uh-zon): The largest commerce portal with more than 500,000,000(five hundred million) monthly users.
3.	App: An application usually loaded onto a mobile device.
4.	Ask.fm: A social media site with 245,000,000 monthly visitors based on asking question and answers.
5.	Asp: Asp is the language for web development.
6.	Attachment (uh-tach-muhnt): A separate item, not in the body of the email.
7.	Average Position: If the average position of an ad is on the front page, then its number is between one and eight.

8.	Bing: Microsoft search engine with more than 285,000,000 monthly visitors.
9.	Bit: A bit is either a 0 or 1.
10.	Blog (blawg): A blog is a constantly updated website written in a casual style. Take a look at my blogs: www.coffeecupclub.blogspot.com, www.americanenglishhollywoodtutor.blogspot.com, www.notsofuturenews.blogspot.com.
11.	Bluetooth (bloo-tooth): A wireless process that uses short wave radio frequencies to interconnect portable devices.
12.	Bookmark: Please remember to bookmark that website, so that it can be found easier next time.
13.	Browser (brou-zer): The browser is an application that allows the user to access (ak-ses) the internet.
14.	Buffer (buhf-er): The video is in the buffer and will download momentarily (moh-muhn-tair-uh-lee).
15.	Byte (bahyt): A single piece of information represented in the binary system.
16.	chemistry.com: The sister dating site of match.com.
17.	Chip (chip): A chip is a small piece of silicon used to convey information.
18.	Christianmingle.com: Dating site with a theme.
19.	ClassMates: Classmates (klas-meyts) is a social media site that connects high school and college friends together with 57,000,000 monthly visitors.
20.	Clicks: The number of times users click through an ad.
21.	Clipboard: The clipboard holds the copy and paste (peystd) document.
22.	Cloud: The cloud located on Earth is a collection of storage devices such as computers, hard drives and servers that share storage space with users to protect and backup against loss of data.
23.	Computer (kuhm-pyoo-ter): The name of the machine that is used to compute.
24.	Cookie (kook-ee): A user's telltale signature on the internet, usually containing an ip address and all the information on all the visits that have been made.
25.	Copy (kop-ee): To reproduce a document, use this command as it will not delete the original.
26.	CPU: The central processing unit is a part of the computer where all the information is processed. The pointer, usually arrow or cross shaped, which is controlled by the mouse.
27.	Crash: When the computer freezes and has a system malfunction and has to be restarted.
28.	Cursor (kur-ser): The cursor is like a finger pointing at a specific letter in the document.
29.	Cut (kuht): When the cut command is used the selected information is deleted and ready to be pasted.
30.	Delicious.com: Delicious (dih-lish-uhs) dot com is a social bookmarking site with approximately 10 million active users.
31.	Desktop: My favorite place to leave important documents on my computer. The place you go when the computer turns on.

32. Digitize: The process of converting linear, analog, or any data into digital data which can be used by the computer.
33. Directory (dih-rek-tuh-ree): The directory organizes all the information on the computer.
34. Download: Download the document to transfer data from the web to the computer.
35. Driver: The driver is the computer program that runs different devices on your computer, when in doubt you can usually download current drivers from a company's website.
36. Drop and drag: On the Mac, a feature which allows one to drag the icon for a document on to the top of the icon for an application, thereby launching the application and opening the document.
37. DSL: A DSL is a digital line used to connect to the internet that runs through a phone line.
38. DVD: Digital video discs are a means for storing and recording digital information.
39. eBay: A leading portal for used as well as new and unusual items to sell. With more than 285,000,000 monthly visitors.
40. Ecommerce (ee-kom-ers): Any business conducted via the internet is referred to as ecommerce.
41. eharmony.com: A top dating site with 1.2 million monthly visitors.
42. Elitesingles.com: A dating site with 54 k monthly visitors.
43. Email: The electronic mail is any messaging system used via the internet.
44. Emoticon: Emoticons are used to convey information via standard keyboard characters. ☺
45. Encryption(en-kript-zhuhn: To prevent the stealing of information, data is coded or encrypted to prevent unauthorized use.
46. Excel (ik-sel): A Microsoft program that is composed of spread sheets and is used in accounting that contains macro programs for complex calculations.
47. Facebook (feys-book): Facebook is the most popular current type of social media with more than 2.6 billion monthly users.
48. FAQ: Acronym for Frequently Asked Questions is always a good place to check when you have a question about a website or product.
49. File: A document with a specific file name that contains information.
50. Firewall (fahyuhr-wawl): A barrier created to protect your computer from the outside.
51. Flash (flash): Flash is a software program used in animation and visual effects.
52. Flash drive: A flash drive is a portable memory device.
53. Flickr: Flickr is an image and video social media web site with more than 112,000,000 monthly users. The largest photo sharing website on the internet.
54. Font (font): The font is a typeface of a specific size and style.
55. **Food delivery apps**: Grubhub.com, Doordash.com, UberEats.com, Postmates.com, Instacart.com, Delivery.com., goPuff.com, ChowNow.com, Grubhub.com,
56. Format painter: Use the format painter to copy formatting from one cell to another.

57.	Gif (jif): A standard format for images and short animations.
58.	Gigabyte (gig-uh-bahyt): A measure of storage capacity equal to roughly a billion bytes.
59.	GoFundme.com: Online fund raising.
60.	Google(goo-guhl): Google is the leading search engine on the internet with 1,600,000,000(one billion, six hundred million) approximate monthly visitors.
61.	Hacker: A hacker is a computer thief that finds a way into computers using programs, software, phishing emails, embedded fonts, etc.
62.	Hard drive: The primary storage device on your computer.
63.	Hardware (hahrd-wair): The actual external devices used with the computer.
64.	Headings: A heading is a title or subtitle for a document.
65.	Home: Let's return to that home page of the website or the main page.
66.	howaboutwe.com: Dating site with a theme.
67.	Html (hypertext markup language): The language used to code instruction for the creation of web pages.
68.	Http (hypertext transfer protocol): The common beginning of URL web addresses.
69.	Hub pages: Is a social media website where you can share with other authors.
70.	I.T: The I.T. person or information technologist is the person responsible for computers, programs, and networking in your office.
71.	Icon (ahy-kon): An icon is a picture or image used to represent a file.
72.	IM: Instant messengering is the kind of online chat which offers real time text transmission over the internet. I'll IM you; you can IM me.
73.	Inbound.org: Inbound.org is a community of marketing professionals.
74.	Instagram: Instagram is a portmanteau of instant telegram mobile photo and video sharing platform with more than one billion monthly visitors. I'm listed under The Hollywood Tutor.
75.	Internet (in-ter-net): The system that connects networks.
76.	IoT: The Internet of things connects all devices.
77.	IP address: The internet protocol (IP) is your specific and traceable internet address of your computer.
78.	iPhone (ahy-fohn): Did you buy a new Apple (ap-uhl) iPhone?
79.	ipod (ahy-pod): A portable video and audio device created by Apple (ap-uhl).
80.	iWatch (ahy-woch): The Apple watch can measure activities like swimming, yoga, walking. Track cadence and pace wirelessly with gym equipment(ih-kwip-muhnt). Rate running information. The optical heart sensor can monitor your heart rate
81.	Keywords: English words you choose so that when users search for those words, your ad may appear higher up in the page.
82.	Kickstarter (kik-stahrt-ter): Kickstarter, a crowd funding company from Brooklyn that has raised more than a billion dollars.
83.	Landing Page: A single web page where information is collected for billing or for marketing purposes.

84.	Landscape (land-skeyp): A document with a landscape view is also known as horizontal orientation.
85.	Laptop (lap-top): A portable computer complete with a built-in keyboard and screen.
86.	lavalife.com: A dating site.
87.	LCD display: The liquid crystal display (LCD) pixels in front of a light source used in imaging in everything from digital watches to flat panel TVs to laptop screens.
88.	LinkedIn (lingkt-in): A business social media site with more than 150,000,000 monthly views, where you can see your business connections and users reviewing you.
89.	Log in: The login is where you enter your personal identification information including password, email address.
90.	MacBook: The new MacBook has a 12-inch retina (ret-n-uh) display for easier viewing.
91.	Mail merge (meyl murj): A term for creating personalized documents combining a list of names from an EXCEL document with a word document to give the appearance of personally addressed correspondences.
92.	Match.com: A top dating site with 3.2 million monthly visitors.
93.	Meetme.com: Dating site with a theme.
94.	MeetMe: With more than 15,500,000 monthly visitors MeetMe is a social media site connecting individuals for various personal meeting opportunities.
95.	Meetup (meet-uhp): A social media site used to create local meetup groups that have similar interests and/ or occupations with 30,300,000 monthly visitors.
96.	Menu bar (men-yoo) (bahr): The menu bar lists various available commands as part of a computer program.
97.	Microphone (mahy-kruh-fohn): The microphone is the device used to record voices usually contained within the computer.
98.	MLA format: The formatting preferred for academic papers with footnotes and proper bibliographic citations.
99.	Modem (moh-duhm): The modem is used to connect the computer to the network and the world.
100.	Motherboard (muhth-er-bawrd): The hardware circuit board inside the computer that holds the major devices such as the CPU and ROM devices.
101.	Mouse (mous): A device used to move the cursor over your computer screen.
102.	Mouse pad (mous-pad): The rubber pad used to help the mouse move effortlessly over your document.
103.	Mp3: It is short for mpeg 1 audio layer 3, it is a compressed audio file.
104.	MSN: A news portal with more than 280,000,000 monthly visitors.
105.	Myspace (mai-speys): Myspace once the leader in social media, is still active and has a more musical audience with bands posting gigs.
106.	Network (net-wurk): A network is a system of computers interconnected.
107.	Okcupid.com: Another match.com dating site.
108.	Operating system: The software that runs a computer.
109.	Ourtime.com: A dating site with 880k monthly visitors.

110.	Password (pass-wurd): Your private coded sign on, phrase or numbers sequence.
111.	Paste (peyst): After copying or cutting the document use paste to transfer the clipboard to the desired location.
112.	PC: Your Personal computer at home.
113.	Pinterest: For quality images and content and to drive traffic with more than 332,000,000 monthly active users.
114.	Pixels (pik-suhlz): The process of using dots to represent images in electronic forms.
115.	plentyoffish.com: Dating site with a theme.
116.	Podcast (pod-kast): Video or audio broadcasting over the internet.
117.	Popup: Ads that automatically appear while you're online.
118.	Port (pawrt): The internal and external terminals to connect devices to your computer.
119.	Portrait (pawr-trit): A document viewed vertically as compare to a landscape (horizontally) viewed.
120.	Printer (prin-ter): The device used to print a copy of your document or item (3-D).
121.	Program (proh-gram): The computer program is a list of instructions and commands written for a particular operating system to perform specific tasks.
122.	Quora: Quora is a quality question and answer website that can drive traffic to your site especially if you are the first to answer the question.
123.	QQ: A Chinese instant messaging chat system with more than 853,000,000 users.
124.	RAM: The Random-Access Memory is the main part of a working memory used to quickly process documents.
125.	Reddit: For sending out viral content, Reddit is a leader in social media. With more than 250,000,000 monthly visitors.
126.	ROM: The Read-Only Memory is the part of the computer's memory that is permanently stored.
127.	Search (surch) engine: The program which searches for requested information on the internet.
128.	Server (sur-ver): The state-of-the-art servers which hosted the websites, filled an entire floor. The servers are computers used to store and retrieve information.
129.	Slashdotslash: Slashdotslash is a user submitted platform for tech and science news.
130.	Software (sawft-wair): Did you download the new software onto the computer?
131.	Spam: Unwanted emails usually characterized by ridiculous offers.
132.	Spyware (spahy-wair): Software that transmit user's information without the owner's knowledge.
133.	Squidoo: Users create content on squidoo in the form of lenses which can be linked to your site.

134.	Streaming (stree-ming): They will be streaming the event, so you will see it live, with no delay.
135.	Stumble upon (stuhm-buhl uh-pon): Stumble upon is a social media website that allows the sharing of content, website, and blogs.
136.	Styles (stahyl): The styles command will help you organize your document headers.
137.	Table of contents: If you set the styles properly, you can just hit a command to create a table of contents.
138.	Technorati (tek-nawr-raht-i): Technorati is a search engine for blogs, which uses tags to help categorize content.
139.	Tic Tok: Is a short form video social media site. Currently very popular with teens with more than 500,000,000 (five hundred million) monthly visitors.
140.	Tinder.com: Dating site with a theme.
141.	Toolbar (tool-bahr): The toolbar has all the icons on it for shortcuts.
142.	Triberr: Triberr is a community of bloggers and writers that share great content.
143.	Tumblr: Owned by Yahoo, with more than 555,000,000 monthly visitors.
144.	Twitter (twit-er): Twitter is the second most popular social media site with more than 68,000,000 monthly visitors.
145.	Upload (uhp-lohd): They uploaded or transferred all the files to the main computers' memory.
146.	URL (universal resource locator): What is your URL? I want to check out your website.
147.	USB (universal serial bus): Let me hook this up to your usb.
148.	Username (yoo-zer-neym): Along with your password, username provides the identity for signing onto websites.
149.	Virus (vahy-ruhs): The computer got infected by a virus and did all sorts of strange things like deleting files and turning itself off.
150.	Webcam (web-kam): Any type of camera system that goes through the internet enabling web broadcasting of events or shows.
151.	Webmaster (web-mas-ter): The webmaster is responsible for the website, please give him a call immediately.
152.	Website (web-sahyt): The location where information is stored on the internet and available for viewing.
153.	What's App: Owned by Facebook since 2014, an instant messaging platform with 1 billion approximate users.
154.	Wi-Fi: The wireless technology term for transmission of data and images between locations and addresses.
155.	Wikipedia: The modern encyclopedia of the internet, Wikipedia has over 20 million articles available for use or review, a great place to start research. With more than 475,000,000 monthly visitors.
156.	Windows (win-dohz): Microsoft operating system used to draft this book.
157.	Wordpress: A commerce site with more than 240,000,000 monthly visitors.

158.	Yahoo (yah-hoo) Yahoo search engine has more than 750,000,000(seven hundred fifty million) users.
159.	YouTube: You Tube is the largest and most popular video sharing website in the universe. With more than two billion (2,000,000,000) monthly visitors. From rare musical performances to complicated "How to" videos YouTube has it all.
160.	Zoosk.com: A dating site with 1.1 million monthly visitors.

12.3 Difficult words and sentences 5

A slightly more challenging list.
Exercise 1: Repeat the word and then the sentence aloud.
Exercise 2: Create a sentence for each new word.

1.	A-cappella (ah- kuh-pel-uh): Jillian always sang a-cappella, which upset the musicians.
2.	Adjective (aj-ik-tiv): What adjective would the student from Italy use to describe Ferraris?
3.	Advisory (ad-vahy-zuh-ree): I asked her to be on the advisory committee for the new land development.
4.	Agglomeration (uh-glom-uh-rey-shuhn): There was an agglomeration of granite (gran-it) in that outcrop.
5.	Ambiguous (am-big-yoo-uhs): Don't be so ambiguous, tell me yes or no.
6.	Antagonist (an-tag-uh-nist): He was a tough (tuhf) antagonist and chased the hero to the bitter end.
7.	Apparatus (ap-uh-rat-uhs): The Hoffman apparatus creates oxygen and hydrogen from water.
8.	Arithmetic (uh-rith-muh-tik): Are they that good in arithmetic?
9.	Articulation (ahr-tik-yuh-ley-shuhn): Practice the articulation of the vowels and consonants in words.
10.	Auditorium (aw-di-tawr-ee-uhm): Which way is the auditorium?
11.	Cafeteria (kaf-i-teer-ee-uh): Is the cafeteria open?
12.	Cantilever (kan-tl-ee-ver): The Engineers built a cantilever bridge, the top half of the bridge builds tension while the lower half holds compression, over the river.
13.	Centenarians (sen-tn-air-eeuhns): They show centenarians on some news shows in the human-interest sections or medical reports since it's rare to be one hundred years old.
14.	Challenge (kaf-i-teer-ee-uh): It was a challenge to bicycle in such heat.
15.	Charming (chahr-ming): She used her charming (chahr-ming) personality to climb (klahym) the ladder of success.
16.	Circadian (sur-key-dee-uhn) rhythms: Circadian rhythms help me maintain my schedule.
17.	Comprehension (kom-pri-hen-shuhn): How is his reading comprehension?

18. Contemplation (kon-tuhm-pley-shuhn): There was deep contemplation before the decision.
19. Criticism (krit-uh-siz-uhm): Constructive criticism always includes a new idea.
20. Daughter (daw-ter): The mother and daughter had new matching outfits.
21. Decathlon (dih-kath-lon): The decathlon is an athletic contest composed of ten events in track and field.
22. Enhance (en-hans): The students will enhance their language skills by reading a dictionary.
23. Fraternity (fruh-tur-ni-tee): In the movie, Animal House, they closed the fraternity on campus due to misconduct.
24. Incident (in-si-duhnt): There was an incident when it started to rain at the picnic.
25. Influence (in-floo-uhns): Celebrities influence how people act, dress, and eat.
26. Interpret (in-tur-prit): We need someone to interpret that contract.
27. Intramural (in-truh-myoor-uhl): Is football an intramural sport?
28. Jewelry (joo-uhl-ree): She inherited (in-her-itd) a lot of antique (an-teek) blue turquoise (tur-koiz) jewelry, including; brooches (brohchs), pins (pinz), necklaces (nek-lises), rings and bracelets (breys-lits) that are family heirlooms (air-loomz).
29. Library (lahy-brer-ee): Have they been to the new library?
30. Maneuver (muh-noo-ver): The running back made a maneuver around the tackle (tak-uhl) in the football game.
31. Masquerade (mas-kuh-reyd): Are they wearing those costumes to the Masquerade Ball?
32. Medieval (mee-dee-ee-vuhl): The European medieval era (eer-uh) is from 467 A.D to 1450 A.D or from the fifth century (sen-chuh-ree) to the fifteenth century.
33. Meditation (med-i-tey-shuhn): Meditation is a great way to quiet the inner monologue.
34. Miniature (min-ee-uh-cher): Did they see that miniature village?
35. Mischievous (mis-chuh-vuhs): Those teenagers were very mischievous when they set free the chickens.
36. Nonagenarian (non-uh-juh-nair-ee-uhn): She's a nonagenarian, she is 92.
37. Octogenarian (ok-tuh-juh-nair-ee-uhn): They called him an Octogenarian since he was in his eighties.
38. Orient (awr-ee-uhnt): The three gyroscopes (jahy-ruh-skohps) orient the satellite each by rotating in their own planes' [x, y, and z].
39. Peanut (pee-nut): President Jimmy Carter was once a peanut farmer; he now helps Habitat for Humanity.
40. Percolator (pur-kuh-ley-ter): Please use the stainless-steel percolator to make the coffee.
41. Protagonist (proh-tag-uh-nist): The protagonist was a true champion and led a charmed life.
42. Prodigy (prod-i-jee): Mozart was a musical prodigy and composed symphonies at the age of five.

43. Robotics (roh-bot-iks):	The biomechanics (bahy-oh-mi-kan-iks) engineering school has a new robotics program.
44. Secretary (sek-ri-ter-ee):	Please call the cadet (kuh-det) secretary.
45. Septuagenarian (sep-choo-uh-juh-nair-ee-uhn):	She is a beautiful Septuagenarian.
46. Serene (suh-reen):	She was pure, bright, clear, and serene.
47. Shortstop (shawrt-stop):	Did he play shortstop in little league?
48. Sorority (suh-rawr-i-tee):	Call the superintendent to gain access to the sorority office.
49. Tetrahedron (te-truh-heedruhn):	In the rare tetrahedron, its six edges and four sides are all equal.
50. Thoroughly (thur-oh-lee):	I thoroughly enjoyed this week's English class.
51. Throughout (throo-out):	They talked throughout the movie, so I have no idea what was said.
52. Treasurer (trezh-er-er):	I think we are going to need a treasurer for that occasion.
53. Variety (vuh-rahy-i-tee):	Variety is the spice of life.
54. Whistle (hwis-uhl):	My best friend taught me how to whistle when I was a kid.

12.4 Dialogue: At the Yogurt Shop

For those that enjoy yogurt and art.

Exercise 1: Repeat aloud the following dialogue. Practice with a friend. Switch characters.
Exercise 2: What items do all yogurt shops have in common? Describe.

Angela:	Hi, I am Angela, welcome to The Silver Cow yogurt shop. What can I get for you?
Eve:	Nice to meet you. What flavors are the best?
Angela:	We have chocolate fudge brownie, upside-down pineapple cake, strawberry shortcake, mango (mang-goh), vanilla (vuh-nil-uh), and peanut butter.
Eve:	Are there toppings?
Angela:	Of course, we have sprinkles, nuts, Reese's, m & ms, just look at all these. Pick anything. Which would you like?
Eve:	Is there hot fudge (fuhj)?
Angela:	Yes, and there is also butterscotch (buht-er-skoch).
Eve:	Can I get some more nuts?
Angela:	Mixed nuts, Almonds (ah-muhnds), or peanuts?
Eve:	Mixed. Thank you. Can I get some whipped cream?
Angela:	Sure, and what else?
Eve:	Is there mango?

Angela:	Absolutely.
Eve:	Can I have a scoop of mango and a scoop of chocolate?
Angela:	Cone or cup?
Eve:	Cone.
Angela:	Sugar or wafer?
Eve:	Sugar, thanks.
Angela:	Enjoy, haven't I seen you at Santa Monica College?
Eve:	Yes, I thought so. What are you studying?
Angela:	Art history the classics like, Albrecht Durer (door-er), Modigliani (moh-dee-lee-ah-nee), Andy Warhol (wawr-hawl), Camille Pissarro (pi-sahr-oh), Caravaggio (kar-uh-vah-joh), Claude Monet (moh-ney), Diego Rivera (ri-vair-uh), Edgar Degas (dee-gas), Edvard Munch (munk), Edward Hopper (hop-er), El Greco (grek-oh), Francis Bacon (bey-kuhn), Frida Kahlo (kah-loh), Gauguin (goh-gan), Braque (brak), Goya (goi-uh), Courbet (koor-be), Gustav Klimt, Hieronymus Bosch (bosh), Jackson Pollock (pol-uhk), Turner (tur-ner), Joan Miro (mee-roh), Vermeer (ver-meer), Leonardo da Vinci (vin-chee), Marc Chagall (shuh-gahl), Matisse (ma-tees), Michelangelo (mahy-kuhl-an-juh-loh), Pablo Picasso (pi-kah-soh), Paul Cezanne (si-zan), Paul Klee (kley), Peter Paul Rubens (roo-buhnz), Pierre Auguste Renoir (ren-wahr), Raphael (raf-ee-uhl), Rembrandt (Rem-brant), Rene Magritte (ma-greet), Rodin (roh-dan), Salvador Dali (dah-lee), Sandro Botticelli (bot-i-chel-ee), Titian (tish-uhn), Vincent Van Gogh (van-goh), Wassily Kandinsky (kan-din-skee), Willem de Kooning (duh-koo-ning).
Eve:	That sounds like a great class. But what's in the smoothie?
Angela:	In our smoothie are 2 1/3 (two and a third) Apples, ½ (one-half) Kiwi, ½ Pineapple, ½ Banana, ½ (one-half) Mango, 20 (twenty) grams Whey and Soy protein, 430 (four hundred-thirty) mgs. (Milligrams) Alfalfa (al-fal-fuh), 80 (eighty) mg (milligrams) Barley grass, 100 (one hundred) mg (milligrams). Broccoli, 54 mg. Ginger, 53 mg. Kale, 54 mg. Parsley, 107 (one-hundred and seven) mgs. Spinach, 1400 (fourteen hundred) mg spirulina (spahy-ruh-lahy-nuh), 100 mg wheatgrass.
Eve:	What about Lou's green shake?
Angela:	It has 1 cup of Nano greens, one scoop pea protein, ½ cup blueberries, ½ cup blackberries, ½ cup raspberries, one banana, 1 T almond butter, 1 T Coconut oil, 1 cup Almond milk, and 1 cup of ice.

12.5 Synonyms 8

Exercise 1: Practice saying the following synonyms aloud. Go across the row.
Exercise 2: Create a different sentence for each word.

Word	Synonym	Synonym
1. Bias(bahy-uhs)	2. Inclination(in-kluh-ney-shuhn)	3. Predisposition(pree-dis-puh-zish-uhn)
4. Pungent(puhn-juhnt)	5. Acrid(ak-rid)	6. Sharp(shahrp)
7. Blend(blend)	8. Combine(kuhm-bahyn)	9. mix(miks)
10. bliss(blis)	11. happiness(hap-ee-nis)	12. joy(joi)
13. bluff(bluhf)	14. boast(bohst)	15. feign(feyn)
16. bold(bohld)	17. daring(dair-ing)	18. fearless(feer-lis)
19. bonus(boh-nuhs)	20. award(uh-wawrd)	21. gift(gift)
22. bother(both-er)	23. annoy(uh-noi)	24. irritate(ir-i-teyt)
25. brief(breef)	26. concise(kuhn-sahys)	27. short(shawrt)
28. brilliant(bril-yuhnt)	29. clever(klev-er)	30. intelligent(in-tel-i-juhnt)
31. brisk(brisk)	32. fast(fast)	33. swift(swift)
34. budget(buhj-it)	35. allot(uh-lot)	36. plan(plan)
37. candid(kan-did)	38. honest(on-ist)	39. truthful(trooth-fuhl)
40. caricature (kar-i-kuh-cher)	41. cartoon(kahr-toon)	42. imitation(im-i-tey-shuhn)
43. casual(kazh-oo-uhl)	44. informal(in-fawr-muhl)	45. natural(nach-er-uhl)
46. category(kat-i-gawr-ee)	47. classification(klas-uh-fi-key-shuhn)	48. division(dih-vizh-uhn)
49. cease(sees)	50. desist(dih-zist)	51. stop(stop)
52. chaotic (key-ot-ik)	53. disordered(dis-awr-derd)	54. messy(mes-ee)
55. cherish(cher-ish)	56. esteem(ih-steem)	57. love(luhv)
58. circumvent (sur-kuhm-vent)	59. avoid(uh-void)	60. dodge(doj)
61. commemorate(kuh-mem-uh-reyt)	62. celebrate(sel-uh-breyt)	63. honor(on-er)

12.6 Dialogue: Grocery Shopping

Grocery shopping is a common experience around the world. Stores and food items may differ, but shopping is similar.

Exercise 1: Repeat aloud the following dialogue. Practice with a friend. Then switch characters.
Exercise 2: Write about a recent shopping experience.
Exercise 3: Create a shopping list after reviewing the refrigerator.

Violet: Can we make some dinner?
Steve: Yes, let's go shopping.
Violet: Do you know where the supermarket is?
Steve: There's a Supermarket down the block but the Gas Station sells burritos.
Violet: Tough choice.
Steve: Gas station?
Violet: No?
Steve: Please!
Violet: What are we cooking?
Steve: Let's make Chicken Marsala (mahr-sah-luh) with spaghetti.
Violet: What do we need?
Steve: Let's buy some chicken, eggs, pasta, mushrooms, breadcrumbs, Marsala Wine, and some parmesan (pahr-muh-zahn) cheese.
Violet: And a salad.
Steve: Let's make some garlic bread too, let's buy some lettuce, carrots and onions, garlic, butter (buht-er) and bread.
Violet: How about a beet salad?
Steve: Alright
Violet: I've changed my mind. I'm now thinking of making salmon (sam-uhn) and brown rice. I'll go over to the fish department.
Steve: Can I get you some rice?
Violet: Sure, I'd like some brown rice or maybe some wild rice.
Steve: Okay.

Violet: Maybe some wild rice mixed with basmati (bahs-mah-tee) rice.
Steve: How about broccoli?
Violet: Did you know broccoli is a combination of Brussels (brush-uhlz) sprouts and cauliflower (kaw-luh-flou-er)?
Steve: No, I had no idea.
Violet: Did you know that Eggplant is a fruit?
Steve: No. Really?
Violet: Do you know where they keep the breadcrumbs?
Steve: Yes, that I do know.
Violet: Do we have everything?
Steve: What about dessert (dih-zurt)?
Violet: Piece of pie?
Steve: What kind?
Violet: Apple (ap-uhl)?
Steve: No.
Violet: Banana Crème?
Steve: No.
Violet: Cherry?
Steve: No.
Violet: Pecan?
Steve: No.
Violet: Chocolate crème?
Steve: No.
Violet: Key lime?
Steve: Yes.
Violet: Wait, what about a dark Chocolate Soufflé?
Steve: Even better idea, this way.

12.7 Dialogue: A Job interview

To prepare for an interview. Be familiar with the company and bring a resume.

Exercise 1: Repeat aloud the following dialogue. Practice with a friend. Then switch characters.

Leigh: Hi, my name is Leigh (lee) Owsley, nice to meet you. I will be interviewing you. What is your name?
Robert: Robert Johnson.
Leigh: Do you have a copy of your resume?
Robert: Yes, here it is.
Leigh: Where did you go to College?
Robert: Santa Monica College.
Leigh: What was your GPA (grade point average)?
Robert: My GPA was 3.8.
Leigh: Tell me about your current job.
Robert: Marketing for an Internet Company.
Leigh: What specifically (spi-sif-klee) do you do?
Robert: Create marketing vehicles.
Leigh: What are some of the tasks you perform?
Robert: I negotiate (ni-goh-shee-yet) agreements between our company and organizations.
Leigh: What is your compensation?
Robert: About twenty dollars per hour plus benefits.
Leigh: How long have you been there?
Robert: Around a year.
Leigh: Why did you leave your last job?
Robert: I moved out of town.
Leigh: Tell me about a time you made a decision that helped the company.
Robert: I wrote the bid that won the city contract for the Metro system.

Leigh: Do you like to work alone or in teams better?
Robert: Teams.
Leigh: What do you like about our company?
Robert: Great reputation.
Leigh: Do you have a list of three references?
Robert: Yes, I can send you one.
Leigh: Have you ever been arrested?
Robert: No.
Leigh: When can you start?
Robert: Two weeks.
Leigh: Where do you live?
Robert: I live in lovely Hollywood, California.
Leigh: Do you have any questions for us?
Robert: Do you have parking?
Leigh: Yes, underground parking. Do you have a ticket?
Robert: Yes, here thank you.
Leigh: Anything else you would like to say?
Robert: Thanks again for the opportunity. When are, you letting, candidates know by?
Leigh: Friday.
Robert: Thank you.

12.8   Dialogue: The Florist Shop

Some of the names of flowers are quite difficult. Go slowly. Switch flowers.

Exercise 1: Repeat aloud the following dialogue. Practice and repeat with a friend.
Exercise 2: Choose a flower and describe its history.

Shopper:	Hi, how are you today, oh is that an Orchid (awr-kid)?
Florist:	Yes, we have several different varieties. We also have lilacs (lahy-luhks), asters, birds of paradise (burds uhv-par-uh-dahys), Asiatic Lily's (ey-zhee-at-ik), mini carnations (kahr-ney-shuhns), tuberoses (toob-roozs), peony's (pee-uh-nees), and snapdragons (snap-drag-uhns).
Shopper:	Can you tell me some prices?
Florist:	The Phalaenopsis(fal-uh-nop-sis) Orchids are $19.99, the Protea are $10.99, the Zinnia(zin-ee-uh) are $5.99 per bunch, the Bells of Ireland (ahyuhr-luhnd) are two for $10.00, the Plumeria are $19.99, the six-inch gardenias(gahr-dee-nyuhs) are $9.99, the Alstroemeria are two for $12.00. We also have Spanish Lavender (lav-uhn-der) for $10.99, the Marigolds (mar-i-gohldz) are $5.99, the Anthurium (an-thoor-ee-uhm) are $11.99, and the Echumeria are $8.99.
Shopper:	What have you got fresh?
Florist:	We have Fuji Mums, they are two bunches for $10.00, and three stem Casablanca's(kas-uh-blanc-kuhs) for $12.99 as well as Gladiolas(glad-ee-oh-luhs), Pom Daisies, Sunflowers, Ecuadorian(ek-wuh-dawrean) Roses, Costa Rican (kos-tuh ree-kuhn) lilies, Fuji Mums, Hydrangeas(hahy-dreyn-juhs) and cushion Chrysanthemums (kri-san-thuh-muhms).
Shopper:	How much for the Hydrangeas (hahy-dreyn-juh)?
Florist:	The Hydrangeas are $13.99; we also have some Goji berry (ber-ee) plants for $24.99.
Shopper:	Do you have roses?
Florist:	Yes. What color would you like? We have red, white, blue, and yellow.
Shopper:	Do you know what a Yucca (yuhk-uh) plant is?
Florist:	Of course, The Yucca is a plant that is a member of the lily family, its spring blossoms are bright white. Early Indians used the plant for food, the roots for soap, the leaves for sandals and, baskets. A single species of moth produces pollination (pol-uh-ney-shuhn).
Shopper:	Really. That sounds great. Can I see a blue rose?
Florist:	Yes, over here. How many would you like?

Shopper:	One dozen and a dozen of the long stem red. Do you have tulips (too-lips)?
Florist:	Yes, we have yellow, pink, purple, violet, white and, orange.
Shopper:	Those white tulips look perfect; can I have a dozen?
Florist:	How would you like them wrapped? Are they to be given right away or later?
Shopper:	Yes, right away. Please add some of that green fern-like filler stuff too.
Florist:	Will do.

12.9 Difficult words and sentences 6

This is a challenging but fun list.
Exercise 1: Repeat the word and then the sentence that follows aloud.
Exercise 2: Create a sentence for each word.

Accessories (ak-ses-uh-rees):	Auto accessories are on the last aisle.
Affidavit (af-i-dey-vit):	I got the affidavit from him right here in the courthouse, so relax.
Agitator: Agitators will be ejected from the conference.	
Aluminum (uh-loo-muh-nuhm):	Did they have any aluminum foil?
Anesthetist (uh-nes-thi-tist):	Get the anesthetist, the feeling is coming back.
Anonymous (uh-non-uh-muhs):	She wanted to remain anonymous and wouldn't take the interview.
Anyway:	He went ahead anyway he could maneuver around the icebergs.
Arctic (ahrk-tik):	The Thing is a classic 1950s Science Fiction movie that takes place in the Arctic, where an Unidentified Flying Object (UFO) is discovered.
Ask (ahsk):	Let me ask.
Asterisk (as-tuh-risk):	Mark the phrase with an asterisk.
Athlete (ath-leet):	He was a great athlete and very athletic, having won all those Olympic gold medals.
Authentic (aw-then-tik):	That will look authentic.
Boysenberry (boi-zuh-n-ber-ee):	I spread boysenberry jam on my biscuit (bis-kit).
Catechism (kat-i-kiz-uhm):	At Church, they had a catechism, and she answered all the questions correctly.
Contaminate (kuhn-tam-uh-neyt):	Don't contaminate the evidence; the forensic scientist screamed.
Controversy (kon-truh-vur-see):	There is great controversy about fracking.
Convection (kuhn-vek-shuhn):	In the interior of stars, convection cells are the most efficient transfer of energy.
Disenfranchisement (dis-en-fran-chahyz-muhnt):	The monster most definitely demonstrated signs of disenfranchisement towards Dr. Frankenstein.

Disguise (dis-gahyz):	The man in the witness protection program wore a costume when he went outside since he was in extreme danger.
Enthusiasm (en-thoo-zee-az-uhm):	The Olympics enthusiasm is contagious (kuhn-tey-juhs).
Equilibrium (ee-kwuh-lib-ree-uhm):	After the fall, it took him a while to gain his balance.
Ethnicity (eth-nis-i-tee):	What is his ethnicity?
Facilitate (fuh-sil-i-teyt):	If he is going to facilitate, please have him stand in front of the classroom.
February (feb-roo-er-ee):	It always snows in February (feb-roo-er-ee), except in warm climates where the succulents grow.
Fool:	Did he find the Fool's Gold?
Gymnastics (jim-nas-tiks):	Gymnastics requires strength, coordination, agility, and stamina.
Hereditary (huh-red-i-ter-ee):	There is an altered chromosome in the genetic link.
Hospitable (hos-pi-tuh-buhl):	Due to its warm climate, Los Angeles is one of the friendliest cities in the world.
Innuendo (in-yoo-en-doh):	An innuendo is a negative insinuation about a person.
Language (lang-gwij):	What is her favorite language?
Literature (lit-er-uh-cher):	To study literature is to study the great writers of our times.
Mind (mahynd):	Will she mind if I sit here?
Murder (mur-der):	He will be "charged with murder" unless he has an alibi (ahl-la-bi) said the Police Captain.
Organizer (awr-guh-nahy-zer):	When Betsy suggested I become an organizer, I asked her if she'd ever seen my desk.
Particularly (per-tik-yuh-ler-lee):	I don't particularly (per-tik-yuh-ler-lee) like it when it rains in Los Angeles, as drivers get incredibly nervous, causing accidents.
Phenomenon (fi-nom-uh-non):	A phenomenon is a type of occurrence. Examples of natural phenomena include biological processes, gravity, tides, oscillation, and erosion.
Philosophical (fil-uh-sof-i-kuhl):	Sometimes, he is very philosophical and at other times he is artistic.
Prejudice (prej-uh-dis):	The hung jury was prejudice towards the teenager.
Prosper (pros-per):	Live long and prosper (pros-per) was Leonard (len-erd) Nimoy's classic line as Spock (spok) in Star Trek.
Provocatively (pruh-vok-uh-tiv-lee):	Basic Instinct is a film about a woman who provocatively manipulates the police in a famous interrogation scene with Sharon Stone.
Rambunctious (ram-buhngk-shuhs):	The new actors got rambunctious when they saw craft service filled with food and accidentally knocked over the lights while running to the table.
Remuneration (ri-myoo-nuh-rey-shuhn):	Juan from Spain joked about the remuneration at the beginning of the session.
Should (shood):	She should listen to her heart.
Stanchions (stuh-tis-tiks):	They attached stanchions to the roof for the solar cells.
Statistics (stuh-tis-tiks):	Can he prove that statement with statistics?

Tassels (tas-uhl):	Those tassels drive him nuts.
Thesaurus (thi-sawr-uhs):	Use a Thesaurus to look up synonyms.
Virulent (vir-yuh-luhnt):	Something or someone that is highly infective, malignant (muh-lig-nuhnt) or deadly. Covid-19 is extremely virulent.
Vulnerability (vuhl-ner-uh-bil-i-tee):	It's the vulnerability as an actor that makes characters real.
Watchful (woch-fuhl):	Be watchful while crossing the street.
Wear (wair):	They usually wear light clothes (klohz) in Hollywood since it's so warm.
Where and Were:	Where were you when the filming took place?
Where (wair):	Where did they put the dark chocolate? It's missing.
Painting:	Besides painting, for an artist, there is drawing, sketching, and sculpting (skuhlpt-ng).
Would (wuhd):	Would you fetch me some wood for the fire?

12.10 Dialogue: Cover letter for Resume

A cover letter is a separate document sent with the resume. It should be well written, with no errors.

Exercise 1: Repeat aloud the following dialogue. Practice with a friend, switch sides.
Exercise 2: Research other cover letters and then create one.

James:	What is the purpose of the cover letter?
Jubilee (joo-buh-lee):	A cover letter aims to get you the interview and, ultimately, the job.
James:	How do I start the letter?
Jubilee:	The opening sentence needs to grab their attention. For example, I saw your ad on Craig's List and would be interested in the position of public relations account executive.
James:	Can you give me another example?
Jubilee:	An opening sentence with a pitch, I called more than five thousand clients in two years and can do the same for you.
James:	What else do I need to include?
Jubilee:	Leave easy, clear contact information, the address is optional at first, but later you might be asked to give all types of documentation and take tests. Do the best you can do on all the tests. Some of these are psychological profiles; some might be math word problems or some specific to a field.
James:	Do I have to take the tests?
Jubilee:	If you want the job, you usually have no choice. So be sure you want the job before giving access. Don't cheat or fake resume details that can easily be checked. It's

	okay to exaggerate (ig-zaj-uh-reyt) a little, but you might be asked to speak those languages you list.
James:	What should I bring?
Jubilee:	For the interview, bring a copy of your resume, be prepared to discuss everything on it, and be appropriately dressed.
James:	When should I arrive for the interview?
Jubilee:	When you are late for the interview, it shows resistance. When you are early for the meeting, it says you are anxious, and when you are precisely on time, it's a sign of obsessive-compulsive behavior.
James:	I guess I'll come early.
Jubilee:	That's usually the best option.

12.11 Difficult words and sentences 7

Exercise 1: Practice reciting the following words and sentences aloud.
Exercise 2: Create a sentence.

1.	Achieve (uh-cheev): May you achieve your dreams and seize all opportunities.
2.	Adapt (uh-dapt): The chameleon (kuh-mee-lee-uhn) adapts to any background color through camouflage (kam-uh-flahzh).
3.	Adopt (uh-dopt): Did she adopt that cute Chihuahua (chi-wah-wah)?
4.	Advice (ad-vahys): Bringing a sweater was good advice, thanks.
5.	Advise (ad-vahyz): If you want to live, I advise you taste the soup before adding salt at the French Restaurant.
6.	Announcement (uh-nouns-muhnt): Congratulations, I heard about the marriage announcement.
7.	Apply (uh-plahy): Did they apply for those great postal jobs?
8.	Awed (awd): They were awed by the fireworks.
9.	Ban (ban): On Halloween to protect the Ocean, there is a ban on using silly string in Hollywood punishable by a $10,000 (ten thousand) dollar fine.
10.	Bang (bang): Did you hear that bang?
11.	Behave (bih-heyv) Try to behave on that flight to Ireland (ahyuhr-luhnd).
12.	Boss (baws): With these new closed-circuit (sur-kit) cameras, the boss is everywhere.
13.	Butler (buht-ler): The butler cleaned the Rolls Royce.
14.	Carrier (kar-ee-er): Did she see the nuclear (noo-klee-er) Aircraft Carrier?
15.	Cooperate (koh-op-uh-reyt): Did they cooperate with the police?
16.	Cord (kawrd): Grab the cord and look out for the buoy (boo-ee).
17.	Duck(duhk): Dabbling duck, Donald Duck, Cold Duck, Domestic Duck, Daffy Duck, Duck L' Orange, Peking(pee-king) Duck, and the Anaheim Ducks.

18. Extinguishers (ik-sting-gwi-shers): Please remember to bring the fire extinguishers (ik-sting-gwi-shers).
19. Fan (fan): Let's get a new fan.
20. Fang (fang): That Cobra had very long fangs.
21. Feudal (fyood-l): During feudal times, villages were established.
22. Freedom (free-duhm): I hope she appreciates the freedom the new schedule allows.
23. Futile (fyoot-l): From that prison, escape is futile.
24. Gnat (nat): That gnat is annoying.
25. Good (good): That's a good decision.
26. Gratitude (grat-i-tood): Please accept (ak-sept) this gift as a gesture of my gratitude.
27. Hurt (hurt): Did the gymnast get hurt after falling off the horse?
28. Life (lahyf): These tools are guaranteed for life.
29. Lower (loh-er): If he gets solar, his electric bills will be lower.
30. Mulch (muhlch): Use the mulch to prevent erosion.
31. Pause (pawz): Where is the pause button (buht-n)?
32. Peace (pees): We prayed for world peace.
33. Pedestrians (puh-des-tree-uhns): Remember to yield for pedestrians and bicycles.
34. Podiatrist (puh-dahy-uh-trist): The Podiatrist examined my feet.
35. Pouch (pouch): Kangaroos are Marsupials (mahr-soo-pee-uhl) and have a small pouch for their young.
36. Predator (pred-uh-ter): Don't thank predators or give them treats; it's the wrong sign.
37. Punctual (puhngk-choo-uhl): The hospital staff was punctual and admitted him on time.
38. Rise (rahyz): I rise with the sun in the morning.
39. Rung (ruhng): The top rung of the corporate ladder is hard to reach.
40. Section (sek-shuhn): Please cut me off a section of that Lasagna.
41. Session (sesh-uhn): I like to take notes during the session.
42. Soil (soil): Try not to lose the topsoil, which takes thousands of years to create.
43. Solitude (sol-i-tood): The hermit (hur-mit) lived a life of solitude and saw no one.
44. Succeed (suhk-seed): If you work hard at something you love, you will succeed.
45. Surf (surf): Did she buy a new surfboard?
46. Syndrome (sin-drohm): This syndrome includes a specific group of symptoms.
47. Tank (tangk): The Army tank guarded the cathedral (kuh-thee-druhl).
48. Told (tohld): I told him not to let the dog loose.
49. Wing (wing): Would they like hot wings for a snack?
50. Wise (wahyz): Be wise, take an umbrella, (uhm-brel-uh) it looks like rain.

12.12 Bartender: Mixed drinks, beers, alcohol, and supplies

Exercise 1: Repeat aloud the name of the drink and the sentences that follow.
Exercise 2: Research and write a sentence or two about the origins of Cognacs, Vodkas and Champagnes.

1. Americano (uh-mer-i-kan-oh): The Americano is made with Campari, sweet vermouth, club soda, and a maraschino cherry.
2. Some popular beer brands include Anchor Steam (ang-ker steem), Belgian White Ale (bel-juhn hwahyt eyl), Blue(bloo) Moon, Brahma(brah-muh), Bud Light, Budweiser, Busch Light, Coors Light, Corona(kuh-roh-nuh), Harbin, Heineken, Keystone Light (kee-stohn lahyt), Kol, Michelob, Miller Genuine Draft (jen-yoo-in drahft), Miller High Life, Modelo, Natural Ice, Natural Light, Rolling Rock (roh-ling rok), Samuel(sam-yoo-uhl) Adams, Shiner Bock (shahy-ner bok), Sierra Nevada (see-er-uh nuh-vad-uh) Pale(peyl) Ale, Snow(snoh), Tsingtao(tsing-tou), Yanjing.
3. Black and tan: To make a black and tan, fill the glass halfway with a Pale Ale and then add a Stout.
4. Blue Hawaiian: Rum, vodka, pineapple juice, blue curacao (koor-uh-sou), ice, garnish.
5. Body: The body is the bottom half of the glass as compared to the head of the beer, which is the top half.
6. Brandy (bran-dee): Brandy is a distilled wine; types of Brandies include Cognacs (kohn-yaks) and Armagnacs (ahr-muhn–yaks).
7. Champagne: Champagne is an actual sparkling wine produced from grapes grown in the Champagne region of France.
8. Cocktails (kok-teylz): A cocktail is usually a generic name for any type of mixed drink, from Screwdrivers to Gimlet, but might also include beers or sake.
9. Cognac (kohn-yak): Made in the town of Cognac in France, brandy is twice distilled in copper pots and aged for at least two years. The grades of Cognac are the following: VS (very special, at least two years old in oak casks), VSOP (very special old pale, at least four years), XO (extra old, at least six years in oak casks and usually much longer).
10. Daiquiri (Dahy-kuh-ree) Great fruity sweet drink with rum, fruit, lemon juice, sugar, and ice then blend. Originally named after a city in Cuba (kyoo-buh).
11. Draft (drahft) or Draught (drahft): Draught beer is on tap and is served from a cask or a keg.
12. Fuzzy navel (fuhz-ee ney-vuhl): The Fuzzy navel is made with 1 oz. peach schnapps, and 2 oz. orange juice.
13. Galliano: Galliano is a sweet liquor originally from Tuscany, made with many ingredients including anise, juniper, lavender, peppermint, cinnamon, and vanilla.
14. Gimlet (gim-let): A Gimlet is made with Vodka (vod-kuh), fresh lime juice, lime roses, and ice.
15. Godiva chocolate and Raspberry Martini (guh-dahy-vuh chaw-kuh-lit and raz-ber-ee mahr-tee-nee): A Godiva Martini is made with Raspberry vodka (vod-kuh), Godiva and dark chocolate liquor (lik-er) and a garnish (gahr-nish).

16.	Grasshopper (gras-hop-er): A grasshopper is a sweet after-dinner drink made with crème de menthe, crème de cacao and fresh crème.
17.	Guinness Stout (gin-is stout): Guinness is a dry stout beer originally made in Ireland, now it is one of the most popular beer brands in the world.
18.	Harvey Wallbanger: A Wallbanger is made with 1 oz. vodka (vod-kuh), 2 oz. orange juice, ½ oz. Galliano and ice. Remember to add the Galliano last and let it float on the surface.
19.	Head (hed): The head is the top portion of a poured glass of beer, usually characterized by foam.
20.	Hurricane: Lime juice, passion fruit syrup, rum, ice, and garnish.
21.	Irish coffee (ahy-rish kaw-fee): A strong drink served on cold nights. Irish coffee is made with ½ oz. Irish whiskey, hot coffee, and a whipped cream garnish.
22.	Kahlua (kah-loo-ah): Kahlua is a coffee-flavored rum-based liqueur from Mexico. Mixed with milk and ice for a drink called a sombrero or mixed with vodka for a white Russian.
23.	Lemon drop Martini (lem-uhn drop mahr-tee-nee): A strong sweet drink for those hot nights, made with vodka (vod-kuh), triple sec, fresh lemon juice and tons of sugar.
24.	Mai Tai: Rum (light and dark), orange curacao, pineapple juice, orange juice, fresh lime juice, grenadine, ice, maraschino cherries, garnish.
25.	Manhattan (man-hat-n): A Manhattan is made with Rye whiskey, Italian vermouth, Angostura, and shaken to perfection.
26.	Maraschino Cherry (mar-uh-shee-noh cher-ee): A candied cherry used in cocktails. One day at the Sharon Osbourne Show, they sent a young intern to go food shopping. He was told to buy fruit for the craft service table; he returned with a gallon of maraschino cherries. That was the last time they sent him out to shop. Why?
27.	Margarita (mahr-guh-ree-tuh): A strong to mild drink very popular in California with Tequila (tuh-kee-luh), triple sec, fresh lime juice, salt, and garnish.
28.	Mint Julep (mint joo-lip): For those days at the Kentucky Derby, made with Bourbon (boor-buhn), fresh mint, simple sugar, club soda, and finely cracked ice.
29.	Mojito (moh-hee-toh): A strong drink sometimes, made with Rum (ruhm), fresh mint, fresh lime juice, and sugar.
30.	Old fashion (ohld fash-uhn): A strong drink, made with Bourbon (boor-buhn), muddle sugar, Angostura bitter, orange slices, club soda, and a Maraschino cherry.
31.	On tap (tap): Beer on tap is usually fresher and less expensive than bottled beers from my experience.
32.	Pina Colada: Pineapple juice, Rum, Coco Lopez coconut cream, mix w crushed ice, garnish w pineapple.
33.	Port (pawrt): Port is a sweet red wine from the Douro Valley (doh-roo val-ee) in Portugal (pawr-chuh-guhl), usually served in a small glass at the end of dinner.
34.	Rum: Rum is a distilled alcoholic beverage made directly from sugar cane products using the processes of fermentation and distillation. Popular uses include Pina Coladas, daiquiris, and mojitos.
35.	Sake (sah-kee): Sake is Japanese fermented rice wine, usually served warm although it is also served cold. To heat sake, take the bottle, open the top, and place in a large 1 quart or

gallon pot of water. Let the water boil and watch as the sake level inside the bottle increases. Usually 5-10 minutes. Take an oven glove or towel and pour it into a cup.

36. Sambuca (sam-byoo-kuh): Sambuca is flavored with essential oils from anise, star anise, licorice (lik-uh-rish) and elderflowers, usually served at the end of dinner with three coffee beans floating at the bottom of a snifter (snif-ter) glass.

37. Scotch (skoch): Scotch whiskey is made from malted barley and must be aged in oak barrels for at least three years in Scotland. Scotch whiskey is broken down into five classes: single malt, single grain, blended malt, blended grain, and blended scotch whiskey. Some single malt brands include Oban, Dalwhinnie, Laphroaig, Balvenie, Ardbeg, Macallan, Lagavulin, Dalmore, Inchgower, Glenmorangie and Jura. Back in the Hollywood Hills days, I would drink Glenfiddich Scotch on the rocks. It had a smooth, rich flavor and was a strong drink.

38. Screwdriver: The classic screwdriver is made with 1 ½ oz. vodka, 6 oz. orange juice and ice cubes.

39. Sea Breeze: A Sea Breeze is made with vodka (vod-kuh), cranberry juice, and ice.

40. Sex on the beach: Vodka, peach schnapps, orange juice, cranberry juice, ice, shaken to finish.

41. Tequila (tuh-kee-luh): Tequila is a distilled beverage made from the Agave plant produced primarily near the town of Tequila in Mexico. Some top brands include Don Julio, Patron, 1800 Tequila, Cabo Wabo, Herradura, Corralejo, Milagro, Tres Generations, Cazadores, El Jimador, Tres Agaves, Ocho, Sauza, Don Ramon, and 1921 Tequila.

42. Tom Collins: To make a Tom Collins add Gin (Jin), fresh lemon juice, club soda, a maraschino cherry, and sugar to taste.

43. Vineyard (vin-yerd): The vineyard is a plantation of grape bearing vines. In California, a vineyard is always a good day trip for a wine tasting experience.

44. Vodka (vod-kuh): Is a distilled beverage composed primarily of water and ethanol, traditionally made from potatoes or cereal grains. Some brands include Belvedere, Poland; Reyka, Iceland; Uluvka, Poland; Snow Queen (kween), Kazakhstan; Russian Standard, Russia; Heavy Water, Sweden; Grey Goose, France; Crystal Head, Canada; Silver Tree, USA; Kauffman Luxury, Russia.

45. Whiskey Sour (hwis-kee sou-er): Sometimes, a whiskey sour is served before dinner. It is made with Whiskey, usually Bourbon, with lemon juice over ice.

46. White Wine: The different types of white wine are the following: Chardonnay (shahr-dn-ey), Sauvignon (soh-vin-yohn) Blanc (blangk), Semillon (sey-mee-yohn), Moscato, Pinot (pee-noh) Grigio, Gewurztraminer (guh-voorts-truh-mee-ner) and Riesling (reez-ling).

47. Red Wine: The different types of red wines are the following: Syrah, Merlot, Cabernet Sauvignon (soh-vin-yohn), Malbec (mael-bek), Pinot noir (pee-noh nwahr), Zinfandel (zin-fuhn-del), Sangiovese (san-geo-veizi) and Barbera (bahr-bair-uh). A great item to bring when visiting a

12.13 Prefixes, Roots and Suffixes 3

The English language is created from many different roots and has many different prefixes (at the front of the word) and suffixes (at the end of the word) or root (in the middle of the word) used in creating words. By studying roots, prefixes, and suffixes the student will improve their ability to quickly understand the meanings of words.

Exercise 1: Repeat aloud the name of the prefix or suffix and the sentences that follow.
Exercise 2: Research and write a sentence or two about the origins of a suffix, prefix, or root.
Exercise 3: Add other prefixes, suffixes, and roots to this list.

Prefix, Suffix, or Root	Meaning	Example words	Sentence
Able	Can do	acceptable, agreeable bearable, capable, comfortable enjoyable, forcible, horrible laughable, manageable portable, reliable, sociable(soh-shuh-buhl) tenable, terrible, .	Is that automobile reliable?
A, ac, ad, af, ag, al, an, ap, as, at prefix	To go forward, to, toward, near, in addition to, by	accompany, adjust, administer, advance, adverb, advocate, affection, affix, aggression, allocate, annihilate, aside, associate, attend.	Tell them they can advance to the next level.
Age	State of,	courage, shrinkage, suffrage, tonnage.	That was very courageous of them.
Ar, er, or	One who does, that which: suffix	Doctor, baker, actor, fighter, beggar, dancer, jester, killer, liar, miser, tractor, barber, wrecker, painter, exhibitor, racer, amplifier, pacifier.	The jester is one who makes the King laugh.
Ary, ery, ory,	Relating to a place where	spectacular, unitary.	They will be able to sleep in the dormitory tonight.

Ate,	Causes, makes,	ameliorate, amputate, candidate, collegiate, delegate electorate, graduate, habitat inviolate.	Don't deviate from the course.
Aud,	Hear	audience, audio, audible, auditorium, audiovisual, audition, auricular.	The lecture will be in the auditorium.
Di	Two, double	divide, diverge, diglycerides.	They are getting a divorce and dividing everything in half.
Dis, dif	Take away	differ, disallow, disarray, disconnect, dismiss, disperse, disproportion, disrespect, dissuade, distemper, divide.	I must disagree with him.
Ec, ef	Out	echo, eclipse, eclectic, ecstasy, eczema.	As an Uncle he is a bit eccentric.
En, em	Into	enamor, embolden, enslave, empower, entangle.	They were encouraged to apply for the job.
en	Made of, make	golden, woolen, silken.	Is that a woolen sweater?
Ex	Out of, away from, lacking, former outside of, beyond	exit, exhale, exclusive, exceed, explosion, ex-mayor external, extrinsic, extraordinary, extrapolate, extraneous, extrovert.	He excelled at the job and was quickly promoted.
Fer	To bring	ferry, coniferous, fertile, defer, infer, refer, transfer.	Did that transfer at the bank go through?
Ful	Full of	mouthful, fanciful.	That horse is a handful.
Ic	Nature of	generic, arithmetic, economics.	The lifesaver was heroic and saved the swimmer's life.
In, ir ible, il, in, im	Not, into, on, near, towards not	convertible, eligible, feasible, flexible, gullible, horrible, illegible, import, impossible, imposter, impregnable, inaction, incredible, innocent, innocuous, instead, intractable,	Where is that Invisible man?

		invincible, inviolate, irresolute, negligible, ostensible, plausible, responsible, reversible, suggestible, susceptible, tangible, terrible.	
Ion, sion, tion	Act or state of Noun: condition or action	abduction, induction, reduction, persuasion, occasion, reception.	His actions are legendary.
Ir	Not	irate, irregular.	Are those irregular sneakers?
Ite	Mineral product Noun: state or quality	graphite, elite, crystallite, vermiculite, stalactite. (stuh-lak-tahyt)	Stalactites are from the ceiling and Stalagmites(stur-lag-mahyt) are from the floors of caves, caverns, etc.
Less	Without	motiveless, lifeless, fearless, timeless.	He was fearless and jumped right off that diving board.
Ly	In the manner, of	fluently.	He shamelessly swept the game.
Ment	State of, results, mind	mental, mention, document.	The agreement continued late into the night.
Nasc, nat	To be born	nascent, natural, native.	She spoke like a native New Yorker.
Ness	The state of being	kindness, happiness, loneliness.	The couple's happiness was contagious.
Non	Not	nonferrous, nonsense, nonabrasive, nondescript.	Such nonsense.
Port	To carry	porter, portable, transport, report, export, import, support, transportation.	The porter will help him with the luggage.
Re	Back again	report, realign, retract, revise, regain.	Did they go to the reunion?
Trans	Across	transform, transoceanic, transmit, transportation, transducer.	Will she be able to translate that document?
Un	Not	unceasing, unequal, unhappy.	He is unable to go swimming.
Vis, vid	Visible	evident, indivisible, provide, providence, review, revise, supervise, video, visible, vision, visit, vista.	The moon is now visible in the Eastern sky.

| Y | Inclined | society, victory, envy, crafty. | Roberto's beagle, Dr. Watson was crafty and found the treats on top of the mosaic(moh-zey-ik). |

Lesson 13

The Moon, Polygons, Prefixes, Hybrids

13.1   Pronunciation Key 18

This is an extensive list of words in the English language. One of the student's favorites. Practice until they are easy and familiar. This is a long list, don't rush.
Exercise: Repeat the words aloud. Then practice the sentence below.

Pronunciation Key

		[practice sentence]
A, as in pat:	plaid (plad), half (haf), halves (havz), laugh (laf)	Don't make me laugh.
A, as in mane:	plain, gauge (geyj), pay, suede (sweyd), bouquet (boh-key), break, vein (veyn), eight (eyt), neighbor	Those are beautiful blue suede shoes.
A, as in care:	aerial (air-ee-uhl), air (air), prayer (prair), there, pear (pair)	I think the pear is ripe.
A, as in father:	balm (bahm), sergeant (sahr-juhnt)	Put some skin balm on.
B, as in bib:	blubber (bluhb-er) cupboard (kuhb-erd), raspberry (raz-ber-ee)	Do we have any raspberry jam left?
Ch, as in church:	cello (chel-oh), Czech (chek), latch (lach), question, denture (den-cher)	Just one more question.
D, as in dark:	muddle (muhd-l), mailed	I mailed that letter a while ago.
E, as in pet:	any (en-ee), aesthetic (es-thet-ik), said, says, thread (thred), heifer (hef-er), leopard (lep-erd), friendly, burial (ber-ee-uhl)	Frank Lloyd Wright had a natural aesthetic.
E, as in be:	Caesar (see-zer), each, beach, beet, conceit (kuhn-seet), people, key, piano, siege (seej), Phoenix (fee-niks)	Let's go to the beach.
F, as in fife:	stiff, enough (ih-nuhf), half, photo, graph.	That's enough ice cream.

G, as in gag:	bragged, ghost, guest, epilogue (ep-uh-lawg)	Did she see the ghost?
H, as in hat:	who, Gila monster (hee-luh mon-ster)	They'll need warm hats.
I, as in pit:	village, climate (klahy-mit), certificate (ser-tif-i-kit), enough (ih-nuhf), been (bin), carriage, sieve (siv), women (wim-in), busy, built, nymph	The climate has changed in the last few years.
I, as in pie:	aisle (ahyl), aye (ahy), Bayou (bahy-oo), height, eye, lie, sigh, right, island, buy, sky, rye	Let's visit the Bayou.
I, as in pier:	here, ear, beer, weird (weerd)	Let's have the picnic here.
J, as in jar:	gradual, lodging, dodge, soldier (sohl-jer), register, gem, vengeance (ven-juhns), exaggerate (ig-zaj-uh-reyt)	I've told him a million times, don't exaggerate.
K, as in kick:	call, ecstasy (ek-stuh-see), account, chaos (key-os), schedule, crack, lacquer (lak-er), talk, plaque (plak)	Let me check my schedule.
Kw, as in quick:	choir (kwahy-uhr), acquire (uh-kwahyuhr)	That school has a beautiful choir.
L, as in lid:	tall, llama (lah-muh), Lloyd (loid), Lhasa (lah-suh)	That is a very tall tree.
M, as in mum:	paradigm (par-uh-dahym), balm (bahm), plumb, hammer (ham-er), solemn	Does he have a hammer and nails?
N, as in no:	gnat (nat), knife (nahyf), mnemonic (ni-mon-ik), pneumonia (noo-mohn-yuh)	Careful she doesn't get pneumonia.
O, as in paw or for:	all, water, talk, Utah(yoo-taw), warm, Arkansas(ahr-kuhn-saw), caught(kawt), gaunt(gawnt), automobile(aw-tuh-muh-beel), awful, awe, Choctaw(chok-taw), oar, broad, bought(bawt), thought(thawt)	I bought a new electric automobile.
Oi, as in noise:	boy, soy, joy, toy	Please no soy sauce.
Ou, as in out:	sauerkraut (souuhr-krout), sauerbraten, hour, bough (bou), sow, scowl	He scowled at the rain.
Oo, as in took:	woman (woom-uhn), wolf (woolf), should, full, cushion (koosh-uhn)	Sorry I took his seat.
Oo, as in boot:	maneuver(muh-noo-ver), shrew, lieutenant (loo-ten-uhnt), do, move, two, canoe(kuh-noo), soup, group, through (throo), rude, blue, flue, fruit, bruise(brooz)	What's his favorite soup?
P, as in pop:	happy (hap-ee), pepper, popular	They were happy with the offer.

R, as in roar:	rhythm (rith-uhm), cherry, write	That song has a complicated rhythm.
S, as in say:	cellar (sel-er) cent (sent), sauce, psalm (sahm), scene (seen), abscess (ab-ses), schism (skiz-uhm), pass	Well how did she like the sauce?
Sh, as in ship:	oceanic (oh-shee-an-ik), chandelier (shan-dl-eer), gracious (grey-shuhs), magician, sugar, conscience (kon-shuhns), schist (shist), nauseous (naw-shuhs), pension (pen-shuhn),	That's a beautiful chandelier.
T, as in tie:	stopped, caught (kawt), Thomas, letter, two	They caught the last flight to the mainland.
U, as in cut:	son, income, does, blood (bluhd), couple, trouble	Did she have any trouble at the DMV?
Yoo, as in use:	beautiful, feud (fyood), pew, adieu (uh-doo), view, cue, suit (soot), you, yule (yool), dew	I need to get my suit dry cleaned.
U, as in fur:	earn, learn (lurn), herd, fern, term, bird(burdz), first, work, journey, journal, scourge (skurj), myrtle (mur-tl)	Have they seen any birds today?
V, as in valve:	of, Steven, Vivian	Vivian drove a Vega.
W, as in with:	one, wonder, world, winter, winner	Is that the number one answer?
Y, as in yes:	onion, hallelujah (hal-uh-loo-yuh)	Would he like a bowl of French onion soup
Z, as in zebra:	czar (zahr), rise, hers, dessert (dih-zurt), xylophone (zahy-luh-fohn) fuzz	Did she try the dessert?
Zh, as in:	garage, mirage (mi-rahzh), pleasure, vision (vizh-uhn).	They will need to get their vision tested this year at the DMV.

13.2 Abbreviations, acronyms, mnemonics

Everyone enjoys abbreviating a word, and with the rise in texting shortcuts are even more important than ever before.

Exercise 1: Create a sentence using each abbreviation
Exercise 2: Add additional abbreviations to the list.

2F4U Too Fast for You	AD Anno Domini, or the Year of Our Lord.
4YEO For Your Eyes Only	
Abbr. Abbreviation (uh-bree-vee-ey-shuhn)	Ad inf. Ad infinitum
	Ad Assistant director
ACK Acknowledgment (ak-nol-ij-muhnt)	Adv. Adverb
	AFAIK As Far As I Know

AKA	Also known As
AM	Ante Meridian (morning)
Anon	Anonymous (uh-non-uh-muhs)
ASAP	As Soon As Possible
Ave	Avenue (av-uh-nyoo)
B	Be
B/C	Because
BA	Bachelor of Arts
BFF	Best Friends, Forever
Blvd	Boulevard (bool-uh-vahrd)
BM&Y	Between Me and You
BRB	Be Right Back
BS	Bachelor of Science
BTW	By the Way
BYOB	Bring your own bottle
c	Cup/cups
C	See
C&P	Copy and Paste
c.	Century (sen-chuh-ree)
CEO	Chief Executive Officer
CFO	Chief Financial Officer
Chap	Chapters
Conj.	Conjunction (kuhn-juhngk-shuhn)
Cons.	Consonant (kon-suh-nuhnt)
CTN	Cannot talk now
CU	See you
CWYL	Chat with You Later
CYT	See You Tomorrow
DC	Doctor of Chiropractic
DDS	Dentist
DIY	Do It Yourself
DJ	Disc Jockey
DOA	Dead On Arrival
DSLR	Digital Single Lens Reflex
DUI	Driving Under the Influence
E123	Easy as 1, 2, 3
Ea.	Each
EM?	Excuse Me?
EOD	End of Day
Eq	Equalizer

Et al.	And others
ETA	Estimated Time of Arrival
Etc.	Et Cetera (and so forth)
EVP	Executive Vice President
Ex	Example
F2F	Face to Face
FAQ	Frequently Asked Questions
FC	Fingers Crossed
FDIC	The Federal Deposit Insurance Corp.
FHA	The Federal Housing Administration
FYI	For Your Information
Gal	Gallon (gal-uhn)
HD	High Definition
I	Eye
IDC	I Don't Care
IDK	I don't know
ISO	International Organization for Standardization
JD	Juris (joor-is) Doctor
KFY	Kiss for You
KO	Knock out
KPC	Keeping Parents Clueless
L8R	Later
Lat.	Latitude (lat-i-tood) (north/south)
Lbs.	Pounds
Ln	Lane
LOL	Laughing out loud
Long.	Longitude (lon-ji-tood) (east/west)
LP	Long Playing
MA	Master of Arts
MD	Medical Doctor
Misc.	Miscellaneous (mis-uh-ley-nee-uhs)
MoF	Male or Female
MPHIL	Master of Philosophy
MYOB	Mind Your Own Business
N/A	Not Available / Applicable
NC	No Comment
NOYB	None of your Business

NP	No Problem
NRN	No Reply Necessary
NSFW	Not Safe for Work
O	Owe
OMG	Oh my God
OMW	On My Way
OTL	Out to Lunch
PA	Personal Assistant, Production assistant
PM	Post meridian (afternoon)
POV	Point of View
Prep.	Preposition
Pron.	Pronoun
PROP(S)	Proper Respect / Proper Recognition
PS	PostScript
Pt.	Pint
QED	Quite Easily Done
Qt	Quart
QT	Cutie
R	Are
Rd	Road
RIP	Requiescat in pace (May he or she rest in peace)
RN	Right Now
ROFL	Rolling on the floor laughing
RSVP	Repondez s'il vous plait (Please reply)
RU	Are You
Rx	Prescription drug
SEP	Someone Else's Problem
SOS	Emergency, Ship in Distress, Call for Help
SOHCAHTOA	Sine Opposite/Hypotenuse Cosine Adjacent/Hypotenuse Tangent Opposite/ Adjacent
SSA	The Social Security Administration.
St	Street
STFU	Shut the F*** Up
Superl.	Superlative (suh-pur-luh-tiv)
SVP	Senior Vice President
TA	Teaching Assistant
TBA	To Be Announced
Tbs (T)	Tablespoon/Tablespoons
TGIF	Thank God, it's Friday
THX	Thanks
TKO	Technical Knock Out
TMI	Too Much Information
Tsp (t)	Teaspoon/Teaspoons
TTYL	Talk to you later
TY	Thank You
U	You
UPS	United Parcel Service
Vb.	Verb
VIP	Very Important person
VP	Vice President
WFM	Works for Me
WRT	With Regard to
WTF	What the F***
WYCM	Will You Call Me?
WYWH	Wish You Were Here
XL	Extra large
XO	Hugs and Kisses
Y	Why?

13.3 The Four Seasons of the Year

Exercise 1: Repeat the seasons and then the sentence aloud.
Exercise 2: What is a favorite sport for each season?
Exercise 3: What is a favorite holiday in each season?

Spring:	The vernal (vur-nl) equinox (ee-kwuh-noks) is March 20th, and that's when spring begins.
Summer:	The summer solstice (sohl-stis) is on June 22nd, and that's when summer begins.
Autumn (fall):	The autumnal equinox is on September 22nd, and that's when autumn begins.
Winter:	The winter solstice is on December 22nd, and that's when winter begins.
Equinox (ee-kwuh-noks):	On the September equinox, there is an equal amount of day and night.
Winter Solstice (sohl-stis):	The December solstice is the shortest day of the year.
Summer Solstice (sohl-stis):	The Summer solstice is the longest day of the year.

13.4 Moon notes

Exercise 1: Practice reciting the moon facts listed below.

Moon details
Waxing = getting bigger.
Waning = getting smaller.
Age: 4.50 billion (bil-yuhn) years
Circumference (ser-kuhm-fer-uhns): 6,780 miles
Gravity (grav-i-tee): 9.81 meters/s² [nine point eight one meters per second squared]
Orbital distance: 238,000 miles
Orbital period: 27.30 days
Radius: 1,080 miles
The Moon is Crescent when less than half is visible.
New moon: day 1, dark night sky
Waxing crescent (kres-uhnt) moon. A very thin sliver of a moon.
Waxing quarter (kwawr-ter) moon: seven days
Waxing gibbous (gib-uhs) moon
Full moon: 14 days: The moon is in the wane (weyn) from full to new moon.
Waning gibbous moon
Waning quarter half moon
Waning crescent moon
New moon: 29 days, 12 hours

Blood moon: A blood (bluhd) moon occurs when there is a total lunar eclipse (ih-klips). The Earth is between the Moon and the Sun. This hides the Moon from the sunlight. Because of this, only light from the edges of the earth's atmosphere gets through, which then has its blue light removed. It is this red spectrum light that's hitting the moon's surface, causing the reddish color.	
Supermoon: A supermoon is when the full moon is at the nearest point in its orbit; this is called the perigee (per-i-jee). It appears larger in the night sky, therefore called a super moon. The furthest point is called the apogee (ap-uh-jee); this is known as a micro moon. A supermoon is 14% bigger and 30% brighter than a micro moon.	
Blue moon: A blue moon is an extra moon in a season of 4 full moons or two moons in one calendar month, occurring every two and a half years.	
Moon bows (moon-bohz) or lunar rainbows are unusual natural phenomena that happen when the light of the Moon becomes reflected and refracted off moisture in the air.	

13.5 Moon idiomatic expressions

Expression	Used in sentence	Idiomatic expression definition
shoot the moon	It's the last hand, let's shoot the moon.	To leave without paying the bill, to bet everything in a card game.
ask for the moon	The celebrity asked for the moon from the studio.	To make unreasonable requests or demands.
many moons ago	I was here many moons ago.	A long time ago.
promise the moon	The presidential candidate promised the moon, but can he deliver.	To offer more than is usually needed.
honeymoon	They went to Tahiti for their honeymoon.	The traditional period after the wedding to celebrate and consummate the marriage.

13.6 Numbers 6: Polygons

Polygons are 2D plane structures with three or more sides.

Exercise 1: Review aloud the following chart.
Exercise 2: Create a list of objects with similar shapes.

Name of polygon(pol-ee-gon)	
Triangle(trahy-ang-guhl)	three sides
Quadrilateral(kwod-ruh-lat-er-uhl)	four sides
Pentagon(pen-tuh-gon)	five sides

Hexagon (hek-suh-gon)	six sides
Heptagon (hep-tuh-gon)	seven sides
Octagon (ok-tuh-gon)	eight sides
Nonagon (non-uh-gon)	nine sides
Decagon (dek-uh-gon)	ten sides

13.7 Numbers 7: Volume 3D shapes

Volume formulas. The volume is generally equated (ih-kwey-td) to the capacity of the container measured in cubic units.

Exercise 1: Review the following formulas aloud
Exercise 2: Add numbers and practice formulas

Key: π = pi = 3.14   ht=height, r=radius, w=width, l=length, V=volume
V sphere (sfeer) = $\frac{4}{3}\pi r^3$: (four thirds pi r cubed)
V cone (kohn) = $\frac{1}{3}(\pi r^2 h)$: (one third pi r squared times height)
V rectangular prism (priz-uhm) = l w h: (length times width times height)
V triangular prism (priz-uhm) = ½ whl: (one half width times height times length.)
V cylinder (sil-in-der) = $\pi r^2 h$: (pi times r sq. multiplied by height)
V pyramid (pir-uh-mid) = $\frac{1}{3}$(lwh): (one third times length width height)
V cube (kyoob) = a^3 (side cubed)
V ellipsoid (ih-lip-soid) = $\frac{4}{3}\pi r1\ r2\ r3$: (four thirds pi times r one times r two times r three)

13.8 Numbers 8: The Decimal point

Keeping track of a decimal point is important. Here are some examples to practice.
Hint: To multiply by ten, move the decimal to the right. To divide by ten, move the decimal to the left.
Exercise 1: Practice saying the following aloud

KEY: [this (=) sign means (equal)] spoken aloud as (5+5=10) (five plus five equals ten).
One trillion (tril-yuhn) = (One followed by 12 zeros) 1,000,000,000,000.
$1,009,000,000,000.00 (one trillion, nine billion dollars)
One billion (bil-yuhn) = (One followed by 9 zeros) 1,000,000,000.
$14,009,500,000.00 (fourteen billion, nine million, five hundred thousand dollars)
One million (mil-yuhn) = (One followed by 6 zeros) 1,000,000.
$2,001,005.00 (two million, one thousand, five dollars)

One thousand (thou-zuhnd) = (One followed by 3 zeros) 1,000.
$1,065.00 (one thousand, sixty-five dollars)
One hundred (huhn-drid) = (One followed by 2 zeros) 100.00
Ten (ten) = (One followed by a zero) $10.00
One (wuhn) =1.00
Zero= 0.0
One tenth= (decimal followed by a one) 0.10(a-tenth) =1/10=0.1
One hundredth= (decimal followed by a zero and one)0.01(a-huhn-dritth) =1/100= 0.01
One thousandth=0.001(a-thousandth) = (decimal followed by two zeros and a one)1/1000= 0.001

13.9 Periodic Table of Elements

This is a remarkable table that contains all the elements. Divided by electron structure. Listed here is only a small portion of the 118 total known elements currently.

Exercise 1: Practice saying the name of these elements and their physical characteristics.
Exercise 2: Create a sentence using the element's characteristics.
Exercise 3: Continue reviewing the full periodic table, up to the last element.

KEY: Density equals-- g/cm3, grams per cubic centimeter.
Atomic number: The number of protons in an atom is its' atomic number. Each element is uniquely defined by its atomic number.
1. H: Hydrogen (hahy-druh-juhn) has 1 proton, it has a density of .09g/cm3 (water is 1.0), Hydrogen comprises .14 % of the Earth's crust and it was discovered in 1776. The most abundant element. In Greek Hydrogen means water former since it produces water when burned.
2. He: Helium (hee-lee-uhm) has only 2 protons, it has a density of .18 g/cm3, Helium comprises 0 % of the Earth's crust and it was discovered in 1895. Helium is named for the Greek god of the sun, Helios. A very rare earth element used for inflating blimps, balloons, and in cryogenics.
3. Li: Lithium (lith-ee-uhm) has only 3 protons, it has a density of .53 g/cm3, and it comprises 0 % of the Earth's crust and was discovered in 1817. The word lithium is from the Greek word litho meaning stone. Also used in treating mental illness.
4. Be: Beryllium (buh-ril-ee-uhm) has 4 protons, it has a density of 1.85 g/cm3, Beryllium comprises 0 % of the Earth's crust and it was discovered in 1797. A very rare element, Beryllium is deadly in a gas form but important in the aerospace industry.
5. B: Boron (bawr-on) has 5 protons, it has a density of 2.34 g/cm3, Boron comprises 0 % of the Earth's crust and it was discovered in 1808. Produced by Cosmic rays, boron is very rare in the solar system and in the Earth's crust.
6. C: Carbon (kahr-buhn) has 6 protons, it has a density of 2.26 g/cm3, Carbon comprises .094% of the Earth's crust. Carbon is the fourth most abundant element in the Universe. From diamonds to coal.
7. N: Nitrogen (nahy-truh-juhn) has 7 protons, it has a density of 1.25 g/cm3, Nitrogen comprises 0% of the Earth's crust and it was discovered in 1772. Nitrogen comprises 78% of the Earth's atmosphere.

8. O: Oxygen (ok-si-juhn) has 8 protons, it has a density of 1.43 g/cm3), Oxygen comprises 46.71 % of the Earth's crust and it was discovered in 1774. Oxygen is partially created through the process of nucleosynthesis (noo-klee-oh-sin-thuh-sis) in Super Nova explosions.

9. F: Fluorine (floor-een) has 9 protons, it has a density of 1.7 g/cm3, Fluorine comprises .029 % of the Earth's crust and it was discovered in 1886.

10. Ne: Neon (nee-on) has 10 protons, it has a density of .9 g/cm3, Neon comprises 0% of the Earth's crust and it was discovered in 1898. That neon light has a reddish-orange glow.

11. Na: Sodium (soh-dee-uhm) has 11 protons, it has a density of .97 g/cm3, Sodium comprises 2.75 % of the Earth's crust and it was discovered in 1807. The metal is highly explosive and must be stored in a water free environment.

12. Mg: Magnesium (mag-nee-zee-uhm) has 12 protons, it has a density of 1.74 g/cm3, Magnesium comprises 2.08 % of the Earth's crust and it was discovered in 1755. A malleable (mal-ee-uh-buhl) metal, magnesium burns with a white-hot light making it popular in incendiary (in-sen-dee-er-ee) devices and flash bulbs.

13. Al: Aluminum (uh-loo-muh-nuhm) has 13 protons, it has a density of 2.7 g/cm3, Aluminum comprises 8.07% of the Earth's crust and it was discovered in 1825. Used in alloys and for lightweight utensils, pots, pans, castings, and aerospace parts. The new Ford 150 is made from Aluminum.

14. Si: Silicon (sil-i-kuhn) has 14 protons, it has a density of 2.33 g/cm3, Silicon comprises 27.69 % of the Earth's crust and it was discovered in 1824. Next to oxygen silicon is the second most abundant element in the earth's crust and is used in the construction of solar cells.

15. P: Phosphorus (fos-fer-uhs) has 15 protons, it has a density of 1.82 g/cm3, Phosphorus comprises .13% of the Earth's crust and it was discovered in 1669. Phosphorus glows in the dark and is used as a tracer for chemical and biochemical research.

13.10 The Solar System

Learning the planets in the Solar System is essential to understanding our position in the Milky Way Galaxy and therefore the Universe.

Exercise: Repeat the name of the planet, its mean distance, period of orbit and the equatorial diameter aloud.
[KEY]
Name of Planet: Mean distance (the average) to the Sun: Period of orbit around the Sun: Equatorial diameter in miles.

Mercury (mur-kyuh-ree):	36 million (mil-yuhn) miles: 87 days: 3,031 miles (mahylz)
Venus (ven-nuhs):	67 million miles: 225 days: 7,519 miles
Earth (urth):	92 million miles: 365 days: 7,927 miles
Mars (mahrz):	41 million miles: 687 days: 4,200 miles
Jupiter (joo-pi-ter):	483 million miles: 11.86 years: 88,846 miles
Saturn (sat-ern):	884 million miles: 29.46 years: 75,060 miles
Uranus (yoor-uh-nuhs):	1,783 million miles: 84.02 years: 29,200 miles
Neptune (nep-toon):	2,793 million miles: 164.79 years: 27,700 miles
Pluto (ploo-toh):	3,690 million miles: 247 years: 1,430 miles

13.11 Cloud types

The following are a list of common cloud types found in the troposphere (trop-uh-sfeer). The troposphere is where cloud formations occur, and weather conditions manifest themselves.

Exercise 1. Recite the following cloud types aloud.
Exercise 2. Identify the clouds in the sky.

High elevation: these form above 20,000 feet.
Cirrus (sir-uhs): above 18,000 feet.
Cirrocumulus (sir-oh-kyoo-myuh-luhs): above 18,000 feet.
Cirrostratus (sir-oh-strey-tuhs):16,500 feet to 45,000 feet.
Middle elevation: 6,500 to 20,000 feet.
Altocumulus (al-toh-kyoo-myuh-luhs): 6,000 to 20,000 feet.
Altostratus (al-toh-strey-tuhs): 6,000 to 20,000 feet.
Multi-level:
Nimbostratus (nim-boh-strey-tuhs): from 2,000 to 18,000 feet.
Cumulus (kyoo-myuh-luhs): below 6,000 feet.
Cumulonimbus (kyoo-myuh-loh-nim-buhs). From ground level to 50,000 feet.
Low elevation: below 6,500 feet.
Stratocumulus (strey-toh-kyoo-myuh-luhs): below 6,000 feet.

> Stratus (strey-tuhs): below 6,000 feet.

13.12　Scientific and Meteorological Terms

This list is a combination of different science terms.

Exercise: Practice reading aloud the following terms and the sentences that follow.

1.	Afternoon (af-ter-noon): The time from noon to evening.
2.	Asteroid (as-tuh-roid): Any of the thousands of rock and iron small bodies that revolve around the sun and usually originate in the asteroid belt, the orbit between Mars and Jupiter. When they impact the Earth, they are called meteorites.
3.	Astronomical (as-truh-nom-i-kuhl): The study of the material world beyond our atmosphere.
4.	Aurora (uh-rawr-uh) Borealis (bawr-ee-al-is): The Aurora Borealis is another name for the Northern (nawr-thern) Lights, an atmospheric phenomenon producing a series of colorful bands of light in the sky. The aurora borealis is caused by solar particles hitting the earth's magnetic field, triggering reactions in the atmosphere from oxygen and nitrogen, which then release multicolored bands of light photons in the night sky.
5.	Barometer (buh-rom-i-ter): Any instrument that measures atmospheric pressure.
6.	Clear (kleer): No clouds. Another bright blue sunny day in Los Angeles in January.
7.	Cloudy (klou-dee): It looks partly cloudy in the Capital of the USA, Washington D.C., today.
8.	Cold Front (fruhnt): I can tell that there is a cold front starting to come in better wear a coat.
9.	Comet (kom-it): A comet is a type of dirty snowball, made of ice and rock orbiting around the Sun. Currently, there are 829,334. (Eight-hundred-twenty-nine thousand three hundred thirty-four) known asteroids. And there are 3,591. (three-thousand five hundred ninety-one known) comets.
10.	Constellation (kon-stuh-ley-shuhn): There are 88 recognized constellations in the sky.
11.	Convex (kon-veks): A surface that is curved outward as contrasted to concave (kon-keyv), a surface that is curved inward. The Hubble Space telescope has a hyperbolic concave lens.
12.	Dawn: The appearance of the day before sunrise. Daybreak.
13.	Dew (doo): Dew are small beads of water which form on cold surfaces in the evening when air condenses.
14.	Drifting snow (snoh): The Mountains in Vermont are covered in drifting snow, ready to ski?
15.	Drizzle (driz-uhl): Light rain. E.g. the drizzle fell lightly, so a raincoat isn't necessary. E.g. it's drizzling outside.
16.	Drought (drout): A period of extended lack of rain. Animals searched for water as the drought went on.

17. Dusk (duhsk): The period after sunset and just before night. The darkest part of twilight before the night begins.
18. Tornado (tawr-ney-doh): Tornadoes intensity is rated by the EF Fujita (foo-jee-tah) scale. The most recent EF scale measures the tornadoes as:

| EF0, wind gusts 65-85 mph (miles per hour). |
| EF1, wind gusts 86-110 mph. |
| EF2, wind gusts 111-135 mph. |
| EF3, wind gusts 136-165 mph. |
| EF4, wind gusts 166-200 mph. |
| EF5, wind gusts over 200 mph. |

19. Evening (eev-ning): The period at the end of the day, usually from about 6 p.m. to bedtime.
20. Exosphere (ek-soh-sfeer): The exosphere is the edge of the earth's atmosphere.
21. Fog (fawg): Fog is made of tiny water droplets.
22. Forecast (fawr-kast): To forecast conditions is to predict the weather in advance by using meteorological information.
23. Freezing rain (reyn): It's that terrible freezing rain that's on the windshield.
24. Frost (frawst): Frost is a narrow layer of ice.
25. Funnel (fuhn-l) clouds: When you see a funnel-shaped cloud projecting from the base of a thundercloud, it's the start of a tornado, time to leave.
26. Galaxy (gal-uhk-see): Astronomers estimate that there are between 200-400 billion stars in the Milky Way Galaxy.
27. Gale (geyl): A gale is a strong wind of 32 to 63 miles per hour.
28. Hailstones (heyl-stohns) Frozen pieces of water that fall from the sky. E.g. The hail came down in the size of golf balls.
29. Haze (heyz): Sun that is covered by thick clouds. Better bring sunscreen even though it's hazy. Otherwise, you might get sunburned.
30. Heat wave (heet-weyv): A heatwave is a long period of continuous above-average temperatures.
31. Heliosphere (hee-lee-uh-sfeer): The solar winds are contained within the heliosphere.
32. Hemisphere (hem-i-sfeer): We live in the northern hemisphere.
33. Hologram (hol-uh-gram): Jay, who bicycled everywhere, mentioned that he knew the inventor (in-ven-ter) of Michael Jackson's hologram. A hologram is a three-dimensional representation produced by an interference of light beams from a coherent (koh-heer-uhnt) light source such as a laser (light amplification by stimulated emission of radiation).
34. Hurricane (huri-keyn): A hurricane is a rapidly rotating storm center from 200-500 miles wide. In the movie, Key Largo, Edward G. Robinson must fight Humphrey Bogart while on a boat and during a hurricane.
35. Kepler's (kep-lers) three laws: The first law is that all planets move about the sun in elliptical (ih-lip-ti-kuhl) circles around the sun as one of the foci (foh-sahy). The second law is any radius (rey-dee-uhs) vector (vek-ter) joining a planet to the Sun

	sweeps out equal areas in equal lengths of time. The third law is that the square (skwair) of the orbital (awr-bi-tl) period of a planet is related to the cube of the semimajor axis (ak-sis) of its orbit.
36.	Meteor (mee-tee-er): A meteor is a piece of mass or matter that, due to frictional heating, produces glowing incandescence (in-kuhn-des-uh ns) upon entering the atmosphere. It is called a falling or shooting star.
37.	Meteorological (mee-tee-er-uh-loj-i-kuhl): Study of the processes in the atmosphere during weather.
38.	Midday (mid-dey): The middle of the day. Lunchtime.
39.	Midnight (mid-nahyt): Twelve midnight. 12:00am.,
40.	Milky Way Galaxy (gal-uhk-see): A spiral galaxy that we live in containing billions of stars and planets, with a supermassive black hole at the center. Diameter is approximately 100,000 light years; thickness is on average 1,000 light years. The Earth is located in the solar system, the solar system is in the Milky Way Galaxy which is located in the Virgo Supercluster. The Milky Way is the second largest galaxy of the local group within the Supercluster.
41.	Morning (mawr-ning): From sunrise to noon. Coffee. Before noon.
42.	Nebula (neb-yuh-luh): A nebula is a cloud of interstellar gas.
43.	Night (nahyt): Night is the dark portion of the day, used for sleeping.
44.	Occluded (uh-klooded): An occlusion is when a cold front, overtaking a warm front, lifts the warm air.
45.	Pouring (pawr-ng): Heavy rain. E.g. it's pouring outside you'll need an umbrella and a raincoat. E.g. it's raining buckets. Or it's raining cats and dogs.
46.	Prominence (prom-uh-nuhns): The solar prominence disturbed cell phone reception for hours.
47.	Rain (reyn): Did you bring an umbrella (uhm-brel-uh)? It looks like rain.
48.	Sandstorm (sand-stawrm): There was a recent sandstorm in Arizona.
49.	Severe (suh-veer) weather: Severe weather has the potential to cause serious social disruption and loss of human life. Each year since the 1800s the number of severe weather episodes has increased. Severe weather includes downbursts, dust storms, excessive precipitation, extratropical cyclones, hail, high winds, ice storms, snowstorms, thunderstorms, tornadoes, tropical cyclones, waterspouts, and wildfires. More big storms each year.
50.	Sleet: A wet mixture of ice, rain, and snow.
51.	Snow (snoh): Hooray, there's plenty of snow for skiing.
52.	Stars (stahr): Stars are classified according to the Morgan-Keenan (MK) system. The system uses the following letter designations O, B, A, F, G, K, and M. The gradient (grey-dee-uhnt) goes from the hottest (O types) to the coolest (M types). Our Sun is rated as a G2V, a star on the main sequence with a temperature of approximately 5,800 degrees Kelvin. One mnemonic device uses the following: OBAFGKM.
53.	Storm (stawrm): A disturbed environment with severe weather.
54.	The Universe (yoo-nuh-vurs): Contains galaxies, planets, black holes, etc. But only five percent is mass, the other 95% of the universe is dark matter, dark energy, and

	interstellar dust. The universe contains more than a hundred billion galaxies. The observable universe is 93 billion light years wide.
55.	Thunderstorm (thuhn-der-stawrm): Did you hear that thunder? I think a storm is coming. A thunderstorm is between 5-15 miles across.
56.	Tremors (trem-erz): Any movement or vibrations, especially after an earthquake, like aftershocks. Also, a fun Kevin Bacon, Reba McEntire movie.
57.	Twilight (twahy-lahyt): After sunset before it is dark. The sun is below the horizon, making the light diffuse and colorful.
58.	Typhoon (tahy-foon): A tropical cyclone (sahy-klohn) in the northwest Pacific is called a Typhoon.
59.	Warm (wawrm): Higher temperature. I can see it's starting to get warm so that I won't need the jacket.
60.	Whirlpool (hwurl-pool): A whirlpool is a small rotating body of water.
63.	Wind: Wind is the movement of air along the earth's surface:

13.13 Chemistry Laboratory

Chemistry can be one of the hardest subjects a student can take. Between electron states, there are calculations of moles with Avogadro's number. This list contains only a few terms found in the lab.

Exercise 1: Repeat the terms aloud.
Exercise 2: Lookup each term and use in a sentence.

1.	Beaker(bee-ker)		13.	Mortar(mawr-ter)
2.	Bell jar(jahr)		14.	Pestle(pes-uhl)
3.	Bunsen(buhn-suhn) burner		15.	Pipette(pahy-pet)
4.	Clamp stand		16.	Rubber tubing
5.	Conical(kon-i-kal)flask		17.	Slides(slahydz)
6.	Electric balance		18.	Stopper(stop-er)
7.	Funnel(fuhn-l)		19.	Test tubes(toobz)
8.	Gas tap		20.	Tongs(tongz)
9.	Lab coat		21.	Tripod(trahy-pod)
10.	Matches(mach-ez)		22.	Wire gauze(gawz)
11.	Measuring cylinder(sil-in-der)			
12.	Microscope (mahy-kruh-skohp)			

13.14 Aviation and aerospace

Here are some of the terms used in aviation (ey-vee-ey-shuhn) and aerospace (air-oh-speys).

Exercise 1: Repeat the phrases and definitions aloud.
Exercise 2: Review a diagram of a jet to locate the parts mentioned.

Aileron (ey-luh-ron): The aileron (ey-luh-ron) is located on the wing, and its function is to change the roll of the plane.
Cockpit (kok-pit): The cockpit is where command and control are located in the front of the plane.
Electromagnetic (ih-lek-troh-mag-net-ik) Propulsion rockets
Elevator (el-uh-vey-ter): The elevator is located on the horizontal stabilizer and is used to change pitch.
Flaps: Flaps are located on the wings and are used to increase lift and drag.
Fuselage (fyoo-suh-lahzh): The fuselage is the central structure of the jet; it holds things together and carries the payload.
Ion (ahy-uhn) Propulsion (pruh-puhl-shuhn) Rockets: Particle accelerators (ak-sel-uh-rey-ters) that release streams of ions out the exhaust (ig-zawst) jet.
Plasma (plaz-muh) Thrusters using an ionized gas with the same number of electrons and positive ions.
Ramjets (ram-jets) Using the compressed forward speed of the aircraft, fuel is injected.
Rudder (ruhd-er): A rudder located on the rear wing changes yaw.
Scramjets (skram-jet): A supersonic (soo-per-son-ik) ramjet engine.
Slats: The slats on the wings increase lift.
Spoiler (spoi-ler): A spoiler changes lift, drag and roll.
Stabilizer (stey-buh-lahy-zer): A vertical stabilizer controls yaw and is located on the rudder on the rear of the plane. The horizontal stabilizer controls pitch.
Turbine (tur-bahyn): The turbine engine generates thrust.
Winglet (wing-lit): A winglet located at the end of the wing decreases drag.
Wings: The wings generate lift.
Yaw (yaw): Turning to the right or left.

13.15 Difficult words and sentences 8

This is an important list of challenging words that came up in tutoring sessions with students and it is in reverse alphabetical order.

Exercise 1: Repeat the words aloud and the sentences that follows.

1.	Wreath (reeth):	On Memorial Day, wreaths are placed on the graves of fallen soldiers.
2.	Wordy (wur-dee):	Was that wordy book worthy of such an award?
3.	Voluptuous (vuh-luhp-choo-uhs): A natural body tone with curves, soft, sexually attractive body. E.g., that voluptuous model is perfect.	
4.	Vegetarian (vej-i-tair-ee-uhn):	Did you order the vegetarian burger?

5. Tremendous (trih-men-duhs):	That performance was tremendous, said the critic.
6. Torn (tawrn):	The tent got torn apart by the sudden storm.
7. Toothpick (tooth-pik):	A toothpick is a small polished piece of wood used to clean debris from teeth.
8. Toothbrush (tooth-bruhsh):	Use a toothbrush after meals and floss every day.
9. Tijuana (tee-uh-wah-nuh):	Did you drive to Tijuana?
10. Thesis (thee-sis):	Is this your thesis?
11. Theme (theem):	The team got a new home theme (theem).
12. Tank (tangk):	The administration sent a thank you note to the Rand Corporation, a think tank.
13. Swollen (swoh-luhn):	The broken foot was very enlarged and swollen.
14. Swelling (swel-ing):	The swelling would decrease with ice.
15. Swell (swel):	During the summer, the wood door would swell.
16. Sweeten (sweet-n):	Let me sweeten that coffee for you.
17. Sweden (sweed-n):	Tom B. moved to the Capital of Sweden, Stockholm.
18. Spot (spot):	Can you spot me?
19. Soliloquy (suh-lil-uh-kwee):	Def. saying aloud your internal thoughts, especially in a play. E.g., He did that Hamlet soliloquy with great conviction.
20. Society (suh-sahy-i-tee):	What kind of society do we live in?
21. Smooth (smooth):	They repaired the street, and now it's smooth.
22. Set (set):	Can we do a quick set?
23. Seen (seen):	Is it the first eclipse you have seen?
24. See (see):	Did you see the eclipse (ih-klips)?
25. Scottsdale (skots-deyl):	Scottsdale, Arizona, is a great place to buy turquoise.
26. Scarsdale (skahrz-deyl):	Have you been to Scarsdale?
27. Saw (saw):	Yes, I saw the eclipse.
28. Rough (ruhf):	The tabletop is rough all over.
29. Rouge (roozh):	Have you seen the film the Moulin Rouge?
30. Rogue (rohg):	Be careful of those rogue ocean waves, they come from out of nowhere and run perpendicular to the shoreline.
31. Rhythm (rith-uhm):	The dancers have an amazing sense of rhythm and syncopated well with the new song.
32. Rhyme (rahym):	What rhymes with your name?
33. Ration (rash-uhn):	Have you gotten your daily ration?
34. Patriarchy (pey-tree-ahr-kee):	When the king is in power, it is a patriarchy.
35. Paella (pay-ey-luh):	Let's split the paella, it's enough for two.
36. Oddity (od-i-tee):	A blue moon is a real oddity and shouldn't be missed.
37. Narrative:	Have you done narrative therapy?
38. Narcolepsy (nahr-kuh-lep-see):	He suffered from narcolepsy and kept falling asleep, so he wasn't allowed to drive.
39. Mythical (mith-i-kuhl):	What is your favorite mythical creature, and why?

40.	Mischief (mis-chif):	Alexandria is always getting into mischief.
41.	Mint (mint):	Do you like mint chocolate?
42.	Meiosis (mahy-oh-sis):	Meiosis is cell reproduction in prokaryotes (proh-kar-ee-ohtz).
43.	Mitosis (mahy-toh-sis):	Mitosis is cell reproduction in eukaryotes (yoo-kar-ee-ohtz).
44.	Matriarchy (mey-tree-ahr-kee):	A matriarchy is a government ruled by women.
45.	Mathematics (math-uh-mat-iks):	Math is the study of numbers, shapes, and patterns.
46.	Liaison (lee-ey-zawn):	She named a liaison to the foreign department.
47.	Jeep (jeep):	She drove a hardtop two-door jeep.
48.	Irony (ahy-ruh-nee):	Do you see the irony in that story?
49.	Iron (ahy-ern):	Iron is magnetic.
50.	Unintelligible (uhn-in-tel-i-juh-buhl):	That recording was unintelligible and had to be redone.
51.	Hors d'oeuvres (awr-durvz):	They serve hors d 'oeuvres or appetizers before dinner at the club.
52.	Horchata:	Have you tried the Horchata at the Mexican restaurant?
53.	Hint (hint):	Maybe just a hint of mint in the hot cocoa (koh-koh).
54.	Hierarchy (hahy-uh-rahr-kee):	The US Army is a hierarchy with the President at top.
55.	Heritage (her-i-tij):	The United States has 22 different Heritage sites.
57.	Heap (heep):	That Jeep looks like a heap.
58.	Gauze (gawz):	She wore a crisp white gauze top.
59.	Gauge (geyj):	Can you gauge if there's still fuel left?
60.	Future (fyoo-cher):	In the future, we will have colonies on Mars.
61.	Foam (fohm):	They used foam on the electrical fire.
62.	Fly (flahy):	Do you like to fly?
63.	Flew (floo):	He flew first-class in that new jet to Beijing, China.
64.	Flee (flee):	It's against the law to flee the scene of an accident.
65.	Feature (fee-cher):	They will feature electrically powered vehicles.
66.	Fathom (fath-uhm):	A fathom is a unit of length 6 feet long, which is used in measuring the depth of water.
67.	Fajita (fah-hee-tuh):	Those fajitas are sizzling, be careful.
68.	Etc., (Et Cetera)	The word et cetera is derived from Latin, which translates to, and the rest.
69.	Essay (es-ey):	Did you author the essay for the class?
70.	Dialogue (dahy-uh-lawg):	The dialogue was so natural and flowed perfectly.
71.	Day:	They went out for the day.
72.	Croissant (kruh-sahnt):	Can I have a chocolate croissant?
73.	Correct (kuh-rekt):	Do you have the correct Powerball numbers?
74.	Conscious (kon-shuhs):	You won't be conscious during surgery.
75.	Conscientious (kon-shee-en-shuhs):	She was a conscientious worker.

76.	Conscience (kon-shuhns):	The hit and run driver's conscience tormented him till he confessed.
77.	Collect (kuh-lekt):	I'm here to collect a debt (det), come on, and fork it over.
78.	Chlorophyll (klawr-uh-fil):	Did you add the chlorophyll to the organic juice?
79.	Cheetah (chee-tuh):	The cheetah is the fastest land animal; it can run 70mph (miles per hour).
80.	Cheaters (chee-ters):	Cheaters will be expelled.
81.	Cheat (cheet):	Don't cheat on that exam.
82.	Cheap (cheep):	That car looked cheap but was expensive.
83.	Caucasian (kaw-key-zhuhn):	He checked the Caucasian box on the census (sen-suhs).
84.	Catastrophe (kuh-tas-truh-fee):	That play was a catastrophe and closed after opening night.
85.	Catamaran (kat-uh-muh-ran):	Let's rent a catamaran when we get to Hawaii.
86.	Camouflage (kam-uh-flahzh):	Have you seen the cephalopod's (sef-uh-luh-pods) camouflage system for blending into the landscape, it's remarkable.
87.	Cage (keyj):	Is the lion in a cage?
88.	Breeding (bree-ding):	The deep breathing during the breeding is legendary.
89.	Both (bohth):	She went to both museums.
90.	Boat (boht):	Have you ever been on a boat in the Pacific Ocean?
91.	Bath (bahth):	Does that apartment come with a bath?
92.	Bat (bat):	The virus was in the bat that was in the cave.
93.	Basil (baz-uhl):	In Basel (bah-zuhl), they use basil (baz-uhl) in the tomato sauce.
94.	Azimuth (az-uh-muhth):	The azimuth is an angular measurement in a spherical coordinate system.
95.	Author (aw-ther):	After the performance, the audience shouted Author! Author!
96.	Algorithm (al-guh-rith-uhm):	An algorithm is a mathematical equation used to model physical behavior.

13.16 Dialogue: At the Post Office

The American Post office is a place where you go to send letters, mail ballots, ship packages and get passports made. You might just have to visit one day. So be prepared.

Exercise 1: Repeat aloud the following dialogue. Practice with a friend. Switch characters.
Exercise 2: Go to the Post Office.
Please remember: Postal prices change over time. These are 2020 prices.

Customer: I want to mail this letter; how much is it going to cost?
Postal Employee: Stamps are fifty-five cents for the first ounce, fifteen cents each additional.
Customer: I need to send this package next day.
Postal Employee: It's $7.35 for priority mail (1-3 days) or $25.50 for next day priority mail express
Customer: My friend had some forever stamps, are they still good?
Postal Employee: Yes, they are good forever.
Customer: That's just amazing; how is it possible?
Postal Employee: It just works out. Would you like delivery confirmation? It's now called Certificate of mailing, and it's only one dollar and forty cents. ($1.40)?
Customer: Why do I need delivery confirmation? I mean, it is going to be delivered, right?
Postal Employee: Of course, this gives you the date and time that it is delivered.
Customer: So, let me see if I got this right, it costs fifty-five cents to mail the letter and a dollar and forty cents to let me know that it was delivered.
Postal Employee: That's it.
Customer: Okay. I have some postcards also.
Postal Employee: Postcards are thirty-five cents.
Customer: How much to tell me if they have been delivered?
Postal Employee: The postcards?
Customer: Never mind. How about an international package?
Postal Employee: Global express is $67.80 (1-3 days guaranteed). Priority mail express international is $44.00 (3-5 days guaranteed), and priority mail international is $25.85(6-10days delivery). It's a dollar and fifteen cents. ($1.15) for a letter.
Customer: I also want to send this priority mail express.

Postal Employee: Priority mail express starts at twenty-five fifty ($25.50) with a money-back guarantee.
Customer: Don't you have something less expensive?
Postal Employee: Yes, you can send it Priority Mail, for a small box, it's $7.35 for two to three days (2-3 days) delivery.
Customer: How about books?
Postal Employee: Media rate.
Customer: Is this a good box?
Postal Employee: Yes.
Customer: Is this scotch tape good?
Postal Employee: No. Here try this tape. Would you like to send this registered? Or Insured?
Customer: Should I?
Postal Employee: Your choice. Would you like a signature required? Is it valuable? Or breakable?
Customer: Do you take credit cards? Can I purchase a money order for $100.00?
Postal Employee: Yes.
Customer: Okay, let's send it Express. Do you know Postman's Motto?
Postal Employee: Yes, let me repeat this for you. We are mothers and fathers and sons and daughters. Who every day go about our lives with duty and pride and neither snow nor rain nor heat nor gloom of night nor the winds of change nor a nation challenged, will stay us from the swift completion of our appointed rounds. Ever.
Customer: Thanks.
Postal Employee: Swipe it here.
Customer: Thank you.
Postal Employee: Here's a survey. Have a great day.

13.17 The Internal Combustion Gas Engine

Using a car requires replacing parts from time to time. Here's a list of almost every item found in a car to review.

Exercise 1: Repeat the word and then the sentence aloud.
Exercise 2: Create a sentence for each word.

1.	Accelerator (ak-sel-uh-rey-ter): Please step on the accelerator also known as the gas pedal to speed up.
2.	Air cleaner (air klee-ner): Your air cleaner smells like pinecone.
3.	Air filter (air fil-ter): Changing the air filter will improve your cars performance.
4.	Air vent (air-vent): Open the air vents to let in the fresh air.
5.	Alternator (awl-ter-ney-ter): Your battery won't hold a charge; did you check the alternator?
6.	Antenna (an-ten-uh): The antenna broke in the car wash.
7.	Antifreeze (an-tee-freez): During extreme weather antifreeze protects your cars' coolant from freezing or boiling.
8.	Axle (ak-suhl) I broke the axle while going over the riverbed.
9.	Backup light (bak-uhp lahyt): When the car is moving in reverse, the backup light comes on to warn drivers.
10.	Battery (bat-uh-ree): The battery is dead; can you give me a jump?
11.	Blinker (bling-ker): Always remember to use your blinkers when making a lane change.
12.	Boot (boot): It's important to wear boots and a helmet while on a motorcycle or a scooter or a Vespa.
13.	Brake (breyk): The brake pedal is to the left of the gas pedal.
14.	Brake fluid reservoir (breyk floo-id rez-er-vwahr): Please check the brake fluid reservoir before going on a long trip.
15.	Brake light (breyk lahyt): The brake light is on; can you check the fluids?
16.	Buckle (buhk-uhl): Always wear your seat belts and buckle up.
17.	Bumper (buhm-per): Bumpers are designed to prevent severe damage from small accidents.
18.	Bumpers (buhm-per): The bumpers protect the car against front or rear end collisions.
19.	Caliper brake kit (kal-uh-per): The calipers squeeze the brake pads against the disc brake rotors to stop the vehicle.
20.	Camshaft (kam-shaft): The camshaft is in the engine block.
21.	Catalytic converter (kuh-tal-lit-ik kuhn-vur-ter): Did you know that your catalytic converter converts pollution into less toxic gases?
22.	Cd player (cd-pley-er): Does this car come with a CD player?
23.	Chassis (chas-ee): The chassis is the frame that holds the car together.
24.	Clutch (kluhch): Please don't ride the clutch, you'll wear it out.

25. Control arm bushings (kuhn-trohl ahrm boosh-ings): That metallic scraping sounds like you need to replace the rubber control arm bushings.
26. Coolant (koo-luhnt): How much coolant does your new car take?
27. Crankshaft (krangk-shaft): The crankshaft is connected to the pistons.
28. Cylinder head (sil-in-der hed): The racing crew replaced the cylinder head for added performance.
29. Dashboard (dash-bawrd): All the gauges are located on the dashboard.
30. Disc brake (disk): Those new disc brakes can stop your car on a dime.
31. Distributor (dih-strib-yuh-ter): The car mechanic had to replace my distributor cap, since it was cracked.
32. Door (dawr): Please open the door for the passenger.
33. Door handle (dawr-handl): The door handles are recessed and are hard to see sometimes.
34. Doors (dawrs): My new Rolls Royce is equipped with suicide doors, which are hinged at the rear.
35. Drive shaft (drahyv shahft): This is the third driveshaft for my new car, what gives?
36. Driver's seat (drahy-ver seet): Did you get a heated driver's seat?
37. Emergency brake (ih-mur-juhn-see breyk): Remember to use your emergency brake and turn your front wheels towards the curb when parking on hills.
38. Engine (en-juhn): Please warm up the engine or motor before driving.
39. Exhaust pipe (ig-zawst): That exhaust pipe has a hole in it and needs to be replaced.
40. Exterior (ik-steer-ee-er): Please be sure to give the exterior a good wash.
41. Flywheel (flahy-hweel): A flywheel is used to store rotational energy.
42. Fog light (fawg-lahyt): The fog lights make driving in fog easier.
43. Front suspension (fruhnt-suh-spen-shuhn): Careful of that pothole it will destroy your front suspension.
44. Fuel filter (fyoo-uhl fil-ter): The fuel filter will remove impurities from the gasoline like water.
45. Fuel injection (fyoo-uhl in-jek-shuhn): My car is equipped with fuel injection.
46. Fuel tank (fyoo-uhl): How many gallons does your fuel tank hold?
47. Gas cap (gas-kap): Don't forget to replace the gas cap after filling up.
48. Gas pedal (ped-l): The gas pedal is used to control the speed of the car.
49. Gas: Please step on the gas, I'm in a rush.
50. Gear (geer): Will you please shift out of first gear?
51. Gear stick (geer-stik): Use the gear stick to shift the car.
52. Glove box (gluhv-boks): Sorry, I left my wallet in the glove box.
53. Grill (gril): Did you smash into the celebrity's Rolls Royce grill?
54. Headlight (hed-lahyt): Did you get the new extra bright halogen (hal-uh-juhn) headlights?
55. Headrest (hed-rest): The headrest is designed to prevent whiplash.
56. Heater (hee-ter): It's freezing, please turn the heater on.

57.	Hood (hood): Don't forget to look under the hood when buying a used car.
58.	Horn (hawrn): That truck is equipped (ih-kwipd) with a very loud air horn.
59.	Hose (hohz): Rubber hoses will eventually get brittle (brit-l) and should be checked during regular maintenance.
60.	Hub cap (huhb-kap): Do you have an extra hub cap; we lost the other one on the freeway.
61.	Ignition (ig-nish-uhn): Insert the key into the ignition and turn clockwise to start the car.
62.	Incline: Be sure to turn your wheels towards the curb when you park on a steep incline.
63.	Interior (in-teer-ee-er): Please make sure they vacuum the interior of the car at the carwash.
64.	License plate (lahy-suhns pleyt): You will get a, "fix it ticket" if you are missing your front license plate.
65.	MacPherson strut (muhk-fur-suhn struht): That sports car is equipped with MacPherson strut suspension.
66.	Master cylinder (sil-in-der): Converts pressure from your foot on the brake pedal to hydraulic pressure to operate the brakes.
67.	Mirrors (mir-er): Please remember to adjust all the mirrors in the rental car.
68.	Motor mount (moh-ter mount): The motor mounts hold the engine in place.
69.	Muffler (muhf-ler): Your automobile sounds like it needs a new muffler.
70.	Odometer (oh-dom-i-ter): The odometer shows the miles driven.
71.	Oil dipstick (oil-dip-stik): To check the oil level in your car use the dipstick.
72.	Oil filter (oil-fil-ter): That oil change includes a new oil filter along with six quarts of synthetic oil.
73.	Oil pan: Careful you don't scrape the oil pan which is the bottom portion of the crankcase on the ramp.
74.	Oil pump (puhmp): The oil pump (puhmp) circulates (sur-kyuh-leyts) the oil through (throo) the motor (moh-ter).
75.	Parking light (par-king lahyt): The parking lights are used to make the car more visible during the day.
76.	Passenger seat (pas-uhn-jer seet): The passenger seat is the seat next to the driver.
77.	Piston (pis-tuhn): The piston rings make the cylinder gas tight.
78.	Power steering reservoir (pou-er steer-ing rez-er-vwahr): Check the fluid level in the power steering reservoir.
79.	Quarter panel (kwawr-ter pan-l): That car will need a new front quarter panel after the accident.
80.	Rack and pinion steering (rak-and pin-yuhn steer-ing): Does your car have rack and pinion steering?
81.	Radiator (rey-dee-ey-ter): I can see the steam coming from your radiator, you must have a leak.
82.	Rear differential (reer dif-uh-ren-shuhl): Did you adjust the rear differential for off road driving?

83. Rear suspension (reer suh-spen-shuhn): That bus needs new rear suspension, it keeps bottoming out.
84. Rear view mirror (reer vyoo mir-er): Can you move to the side; you're blocking the rear-view mirror.
85. Rear window (reer-win-doh): Hitchcock's film, Rear Window, is an amazing thriller.
86. Reflector (ri-flek-ter): The reflectors help to illuminate the car.
87. Registration (rej-uh-strey-shuhn): The police will usually ask you for your license and registration, so keep it handy.
88. Rim (rim): Those new black rims look great.
89. Seals and gaskets (seels and gas-kits): The engine is going to need a set of seals and gaskets.
90. Seat (seet): Does that car come with bucket seats?
91. Seat belt (seet-belt): Wearing your seatbelt prevents serious injuries in case of an accident.
92. Sensors (sen-sawrs): That idiot light indicates that the oxygen sensors need to be replaced.
93. Shock absorber (shok-ab-sawr-ber): The car's ride will be much smoother with the new shock absorbers.
94. Spark plugs (spahrk-pluhg): Your spark plugs are all worn out which are causing the engine to misfire.
95. Steering wheel (steer-ing hweel): Keep both hands on the steering wheel in case of emergency.
96. Sunroof (suhn-roof): Can I order the coupe with a sunroof?
97. Suspension (suh-spen-shuhn): The bus is equipped with air suspension.
98. Tail gate (teyl-geyt): Don't tailgate and remember to leave at least one car length for every ten miles per hour.
99. Taillights (teyl-lahyts): The police gave me a "fix it ticket" for the busted taillight.
100. Timing belt (chain) (tahy-ming belt): An endless belt or chain used to synchronize the motor.
101. Tire (tahyuhr): Did you kick the tires?
102. Tire inflation (tahyuhr in-fley-shuhn): Low tire inflation reduces gas mileage.
103. Transmission (trans-mish-uhn): Does your new car have automatic or manual transmission?
104. Transmission filter (trans-mish-uhn fil-ter): Did you even know that there is a transmission filter in your car?
105. Trunk (truhngk): Did you remember to put the luggage in the trunk?
106. Turbocharger (tur-boh-chahr-jer): I just got a new turbocharged Porsche, want to go for a ride?
107. Turn signal (turn sig-nl): The turn signal indicates which way the car is turning.
108. Undercarriage (uhn-der-kar-ij): On the East coast, they apply a special sealant to the undercarriage to protect against the corrosive (kuh-roh-siv) forces of road salt.

109.	Upper ball joint (uhp-er bawl-joint): Upper ball joints are spherical (sfer-i-kuhl) bearings (bair-ings) that connect to the control arms and are used to steer the vehicle.
110.	Valve cover (valv-kuhv-er): Did you order the chrome valve covers?
111.	Valves (valv): You might need a 60,000-mile valve adjustment.
112.	Vehicle identification number (VIN) (vee-i-kuhl ahy-den-tuh-fi-key-shuhn nuhm-ber): The individual VIN number contains the following information: Manufacturers code, model code, restraint system code, check digit, model year, and plant of manufacture. The VIN is stamped on body components, engine, and transmission.
113.	Wheel (hweel): Please keep your hands on the wheel and remember no texting.
114.	Window frame (win-doh freym): Can you fill that window frame with glass? In other words, close the window.
115.	Windshield (wind-sheld): Please replace that cracked windshield to avoid getting a ticket.
116.	Windshield washer (wind-sheld): Use the windshield washer to clean away the mud from the vehicle's windshield.
117.	Windshield wiper (wind-sheeld wahy-per): Please replace the windshield wipers when you bring the car in for service they are starting to streak (streek).

13.18 Electric and Hybrid Cars

Just like owning a gas car, having an electric car requires replacing parts from time to time. Here's a brief list of parts to review.

Exercise 1: Repeat the word and then the sentence aloud.
Exercise 2: Describe the difference in driving a gas vehicle compared with an electric vehicle.

All Electric Vehicle Components
1. Battery(bat-uh-ree) pack: This battery holds power created using regenerative braking and adds additional power to an electric traction motor.
2. Battery: In the electric drive vehicle, the battery (an auxiliary) provides power to start the car as the other battery (traction) is connected while powering the vehicles' accessories.
3. DC/DC converter (kuhn-vur-ter): This device changes the power from a traction battery pack to the lesser DC power needed to run the car's devices and charges the auxiliary storage battery.

4. Electric traction (trak-shuhn) motor (FCEV): Using energy from a fuel cell and energy generated by this motor powers the vehicles' wheels. Some cars use engine generators to power both drive and regeneration functions.

5. Fuel cell stack: A collection of singular electrodes (ih-lek-trohds) that use oxygen and hydrogen to create electricity.

6. Fuel filler: This is where fuel is added to the car.

7. Fuel tank (hydrogen): Holds the hydrogen gas until ready to use.

8. Power electronics controller (FCEV): This controls the amount of electrical energy determining the velocity (vuh-los-i-tee) of the motor.

9. Thermal (thur-muhl) system (cooling) - (FCEV): This device controls the temperature in the fuel cell, the electric motor, and all of the other power electronics.

10. Traction (trak-shuhn): The friction of one body on another as in a tire on a highway or a runner on a track.

11. Electric Transmission: This transfers energy to drive the wheels.

Hybrid Electric Vehicle Components

1. Battery auxiliary (awg-zil-yuh-ree)
2. DC/DC converter
3. Electric generator (jen-uh-rey-ter)
4. Electric traction motor
5. Exhaust system
6. Fuel filler
7. Fuel tank (gasoline)
8. Internal combustion engine (spark ignited)
9. Power electronics controller
10. Thermal system (cooling)
11. Traction (trak-shuhn) battery pack
12. Transmission

13.19 Compare and Contrast 6

Compare and contrast the following words, some of them are homonyms and sound the same and some are near homonyms and sound very near the same. In any case this is a really great list of words, it would be worthwhile to learn this list.

[KEY]
v= verb, adv=adverb, n=noun, pn=pronoun, adj=adjective, con=contraction, prep=preparation

Exercise 1: Repeat the following groups of words, note the differences in pronunciations and definitions.
Exercise 2: Create a sentence for each one.

Advice (ad-vahys) Written guidance or recommendations concerning prudent future action, typically given by someone regarded as knowledgeable or authoritative. E.g., listen to my advice.
Advise (ad-vahyz) v, an offer, or suggestions about the best course of action for someone. The president was advised not to speak with the press corps (kawr).

Breath (breth) n: Air is taken in or expelled from the lungs. Take a deep breath.
Breathe (breeth) v: The process of taking in air and expelling it out through the lungs. Please breathe in and out.

Confidant (kon-fi-dant) n. An individual that has chosen to share some very personal information.
Confident (kon-fi-duhnt) adj., Feeling, or showing confidence in oneself; self-assured.

Farther (fah-ther) adv. Farther refers to physical distance. The distance from one thing to another. Hamilton can run farther than Monroe.
Further (fur-ther) adj. Further means added or more of what already exists or has already taken place, been done, or been accounted for. A metaphorical distance, meaning added or more. E.g., please give me further information about the best route to Hermosa Beach.

Lightening (lahyt-n-ing) v. To reduce the weight of. They will need to lighten the load on the helicopter.
Lightning (lahyt-ning) the electrical discharge in the sky. The sky is lite with lightning.
Lighting (lahy-ting) Illumination by electrical bulbs.

Amoral (ey-mawr-uhl) (adj) Lack of a moral sense; unconcerned with the rightness or wrongness of something.
Immemorial (im-uh-mawr-ee-uhl) Immemorial refers to that which is beyond time, ancient.
Immoral (ih-mawr-uhl) Immoral means unethical, X-rated.

Immortal (ih-mawr-tl) Immortal describes things that live forever.	
Moral (mawr-uhl) Conscience is an inner, moral guide. Ethical.	
Morale (muh-ral) n. A feeling of confidence with an individual or team.	

Principal (prin-suh-puhl) adj., the most important. The head of a school first in rank. E.g., the student's parents had to have a meeting with the principal.
Principle (prin-suh-puhl) n., a fundamental rule, truth, or belief.

Veracious (vuh-rey-shuhs) adj. Speaking or being the truth.
Voracious (vaw-rey-shuhs) adj. wanting or devouring great quantities of food.

Country (kuhn-tree) n, a nation with its government, occupying a territory.
County (koun-tee) n, a political and administrative division of a state in the USA, giving certain local governmental services and forming the central unit of regional power.

Dual (doo-uhl) having two parts.
Duel (doo-uhl) a fight or contest between two people. Hamilton lost the duel.

Envelop (en-vel-uhp) to cover or surround. She enveloped him in her arms.
Envelope (en-vuh-lohp) a paper container for a letter.

Later (lei-ter) afterward. E.g., come later than nine o'clock.
Latter (lat-er) the last of two things mentioned. E.g., if I must choose between brains or beauty, I'll take the latter.

Medal (med-l) n., Made with precious materials and metals usually in the form of a round disk with an inscription honoring a special event or a hero. An Olympic medal.
Metal (met-l) n., a solid material (an element or alloy) that is hard, shiny, malleable, fusible, and ductile with electrical and thermal conductivity.

Picture (pik-cher) n., a painting or drawing. E.g., Can she draw me a picture of a great white shark?
Pitcher (pich-er) n., A container, typically earthenware, glass, or plastic, with a handle and a lip, used for holding and pouring liquids.

Than (than) con., a conjunction used to introduce the second member of an unequal comparison. E.g., my right ear is larger than my left ear, oh my.
Then (then) adv., then is a word to describe a time that is not now. At that time. E.g., Luis prefers Fridays, and it would be better to meet then.

Ware (wair) n. is an article of merchandise, a product usually used in the plural. E.g., the artist displayed her wares on a wooden stand.
Wear (wair) v, A verb (wear, wore (wawr), worn (wawrn)), meaning to have clothing on. E.g., Rudolph Porter always wore red silk paisley ties.
We're (weer) v, con. We're is the contraction of two words, we and are. E.g., we're going to the Dodger game this weekend.
Were (wur) v. The past tense of are, e.g., Marty and Dee Dee, were at the airport last weekend.
Where (hwair) adv., in or to what place, location, or position. E.g., where are we?

Adduce (uh-doos) v. To give as evidence. E.g., the team used many relevant examples to adduce the situation.
Deduce (dih-doos) v. To arrive at a fact or a conclusion by reasoning; draw as a logical conclusion.
Induce (in-doos) v. To succeed in persuading or influencing someone to do something.
Infer (in-fur) v. To deduce something that hasn't been said directly.

Abjure (ab-joor) v., to solemnly renounce a belief, cause, or claim.
Adjure (uh-joor) v., an urge or request for someone to solemnly or earnestly do something.

Admission (ad-mish-uhn) n., a statement acknowledging the truth of something.
Admittance (ad-mit-ns) n., the process or fact of entering or being allowed to enter a place or institution.

Afterward (af-ter-werd) adv. At a later or future time, after.
Afterword (af-ter-wurd) n. A concluding section in a book, typically by a person other than the author.

Allude (uh-lood) v. To suggest indirectly. E.g., Gwen can't speak to her husband without alluding to his affair with their housekeeper, Bunny Blue.
Elude (ih-lood) v. To dodge or escape. E.g., serious friendships always seemed to elude him.
Illude (ih-lood) v. To trick. E.g., he had allowed his imagination to illude him.

Altogether (awl-tuh-geth-er) Means wholly or entirely. Space X rocket engines have an altogether different approach to propulsion.
All together (awl tuh-geth-er) Applied to people or things that are being treated as a whole. E.g., we always had fun when we were all together.

Ambiguous (am-big-yoo-uhs) adj, Ambiguous is a phrase or acts with more than one meaning. The ending of the horror movie is ambiguous; we don't know if he got eaten by the zombies.
Ambivalent (am-biv-uh-luhnt) adj, Ambivalence is uncertainty and having conflicting attitudes and feelings. E.g., he was ambivalent as to which candidate to vote for in the election.

Anyone (en-ee-wuhn) p, anybody, any person at all. E.g., anyone can volunteer to help.
Any one (en-ee wuhn) any one person. E.g., any one of you may go, but not all of you.

Appraise (uh-preyz) v. To assess or estimate the worth of something or someone. E.g., to appraise a diamond.
Apprise (uh-prahyz) v. Is to inform or notify. E.g. the officer apprised us of our rights.

Avenge (uh-venj) v. To inflict harm in return for an injury or wrong done to oneself or another in the past. To exact satisfaction against someone.
Revenge (ri-venj) v. The action of giving hurt or harm on someone for an injury or wrong suffered at their hands.

Biannual (bahy-an-yoo-uhl) something is occurring twice a year. E.g., The biannual meeting of the planning committee. My trip to Hawaii is a biannual event.
Semiannual (sem-ee-an-yoo-uhl) adj., something is occurring twice a year. E.g., Welcome to the semiannual sales meeting.
Biennial (bahy-en-ee-uhl) n, every two years. E.g., these flowers are biennial, and they bloom every two years.

Compelled (kuhm-peld) v. Being forced or coerced to do something. They were compelled to join the army.
Impelled (im-peld) v. An urge to do something based on an incentive.

Complacent (kuhm-pley-suhnt) adj, showing smug, or uncritical satisfaction with oneself or one's achievements.
Complaisant (kuhm-pley-suhnt) adj, a firm willing to please.
Compliant (kuhm-plahy-uhnt) adj. someone who generally agrees to follow the rules.

Complement (kom-pluh-muhnt) n. To add or to improve, an addition that enhances something.
Compliment (kom-pluh-muhnt) n. To praise or express approval, an admiring comment. That's a great compliment.

Consequent (kon-si-kwent) adj. something following as a result or effect. Let's play truth or consequences.
Subsequent (suhb-si-kwuhnt) n. coming after something in time, the next event.

Corollary (kawr-uh-ler-ee) n, adj. As that follows from and is often updated or added to something already proved.
Correlation (kawr-uh-ley-shuhn): A mutual relationship or connection between two or more things.

Disk (disk) n. A flat, thin, round object, like a Frisbee.
Disc (disk) n. A variant of the disk, a discus.

Elicit (ih-lis-it) v. To draw out a reply or reaction, to evoke. The press elicited answers from the cabinet.
Illicit (ih-lis-it) adj. Not allowed by law or rules. They must stop that illicit activity, said the officer.

Assure (uh-shoor) v. To have confidence or trust. To put one's mind at rest.
Ensure (en-shoor) v. To make sure that something will happen.
Insure (in-shoor) v. To give compensation if a person dies or if a property is damaged.

Epidemic (ep-i-dem-ik) n. A widespread incident of an infectious disease in a community at a specific time.
Endemic (en-dem-ik) adj, n. A disease or condition regularly found among people or in a certain area.

Grisly (griz-lee) adj. A gruesome, revolting causing horror or disgust (dis-guhst, dih-skuhst).
Gristle (gris-uhl) n. Cartilage, especially when found as tough, inedible tissue in meat.
Grizzled (griz-uhld) adj, n, v. Having or streaked with gray hair.
Grizzly (griz-lee) adj., n. An animal of a large race of brown bear native to North America.

Emigrate (em-i-greyt) v. To move away from a city or country and to live somewhere else. E.g., Donald's grandfather emigrated from Germany sixty years ago.
Immigrate (im-i-gruhnt) v. To move into a country from somewhere else. E.g., her family immigrated to the United States four generations ago. Anna Marie immigrated to America.

Odious (oh-dee-uhs) adj. extremely unpleasant, repulsive.
Odorous (oh-der-uhs) adj. Having or giving off a smell.

Ought (awt) aux v, n, adv. ought to be used to indicate duty or correctness, typically when criticizing someone's actions. E.g., they ought to use less salt.
Should (shood) v. should is used to indicate obligation, duty, or correctness, typically when criticizing. He should come in early tomorrow.

Stationary (stey-shuh-ner-ee) adj, n. something that is not moving, geostationary.
Stationery (stey-shuh-ner-ee) n. Writing materials, such as pencils, envelopes, paper, and pens.

Capital (kap-i-tl) n, adj. Capital is a seat of government, generally a city.
Capitol (kap-i-tl) n. The capitol is the building used for governmental meetings.

Carat (kar-uht) n. A carat is the weight unit of a gemstone.
Karat (kar-uht) n. Measures the purity of gold with pure gold being 24 karats fine.
Caret (kar-it) n. The mark where content is being inserted.
Carrot (kar-uht) n. From the parsley family, the yellow-orange root being the edible portion.

Accept (ak-sept) v. To agree to receive or do. I accept that invitation.
Except (ik-sept) prep., conj., v. Not including. E.g., anyone can attend, except for first-year students.

Adverse (ad-vurs) adj. Unfavorable, harmful.
Averse (uh-vurs) adj. Strongly disliking; opposed or opposition.

Along (uh-lawng) prep, adv. Moving or extending horizontally. E.g., Paint a stripe along the dock.
A long (uh-lawng) Referring to something of considerable length.

Balmy (bah-mee) adj. pleasantly warm. I like this balmy weather.
Barmy (bahr-me) adj. Foolish, crazy. After working without a break, the staff became quite barmy.

Berth (burth) n. A bunk in a ship, train, etc. I want the top berth.
Birth (burth) n. The release of a baby from the womb. That was a natural birth.

Bough (bou) n. The main branch of a tree.
Bow (bou) (rhymes with cow). V. n. To fold at the waist or the front of a ship.
Bow (bou) (rhymes with toe) E.g., That's a great looking bow tie.

Breach (breech) v, n. To break through or break a rule. The heavy rain breached the dam.
Breech (breech) v, n. The lower part of anything, the back part of a gun barrel.

Broach (brohch) v. To raise a subject for discussion. I want to broach a conversation on world peace.
Brooch (brohch) n. A piece of jewelry with a clasp.

Canvas (kan-vuhs) n. A dense, tightly woven cotton, hemp, or linen, used for tents, sails, etc.
Canvass (kan-vuhs) v. To seek people's votes. The students canvassed the neighborhood.

Censure (sen-sher) v, n. To criticize strongly.
Censor (sen-ser) n, v. To ban or alter parts of a book or film, or a person who does this. That film was censored.

Cereal (seer-ee-uhl) n. Breakfast food made from grains. Some popular serials include Apple Jacks, Cap 'Crunch, Cheerios, Chex, Donkey Kong Crunch, Franken Berry's, Froot Loops, Frosted Flakes.
Serial (seer-ee-uhl) adj. A story that is appearing in multiple episodes. E.g. The Sopranos, the HBO series that lasted for six seasons, produced 86 episodes.

Climactic (klahy-mak-tik) adj. forming or coming to a climax. The climactic part of the play.
Climatic (klahy-mat-ik): adj. relating to climate.

Cue (kyoo) n., anything said or done on or off stage that is followed by a specific action, a signal for action; also, a wooden rod with a leather tip that is used to strike the ball in billiards or pool.
Queue (kyoo) n., a line of people or vehicles, a braid of hair.

Curb (kurb) n. To keep something in check, control, or limit. Curb that behavior.
Kerb (kurb) British English

Currant (kur-uhnt) n. A small seedless raisin, dried grape.
Current (kur-uhnt) adj, n. something that is happening or occurring at this moment.

Defuse (dee-fyooz) v. To make a situation less tense, to remove the fuse.
Diffuse (dih-fyooz) v, adj. To spread over a wide area, to disseminate.

Discreet (dih-skreet) adj. Careful not to attract attention, judicious. Please be discreet.
Discrete (dih-skreet) adj. Separate and distinct.

Disinterested (dis-in-tuh-res-tid) adj. Impartial.
Uninterested (uhn-in-ter-uh-stid) adj. Not interested.

Draw (draw) v. A tie or even score at the end of a game. Or to cause or move in a direction.
Drawer (drawr) n. A sliding storage compartments. It's in the top drawer.

Exercise (ek-ser-sahyz) n, v. A physical activity; to do physical activity. Walking is an excellent method of exercise.
Exorcize (ek-sawr-sahyz) v. To drive out an evil spirit.

Fawn (fawn) n, v. A young deer with a light brown color.
Faun (fawn) n. A mythical being, part man, part goat (ears, horns, tail, hind legs).

Flaunt (flawnt) v. To display or parade ostentatiously or boldly.
Flout (flout) v. To disregard a rule, to treat with disdain.

Flounder (floun-der) v. To struggle or stagger helplessly or clumsily in water or mud.
Founder (foun-der) n, v. A person who manufactures articles of cast metal. The owner or operator of a foundry.

Forbear (fawr-bair) v. Politely, or patiently restrain an impulse from doing something, refrain.
Forebear (fawr-bair) n. Ancestor, forefather, antecedent, progenitor, primogenitor.

Antecedent (an-tuh-seed-nt) adj, n. something that existed before or logically preceded another.
Precedent (pres-i-duhnt, pri-seed-nt)) n. An earlier event, action, or decision that is regarded as an example or guide to be considered in subsequent similar decisions.

Imply (im-plahy) v. strongly suggests the truth or existence of something not expressly said.
Infer (in-fur) v. To deduce or conclude from evidence and reasoning rather than from explicit statements.

Loath (lohth) adj. Reluctant, unwilling, disinclined, ill-disposed, averse, opposed, resistant.

Loathe (lohth) v. A feeling of intense dislike or disgust.

Mitigate (mit-i-geyt) v. To make less severe, dangerous, or painful.
Militate (mil-i-teyt) v., to weigh heavily, a fact or circumstance to be a compelling or conclusive factor.

Petal (pet-l) n., Colored segments of the corolla of a flower.
Pedal (ped-l) n. v. A foot-operated lever or control for a vehicle, musical instrument, or other mechanisms.
Peddler (ped-ler) n. To sell (something, especially small goods) by going from house to house or place to place.

Pole (pohl) n. A cylindrical round-shaped piece of metal or wood to hold something up. The telephone pole held the phone wires.
Poll (pohl) n, v. The process of voting in an election. E.g., the country went to the polls.

Prescribe (pri-skrahyb) v. For a Doctor, to order the taking of a drug in writing.
Proscribe (proh-skrahyb) v. To forbid, especially by law.

Skeptic (skep-tik) n. An individual who is reluctant to accept (ak-sept) ideas or opinions.
Septic (sep-tik) adj. A condition created by sepsis or infection.

Sight (sahyt) n. The faculty or power of seeing eyesight, vision, eyes, faculty of sight, visual sense.
Site (sahyt) n. A location for the construction of any kind.

Titillating (tit-l-ey-ting) adj., to stimulate or excite someone, especially in a sexual way. E.g., these journalists are paid to titillate the public.
Titivate (tit-uh-veyt) v., to groom or freshen up. E.g., she slapped on her war paint and titivated her hair.

Tortuous (tawr-choo-uhs) adj. containing a zigzag of turns. Of twists and turns, e.g., the route (root, rout) is remote and tortuous.
Torturous (tawr-cher-uhs) adj. Characterized by, involving, or causing excruciating pain or suffering.

Wreath (reeth) n. A wreath is a collection of leaves and twigs shaped like a ring placed on a grave.
Wreathe (reeth) v. To cover, surround, or encircle something. He sits wreathed in air pollution.

Allusion (uh-loo-zhuhn) n. The mention of an idea or remark. In books, allusions are used to connect ideas that the reader already knows, with themes discussed in the story. E.g., He drove his car like Steve McQueen in Bullitt.

Illusion (ih-loo-zhuhn) n. An illusion is anything that looks or seems different from what it is. The magician used the illusion to keep the secret from the audience.

Awhile (uh-hwahyl) adv. Awhile is a brief period. E.g., it has been a while since it rained last.

A while (hwahyl) determiner. A while describes a time, a noun. I will be a while at the dentists.

Dessert (dih-zurt) n. A dessert is a sweet confectionery food that completes the main meal.

Desert (dez-ert) v., to abandon, a person, cause, or organization in a way considered disloyal or treacherous.

Their (thair) pn. Their shows possession. It is just like my, his, her, and ours. E.g., This is their house.

They're (thair) con. There is a contraction of (they are).

There (thair) adv. Directs our attention to a specific location. As in, there's the car I bought.

Hone (hohn) v., n. A whetstone of fine, compact texture for sharpening razors. When you hone a blade, you sharpen the blade. E.g. He was carefully honing the curved blade with a whetstone of fine, compact texture

Home (hohm) n, adj, adv, v. A home is the place where one lives permanently, primarily as a member of a family or a household.

Among (uh-muhng) prep. During or surrounded by.

Amongst (uh-muhngst) The British version of among.

Inquiry (in-kwahy-uh-ree) n. An act of asking for information.

Enquiry (en-kwahy-uh-ree) n. British term for inquiry.

Gaff (gaf) n. A gaff is a pole with a metal hook for landing large fish also a cheat or fixes as in at a Carnival game, as well as harsh treatment someone takes.

Gaffe (gaf) n. A gaffe is a verbal blunder. E.g., He's not the waiter, sorry.

Gag (gag) n, v. A gag is a joke or a comic routine or something that prevents someone from talking.

Historic (hi-stawr-ik) adj. someone who is famous or important in history, or potentially so.

> Historical (hi-stawr-i-kuhl) adj. concerning history, concerning past events.

13.20 Clichés, Idiomatic expressions and Proverbs 4[M-S]

Exercise 1: Repeat each phrase and then the sentence that follows aloud.
Exercise 2: Create a sentence with each phrase and practice saying the sentence aloud.
Exercise 3: Research each phrase and write a sentence on the origins and etymology (et-uh-mol-uh-jee) of the words.

1.	May I accompany you: It's late, may I accompany you to your car?
2.	May I ask what happened? I know it's none of my business, but may I ask what happened?
3.	Middle of the road: He's a real middle of the road kind of candidate.
4.	Misery loves company: I must stay late at work too but don't worry, misery loves company.
5.	Misfortunes seldom come alone: That person lost his job, his wife, and his life.
6.	Monday morning quarterback: As a Monday morning quarterback, I have a list of suggestions for last weeks' game.
7.	Money does not grow on trees: We are going to have to cut back, since money does not grow on trees.
8.	Monkey business: No monkey business and stop fooling around, said the counselor to the campers.
9.	More holes than Swiss cheese: The detective said that the story has more holes than Swiss cheese.
10.	Movers and shakers: When Jeff Bezos stopped by my desk, I gave him a business card, since he is a mover and shaker as well as the richest man in the world.
11.	Mums the word: Remember, don't say anything about the accident, and mums the word.
12.	Necessity is the mother of invention: Def. The mother or creative force is a strong need.
13.	Never fry a fish till it's caught: Wait till the contest is over, you might not win, remember, and never fry a fish till it's found.
14.	Never look a gift horse in the mouth: Thank them, no matter what, and never look a gift horse in the mouth, no complaints about gifts.
15.	Never put off until tomorrow what you can do today. Def. Avoid procrastination, the disease of tomorrow.
16.	New kid on the block: Can you explain everything to me? I'm the new kid on the block.
17.	No news is good news: I paid all those bills, and never heard back, but as they say, no news is good news

18.	Not a second too soon: Randee made it to the hospital, not a second too soon, her water burst in the lobby, and Morgan was born.
19.	Not up to par: When a standard is not met.
20.	Nothing hurts like the truth: Finding out the truth is often unpleasant and hurts.
21.	The fats in the fire. Now that I've submitted the estimate, the fats in the fire. Let's see if we get the job.
22.	Nutty as a fruit cake: That clown at the circus is nutty as a fruit cake
23.	Off the hook: Getting out of trouble, free of responsibility or accountability.
24.	Off the record: I told the reporter that my comments are not quotable and completely "off the record."
25.	Old habits die hard. The longer a pattern lasts, the harder it is to stop, since old habits die hard. See the movie Ronin, for example, its proper use.
26.	On cloud nine: The Newlyweds were on cloud nine during their Honeymoon.
27.	On the wagon: Def. He hasn't had a drink in months. , He's on the wagon of sobriety.
28.	On the warpath: Lookout for the boss, she's on the warpath.
29.	She is once bitten, twice shy: Def. An unpleasant experience induces caution. After getting bitten by the shepherd, she was scared of dogs.
30.	Once in a lifetime: Riding the elevator up with Ted Turner, talking about bookstores, was a once in a lifetime experience.
31.	One in a million: Your odds of getting a free ticket are one in a million.
32.	Out of darkness: It took a while, but out of the night came to light.
33.	Out of sight, out of mind: Stay close so that we can keep in touch cause out of sight is out of mind.
34.	Out of the blue: I was in your area, so I decided to stop by out of the blue.
35.	Over my head: This project is way too complicated; I'm in over my head.
36.	Paddle your own canoe: Mind your own business. Don't worry about me; I can paddle my boat.
37.	Paint the town red: I just won the lottery, let's paint the town red.
38.	Pass the buck: Don't pass the buck, take responsibility for your actions.
39.	Pay through the nose: Def. Pay an excessive amount for something, as in, we paid through the nose for that vacation.
40.	Pie in the sky: That project is pie in the sky and will never get funded.
41.	Piece of cake: That quiz was so easy, it was a piece of cake.
42.	Pipe dream: Don't let that become a pipe dream, make it happen.
43.	Pissing contest: Remember, in Corporate America, no one ever wins an argument or a pissing contest.
44.	Play by ear: I'm not sure when we can meet, let's play it by ear.
45.	Plead the fifth: When you decide not to give self-incriminating information.
46.	Pull the wool over your eyes: Don't let them pull the wool over your eyes, stay alert.
47.	Put a sock in it: Hey put a sock in it, I've heard enough.

48.	Raincheck: Sorry I missed your sale; can I have a rain check; I'll come back later and buy the item.
49.	Raining cats and dogs: You'll need an umbrella; it's raining cats and dogs.
50.	Red herring: Def. A red herring is anything that distracts from a relevant or important issue.
51.	Reinventing the wheel: When you duplicate a primary method that has already previously been created or optimized by others.
52.	Ride the tide: That movie sold that car; we can ride the tide for a while.
53.	Right under his nose: They drilled a tunnel, right under our noses, said the investigator.
54.	Ripe old age: The people who live on mountaintops always live to a ripe old age, unless they fall off.
55.	Rome wasn't built in a day: The new museum will take some time after all; Remember Rome wasn't built in a day.
56.	Room and board: The scholarship covers room and board, but not tuition.
57.	Saddle up: The sun has risen; let's saddle up and get going, said the cowboy.
58.	Saved by the bell: When a phone or bell rings, interrupting an event, altering the situation in either a positive or negative manner.
59.	Say uncle: When wrestling an opponent, saying Uncle means, to give up.
60.	Second banana: A person who works in a supporting, secondary capacity.
61.	See red: To become very angry.
62.	Nip it in the bud: See the dentist right away for that pain, better to nip it in the bud, then have some big problem later.
63.	Separate the wheat from the chaff: To be able to discern between valuable people or ideas from worthless ones.
64.	Shady: That guy in front of the bar looks shady.
65.	Shake a leg: Start moving, come on and shake a leg, or we'll miss the train.
66.	Shoot the breeze: We'll shoot the breeze until she's ready.
67.	A sigh of relief: She let out a sigh of relief after the doctor's call.
68.	Sick: Something good. That movie is sick.

Lesson 14

Beauty Salon, Jazz, Cliches, Derivatives

14.1 Pronunciation Key 19 and sentences

Exercise: Repeat the words and sentences aloud.
These are all the sounds of the English language using different words and sentences.
Practice until they are easy and familiar.

Word (phonetic spelling)	Phonetic sound	Sentence
	key: long/short (actual sound) with (actual letters)	Find the key word in each sentence to stress.
badge, sage, cage	short [a]	May I see the badge?
cake, make, Drake	long [a]	Where is the chocolate cake?
bench, stench, mensch	short [e]	Where is the bench?
wheel, heel, meal	long [e]	Both hands on the wheel.
hippo, zippo, crip	short [i]	Hippos are not usually friendly.
kite, fight, might, sight	long [i]	Can they get the kite out of the tree?
dog, bog, fog, cog	short [o]	What is his dog's name?
home, gnome, drone	long [o]	Home is where the heart is.
crunch, lunch, munch	short [u]	What is for lunch?
juice, caboose, noose	long [u]	Does he sell carrot juice?
cymbal, gym, bicycle	[y] short [i] sound	I want a blue bicycle.
dry, fly, sky	[y] long [i] sound	Where is the fly swatter?
happy, party, puppy	[y] long [e] sound	What a cute puppy.
tube, kite, rope, huge, cape, pine, tape, note	silent [e] creates long vowel sound	Would he like some pine nuts?
rain, daisy, hay, break, sleigh, they	long [a] sound digraphs (ai, ay, ea, ei, ey)	Let's go sleigh riding.

paw, saw, draw	long[aw]	The Rottweiler (rot-wahy-ler) has large paws to help support its weight.
autumn, haul	long[au]	Did Morgan and Hunter rent a U-Haul?
bee, teeth, bee	long[e] sound with [ee]	Is that a bumblebee?
leap, speak, seal, pea, bead	long[e] sound with [ea]	The orca ate the seal.
head, thread, spread, bread	short[e] sound with [ea]	Spread the butter on the bread.
build	short[i] sound with [ui]	Did she build that?
chief, thief, grief, siege	long[e] sound with [ie]	Heba was filled with grief upon learning of her Aunt's death.
buy, sight, might, bind, night, mind	long[i] sound with [uy], [ind], [ight]	Rusty might read that script.
blow, flow, grow, low, mow, snow	long[o] sound with [ow]	Will he mow my lawn?
float, goat, moat, road,	long[o] sound with [oa]	Hawks can knock goats off of mountains.
boil, coil, coin, point, toil	long[o] sound with [oi]	Coin collecting is a fun hobby.
ahoy, boy, joy, royal	long[o] sound with [oy]	"Joy to the World" is a wonderful happy song by Three Dog Night that went gold when 1,000,000 units across the United States were sold.
moon, foot, book	long [u] sound with [oo]	Bookbinding is a lost art.
grew, blew	long [u] sound with [ew]	She blew out the candles on her birthday cake.
true, blue	long [u] sound with [ue]	What a beautiful blue sky.
view	long [u] sound with [iew]	How's the view from, up there?
ball, bat, bear, bath,	[b] sound	Was that a brown bear?
cent, circus, cereal, cow, center, cycle, circle, cement	Soft [c]	Stand inside the circle.
cake, carrot, cow, crown, coat, cookie,	Hard [c]	The king wore a gold crown.
chair, cheese, cherry, chalk, chalk,	[ch] sound	She would like some dark chocolate cherries.
clock, chick, tack, lock,	[ck] sound	Remember to lock the doors.

The Hollywood Tutor's AMERICAN ENGLISH © 2020 Mitch Rubman. All rights reserved. No part of this publication may be reproduced or distributed in any form or by any means without the written permission of the copyright owner

desk, dish, doll, dog, dress, drum, duck, dragon	[D] sound	These treats are for the dog.
fan, fox, fat, fin, fish, five, flag, flute, flower.	[f] sound	Flags have many symbols in them.
goat, game, goose, grapes, gift, green	hard [g] sound	Those grapes are sweet.
germ, gym, gentle, giant.	soft [g] sound	That dog is gentle.
cough, rough, tough	[gh] sound [f]	It's going to be a rough night.
high, sleigh, dough, right, light, weight, fright	[gh] silent	The answer is right around the corner.
hand, hat, hay, helmet, hen, hippo, home, horn, horse, house	[h] sound	She liked to blow her own horn.
jack, jade, jump, jelly, jab, job, jam, jog	[j] sound	Does he like peanut butter and jelly?
kiss, kitchen, kitten, kick, kettle, kangaroo, keep, kite	[k] sound	The kitten is under the sofa.
knack, knee, kneel, knife, knight, knit, knock, knot, know.	[kn] sound [n]	Knock first before entering the office.
ladder, ladybug, lake, leaf, lion, limb, lock, lollipop	[L] sound	Tracy fell out of bed and broke her leg.
mint, mirror, monkey, mop, mushroom, music, mouse	[m] sound	There are many mushrooms that are good to eat.
nail, napkin, nest, net, news, night, nine, nurse, nuts	[n] sound	Nuts are healthy to eat.
pair, paper, panda, peanut, pear, pencil, pig, pony	[p] sound	Pandas are the prize of the zoo.
phone, phrase, phase, gopher, elephant, phonics, photograph	[ph] sound [f]	The gopher chewed through the wires.
banquet, quilt, queen, question, squirt, quiz, quail, quick, quarter	[kw] sound with [qu]	Quilts are often made for newly married couples.
rabbit, rectangle, read, rocket, road, rainbow, rope, radio	[r] sound	The Space X rocket is ready for testing.
spider, snake, sun, soda, seal, soap	[s] sound	Here comes the Sun.

scene, scent, science, scissors,	[sc]sound[s]	Is this the Arts & Sciences building?
scan, scale, scare, scrap, screen, escape	[sc]sound[sk]	The screen needs to be repaired.
shoe, trash, ship, splash, shell, flash	[sh]sound[sh]	There are millions of shells on the beach.
tap, tub, nut, tube, toy, train	[t] sound	What is her favorite nut?
third, thaw, thing, thimble, thought	[th soft sound]	Use a thimble to protect the finger.
these, those, they, weather, bother,	[th hard sound]	How's the weather today?
switch, match, hatch, catch, watch,	[tch] sound[ch]	That hatch leads to the engine room.
van, vine, vase, vowel, vent, vane, vote, vast, verb	[v] sound	The vowels are the most important.
wagon, walrus, water, wafer, wear,	[w] sound	The walrus gave the polar bear a hard time.
white, whale, wheel, what, when, why, wheat	[wh]sound [w]	The blue whale is the largest marine mammal that has ever existed.
who, whom, whole	[wh] sound [h]	I'll take the whole pie.
ax, box, exam, exit, extra, ox,	[x] sound [x]	The exam will start in one hour.
xenon, xylophone	[x] sound [z]	Can she play the xylophone?
yet, yellow, yak, yogurt, yeast, yell, yolk	[y] sound [y]	Yogurt has active cultures.
zipper, zebra, buzz, zoom	[z] sound [z]	The zebra's stripes are unique.
hose, weasel, easel, rise	[s] sound [z]	The weasel is under the house.

14.2 Pronunciation Key 20

Exercise: Repeat the words and sentences aloud. These are the sounds of the English language. Practice until easy.

Word	Sound	Example sentence
1. Artistic(ahr-tis-tik)	A	She's is very artistic (ahr-tis-tik).
2. Art(ahrt)	A	Art: Have they been to the new art museum?
3. Fat(fat)	A	Fat: Please trim off the fat, I like it extra lean.
4. Fare(fair)	A	Fare: The bus fare for Metro right now is $1.75 per ride or $7.00 for a full day unlimited or $25.00 for a week unlimited or $100.00 for a month unlimited.
5. Get(get)	E	Get: Let's get out of here.
6. Prey(prey)	E	Prey: Be careful the pets don't become prey to coyotes (kahy-oh-tyeez).

7.	Hit(hit)	I	Hit: He got a hit his first-time at-bat.
8.	Suffice(suh-fahys)	I	Suffice: How's the Lamborghini, does it suffice?
9.	Obey(oh-bey)	O	Obey: Remember to obey the rules of the road and always signal when making a lane change.
10.	Go(goh)	O	Go: Which way does he want to go?
11.	Not(not)	O	Not: I told him I'm not diving off that diving board.
12.	Or(awr)	O	Does he want soup or salad?
13.	Full(fool)	U	Full: I'm full, no more Indian buffet.
14.	Rule(rool)	U	Rule: What was that rule about talking in the library?
15.	Burn(burn)	U	Burn: Let the fire burn out.
16.	Aisle(ahyl)	Ai	Aisle: They took their wedding vows after walking down the aisle.
17.	Sauerkraut (sou-uhr-krout)	Au	Sauerkraut (sou-uhr-krout): Would he like sauerkraut on that frankfurter (frangk-fer-ter)?
18.	Duration(doo-rey-shuhn)	U	Duration: Will she be here for the duration of the race?
19.	Feud(fyood)	U	Feud (fyood): That feud went back hundreds of years.
20.	Oil(oil)	Oi	Oil: Remember to oil that door at least once a year.
21.	Cat(kat)	K	Cat: Is that a Siamese (sahy-uh-meez) cat?
22.	Kaleidoscope(kuh-lahy-duh-skohp)	K	Kaleidoscope (kuh-lahy-duh-skohp): Take a look through the kaleidoscope.
23.	Gopher(goh-fer)	G	Gopher: Did the gopher eat that carrot?
24.	Sing(sing)	Ng	Sing: Would Joe Barile like to sing tonight?
25.	Thin(thin)	Th	Thin: He is looking very thin; has he been running marathons?
26.	This(this)	Th	This: Let's get this straight, what time is the flight?
27.	So(soh)	S	So: So, what time is dinner?
28.	Zest(zest)	Z	Zest: She had a zest for life that was contagious.
29.	Church(church)	Ch	Church: The choir sang in a beautiful church.
30.	Jet(jet)	J	Jet: Was that a Jet or a UFO that I just saw zigzag over the sky in Santa Monica?
31.	Ship(ship)	Sh	Ship: The Harmony of the Seas is the world's largest ship.
32.	Vision(vizh-uhn)	Zh	Vision: What's your vision?

14.3 Irregular plural nouns

This is a difficult list. The irregular nouns are important variations of some commonly used words. Some of these nouns are not very well known, so take your time learning them.

Exercise 1: Read aloud and across the line.
Exercise 2: Create a sentence for each singular and plural word.

Singular	Plural
1. alumnus(uh-luhm-nuhs)	2. alumni(uh-luhm-nahy)
3. analysis(uh-nal-uh-sis)	4. analyses(an-l-ahyz)
5. appendix(uh-pen-diks)	6. appendices(uh-pen-duh-seez)
7. axis(ak-sis)	8. axes(ak-seez)
9. bacterium (bak-teer-ee-uh m)	10. bacteria(bak-teer-ee-uh)
11. basis(bey-sis)	12. bases(bey-seez)
13. beau(boh)	14. beaux(bohz)
15. cactus(kak-tuhs)	16. cacti(kak-tahy)
17. corpus(kawr-puhs)	18. corpora(kawr-per-uh)
19. crisis(krahy-sis)	20. crises(kreez)
21. criterion(krahy-teer-ee-uhn)	22. criteria(krahy-teer-ee-uh)
23. curriculum(kuh-rik-yuh-luhm)	24. curricula(kuh-rik-yuh-luh)
25. datum(dey-tuhm)	26. data(dey-tuh)
27. diagnosis(dahy-uhg-noh-sis)	28. diagnoses (dahy-uh g-noh-seez)
29. ellipsis(ih-lip-sis)	30. ellipses(ih-lip-seez)
31. focus(foh-kuhs)	32. foci(foh-sahy)
33. foot(foot)	34. feet(feet)
35. genus(jee-nuhs)	36. genera(jen-er-uh)
37. goose(goos)	38. geese(gees)
39. hypothesis(hahy-poth-uh-sis)	40. hypotheses(hahy-poth-uh-seez)
41. index(in-deks)	42. indeces(in-duh-seez)
43. matrix(mey-triks)	44. matrices(mey-tri-seez)
45. medium(mee-dee-uhm)	46. media(mee-dee-uh)
47. memorandum(mem-uh-ran-duhm)	48. memoranda(mem-uh-ran-duh)
49. oasis(oh-ey-sis)	50. oases(oh-ey-seez)
51. paralysis(puh-ral-uh-sis)	52. paralyses(puh-ral-uh-seez)
53. parenthesis(puh-ren-thuh-sis)	54. parentheses(puh-ren-thuh-seez)
55. phenomenon(fi-nom-uh-non)	56. phenomena(fi-nom-uh-nuh)
57. radius(rey-dee-uhs)	58. radii(rey-dee-ahy)
59. stimulus(stim-yuh-luhs)	60. stimuli(stim-yuh-lahy)
61. stratum (strey-tuhm)	62. strata(strey-tuh)
63. synopsis(si-nop-sis)	64. synopses(si-nop-seez)
65. tableau(ta-bloh)	66. tableaux(ta-blohz)
67. thesis(thee-sis)	68. theses(thee-seez)
69. tooth(tooth)	70. teeth(teeth)

14.4 Dialogue: The Beauty Salon

For those of you that wish to get your hair done, here is one such experience.

Exercise 1: Practice this dialogue aloud, switch sides and try again.

Employee:	Welcome to the new and improved original Beverly Hills Salon (suh-lon), Spa and juice bar, how may we serve you?
Customer:	I'd like to get a cut and a color with layers.
Employee:	Here is our cutting menu; for a senior stylist, its $120.00 for the cut, which includes a consultation with a TV stylist, herbal (ur-buhl) shampoo massage (muh-sahzh), fat-free organic conditioner (kuhn-dish-uh-ner) and full finish.
Customer:	Does that include a blow-dry?
Employee:	That's another $65.00.
Customer:	Do you do flat iron (ahy-ern)?
Employee:	Yes, that's another $25.00, if we do just a blow dry, we can also offer a treatment cut for only $30.
Customer:	What about bleach and toner?
Employee:	That's $120 for a top colorist or $75 for a color change.
Customer:	How about my full head, a total redo with panels, highlights, and lowlights?
Employee:	That's about $200.
Customer:	How about extensions (ik-sten-shuhns)?
Employee:	That's around $160, depending on which staff member is used.
Customer:	I'd like it short in the front with maybe bangs.
Employee:	We can take you now.
Customer:	Thanks, I'm in a rush. Can I ask you about the spa also?
Employee:	Sure, what questions can I answer for you?
Customer:	What's a proper spa treatment for a beginner?
Employee:	We have a basic spa package which includes a Eucalyptus (yoo-kuh-lip-tuhs) steam, a one-hour Swedish massage and aromatherapy (uh-roh-muh-ther-pee) facial for $200.
Customer:	What about for guys?

Employee:	A man's cut starts at $65.00.
Customer:	Do you have anybody wraps?
Employee:	Yes, we have cocoa (koh-koh) butter wrap for $85 for one hour or a wax wrap for $100 or a seaweed wrap for $120. We even do foot massages for $50, which includes a unique collagen (kol-uh-juhn) cream, and we also do all types of waxing in case you are interested.
Customer:	Waxing? Yes, can you tell me the prices?
Employee:	Sure, the prices are the following; $10 for eyebrows, $8 for cheeks, $10 for chin, $15 for sideburns, $10 for the neck, $40 for the breast line, $28 for full arms, $15 for half arms, $25 and up for hands and fingers, $8 for a regular bikini, $60 for buttock(buht-uhk) without bikini, $32 for a full leg, $4 for a thigh, $8 for a stomach line, $8 for the lower lip, $15 for ears, $55 for a full face, $15 for chest, $8 for nipples, $15 for underarms, $30 for a full back, $5 for feet, $5 for toes, and for men it's a minimum of $55 for the back.
Customer:	How about a manicure?
Employee:	It's $15 for a manicure and $25 for a pedicure.
Customer:	Do you take credit cards?
Employee:	Of course.
Customer:	Be right back.

14.5 Difficult words and sentences 9

These words might be more challenging than others.

Exercise 1: Repeat each word and then the sentence that follows aloud.
Exercise 2: Create a sentence with each new word and practice saying the sentence aloud.

Abuse(uh-byooz):	Don't abuse that rental car.
Ancestor (an-ses-ter):	Is he an ancestor?
Anise (an-is):	The black licorice (lik-er-ish) is made with anise.
Anxiety(ang-zahy-i-tee):	Getting that speeding ticket gave me a lot of anxiety.
Apostrophe (uh-pos-truh-fee):	Please use an apostrophe to indicate possession.
Applaud (uh-plawd):	I must applaud that decision.
Applause (uh-plawz):	Loud applause followed her performance on the piano.
Argyle (ahr-gahyl):	Did she like the diamond geometric patterns of the argyle socks?
Available(uh-vey-luh-buhl):	Is the Doctor available?
Axe (aks):	Did he get the axe at work?
Bolt(bohlt):	Did that lightning(lahyt-ning) bolt split the tree in half?
Bomb(bom):	The bomb was found in the bottle(bot-l) of champagne(sham-peyn).

Bottom(bot-uhm):	I'll get to the bottom of this if it's the last thing I do, is a famous saying.
Bowl(bohl):	Bowl of brown rice.
Britain (brit-n):	Have they been to Great Britain?
Cavalry (kal-vuh-ree):	Here comes the cavalry.
Celery(sel-uh-ree):	Does she want celery in that Bloody Mary?
Chair(chair):	Use this chair.
Chandelier (shan-dl-eer):	That's a beautiful chandelier over the table.
Chaos (key-os):	It is said that the universe tends towards chaos or disorderliness.
Chauffer (shoh-fer):	What time will the limousine and the chauffer be here?
Childhood(chahyld-hood):	Let's talk about childhood.
Chronological (kroon-l-oj-i-kuhl):	Please list references in chronological order.
Clothes (klohz):	Let's buy some new clothes.
Complacency (kuhm-pley-suhn-see):	Don't let complacency get to them, keep on moving forward.
Concussion(kuhn-kuhsh-uhn):	The NFL (National Football League) initiated a concussion management program.
Conflagration (kon-fluh-grey-shuhn):	There was a terrible conflagration on the Steamboat Lexington.
Consultant (kuhn-suhl-tnt):	I was hired as a consultant, not an employee.
Context(kon-tekst):	Put the new words in the proper context.
Cousins (kuhz-uhns):	Have you met my cousins David, Lou, or Devorah?
Discipline (dis-uh-plin):	Getting a black belt in Tae-Kwon-do requires a lot of discipline.
Donation(doh-ney-shuhn):	Please make your donations.
Drought(drout):	Only the durable succulents can make it through the drought (drout).
Eliminate(ih-lim-uh-neyt):	They had to eliminate the leak and hired a roofer.
Eminent (em-uh-nuhnt):	They tore down my apartment complex after the court ruled in favor of eminent domain for the new Highway.
Enervate (en-er-veyt):	The instructor enervated me with that exercise, I'm going to need lunch.
Extract (ex-strakt):	That great manager Walter T. will need vanilla extract for those cookies.
Extremely(ik-streem-lee):	I am extremely happy about the new job.
Flesh(flesh):	The zombies especially enjoyed the human flesh.
Foreign (fawr-in):	Does he prefer foreign or American made cars?
Freight (freyt):	That furniture will be shipped by freight.
Gravitas(grav-i-tahs):	The voice of James Earl Jones added gravitas to the role of Darth Vader in Star Wars.
Illuminating(ih-loo-muh-ney-ting):	That was a very illuminating lecture on the Greenhouse effect.
Independence(in-di-pen-duhns):	They can view a copy of the Declaration of Independence at the Smithsonian Institute in Washington, D. C.

Individuality(in-duh-vij-oo-al-i-tee):	He developed his individuality at college.
Intention(in-ten-shuhn):	They had good intentions but arrived too late.
Itch(ich):	That poison ivy made me itch.
Jealous(jel-uhs):	He was jealous of the first-place winner.
Knickerbocker (nik-er-bok-er):	I stayed at the Knickerbocker Hotel in Chicago.
Knife(nahyf):	Please sharpen the knife before carving.
Laryngitis (lar-uhn-jahy-tis):	When the opera singer came down with laryngitis, they had to call on the understudy to rise to the occasion.
Least(leest):	At least bring some wine to the party.
Macramé (mak-ruh-mey):	The art of creative knotting is called macramé.
Meant(ment):	Is that what he meant?
Merger(mur-jer):	Please call the Mergers and Acquisitions attorney.
Method(meth-uhd):	Though this is madness, yet there be method in it, Hamlet, Shakespeare.
Moaning(mohn-ng):	The organ made a moaning sound when the wind went through it.
Notwithstanding(not-with-stan-ding):	The car is his, notwithstanding the driver's license.
Obligatory (uh-blig-uh-tawr-ee):	An answer to the text is helpful, but not obligatory.
Ordinarily (awr-dn-air-uh-lee):	Those boxes get recycled ordinarily.
Overwhelmed(oh-ver-hwelm):	They were overwhelmed at the response to the ad.
Paints(peynts):	He paints every day at the seashore using oil.
Patience:	Taking painting lessons requires patience, especially if painting with gouache (gwahsh).
Persistence (per-sis-tuhns):	The persistence paid off for the athlete when he won the race.
Phillips(fil-ips):	I think that they will need a Phillips head screwdriver to assemble that desk.
Pliers (plahy-ers):	Use the needle nose pliers for small delicate jobs.
Plumber (pluhm-er):	Call the plumber, the sewer (soo-er) pipes (pahyps) broke.
Pneumonia (noo-mohn-yuh):	Be careful not to get pneumonia during the winter.
Poem (poh-uhm):	Did she get her poem published?
Prairie (prair-ee):	Life on the prairie was tough for the early settlers.
Prefer(pri-fur):	Does he prefer white or dark meat turkey, they asked at the Laugh Factory for their free Thanksgiving dinner.
Prestige(pre-steezh):	The Mercedes Benz has a higher prestige value, and the valets (va-leyz) will be expecting a larger tip.
Profession(pruh-fesh-uhn):	What did she say her profession was?
Prove(proov):	Can he prove that answer?
Quotation(kwoh-tey-shuhn):	That's my favorite book on Historical Quotations.
Racer(rey-ser):	Is he a drag racer?
Rack(rak):	We need a ski rack for this trip.
Razor(rey-zer):	I need a new razor; this one is dull.
Recognize(rek-uhg-nahyz):	The tiger recognized his feeder.

Regime (ruh-zheem):	That regime change was sudden.
Ridiculous (ri-dik-yuh-luhs):	Stop being ridiculous, eat the broccoli.
Rosetta (roh-zet-uh) stone:	The Rosetta Stone was discovered in 1799, it has the same inscription in three languages; the top register is ancient Egyptian hieroglyphs (hahy-er-uh-glif-iks), the second Egyptian demotic script and the third in Ancient Greek. With its three languages, it is the key to deciphering ancient Egyptian. It weighs approximately 1,680 lbs. and was created in the year 196 BC. It is on display at the British Museum.
Salary (sal-uh-ree):	Remember to ask for a higher salary.
Salmon (sam-uhn):	Let's order the salmon with wild rice.
Screwdriver (skroo-drahy-ver):	They will need a screwdriver to assemble that desk.
Sequestration (see-kwes-trey-shahn):	The jury of the murder (mur-der) case was put in sequestration for the duration of the trial.
Slowly (sloh-lee):	Slowly, I turned, step by step, inch by inch.
Spontaneous (spon-tey-nee-uhs):	Can we be spontaneous and not plan the vacation?
Statue (stach-oo):	Did she have a chance to visit the Statue of Liberty in New York harbor? It's a giant copper statue presented to the United States by France.
Strength (strengkth):	He didn't know his strength and broke his bat into splinters.
Subordinate (suh-bawr-dn-it):	A subordinate clause cannot be used as a sentence since it does not contain a complete thought.
Subordination (suh-bawr-dn-ey-shuhn):	Use of a subordinate at the end of a sentence weakens it.
Subtle (suht-l):	The difference between the two shades is quite subtle and almost impossible to see.
Suffering (suhf-er-ing):	The suffering must stop.
Technique (tek-neek):	She had great method and bowled a perfect game.
Telepathy (tuh-lep-uh-thee):	The psychic used telepathy to communicate.
Theme (theem):	What is the idea of the script?
Trench (trench) coat (koht):	The trench coat was first used during World War One.
Volunteers (vol-uhn-teer):	They can always use volunteers at the Hospital.
Whenever (hwen-ev-er):	I like to walk whenever I get the chance.
Wrench (rench):	Please hand me the 3/8" wrench.
Yacht (yot):	Would he like to go out to sea in my new Yacht?
Yams (yams):	I like yams with my Turkey

14.6 Slang Spoken Contractions:

Slang expressions eliminate words, letters and speed up the process of communicating.
They are used most often for casual conversations with friends, and not usually written out.

Exercise 1: Practice the following slang expressions.
Exercise 2: Create a slang sentence.
[KEY]

Slang word (phonetic spelling) (formal spelling)	Slang example used in a sentence.
Dunno(duh-noh) (don't know)	I dunno.
Gonna(gaw-nuh) (going to)	I'm gonna be late.
Gotta(got-uh) (got to)	I gotta make a phone call.
Hafta(haf-uh) (have to)	I hafta be home by six o'clock.
Hasta(haz-tuh) (has to)	The lion hasta be fed twice a day.
Kinda(kahyn-duh) (kind of)	I kinda like the Ferrari better than the Lamborghini.
Outta(out-uh) (out of)	She's outta bananas.
Wanna(won-uh) (want a)	Wanna cup of coffee?

14.7 Clichés, Idiomatic expressions and Proverbs 5 [S-W]

Just a few favorites of the many idiomatic expressions used in conversation.
Some phrases have sentences demonstrating use, others have short definitions.
[Key] Def: Definition

Exercise 1: Repeat aloud the phrase and then the sentence that follows.
Exercise 2: Research the origins of the phrase.

1.	Social butterfly:	E.g. She is such a social butterfly, how many birthday cards arrived today?
2.	Still waters run deep:	E.g. Inscribed on Sid's tombstone, Still waters run deep.
3.	Stockholm syndrome:	Def. When hostages are sympathetic to their captors.
4.	Stopped dead in his tracks:	E.g. He stopped dead in his tracks after he heard the good news.
5.	Straight from the horse's mouth:	E.g. I know it's true because I got it from the horse's mouth.
6.	Sweet:	Def: Something that is good.
7.	Take the bull by the horn:	E.g. It's a big project, so they'll need to take the bull by the horn.

8.	Worth her weight in gold: E.g. That new assistant finished all of my reports on time and is worth her weight in gold.
9.	The acid test: E.g. The acid test will be if the car starts.
10.	The apple doesn't fall far from the tree. Def: Children are usually like their parents.
11.	The best things in life are free: Def. This proverb means those things that cost money should not be prioritized over free things like family and friends. Those free things are, in the end, worth more than anything money could buy.
12.	The bigger they are, the harder they fall. Def: Sometimes size works against you.
13.	The birds and the bees: E.g. Son, I think it's time we have a talk about the birds and bees.
14.	The customer is always right: E.g. Don't argue with the patrons, remember the customer is always right.
15.	The heat of battle: E.g. In the heat of battle, many unexpected things can happen.
16.	The jury is still out: E.g. The jury is still out on which house to buy.
17.	The long arm of the law: E.g. Never underestimate the long arm of the laws' reach.
18.	Rule of thumb: E.g. The runner calculated all the distances using rule of thumb, so it's not perfectly accurate.
19.	The world's my oyster: Def. From Shakespeare, meaning, we all have the ability or opportunity to achieve anything we want in life. Take the opportunities as they come.
20.	There are plenty of fish in the sea: Def. There are many other people that can be met and dated.
21.	Thick as thieves: Def. Old friends that are very close.
22.	Three Dog Night (1967-) Two different definitions. An American Rock Band. Founding members include vocalists Danny Hutton, Cory Wells and Chuck Negron. The Band had 21(twenty-one) Billboard top 40(forty) hits and 3(thre) number 1's.(ones) Their songs include Joy to the World, Eli's coming, and Black & White. Another definition of [3] Three dog night is as a temperature gauge. Dogs companioning humans at night. One dog is slightly cold, two dogs are really cold, and three dogs are freezing.
23.	Threw the book at him: E.g. the Judge threw the book at him.
24.	Through thick and thin: Def. Through hard and easy times. E.g. they stayed together through thick and thin.
25.	Throw a monkey wrench into something. Def. To stop the flow of something.
26.	Throw caution to the wind: Def. To go fully into an event or circumstance.
27.	Tinsel town: Welcome to Hollywood, also known as Tinsel town. Tinsel is a metallic like decorative material that mimics the effect of ice, consisting of thin strips of sparkling material attached to a thread. When in long narrow strips it is called, lametta and emulates icicles. It was originally a metallic garland for Christmas decorations.
28.	To be in: Def. When you are included in the discussions.

29.	To burn one's bridges: Def. When an opportunity ends with you destroying your chance to return. Just like if you burn down the bridge that you crossed to go somewhere; you won't be able to go back over that bridge.
30.	To have a blast: Def. To have a fun time at something.
31.	To have the best of both worlds: Def. A situation wherein one can enjoy two different opportunities.
32.	To make a long story short: Def. To tell a more concise version of a long story. E.g. To make a long story short, we won the game.
33.	To play ball: Def. To join whatever is going on.
34.	To the bitter end: E.g. They had to stay on the set till the bitter end, since they were in all those scenes.
35.	Trickle of rain: E.g. was that a trickle of rain that I just felt?
36.	Twist someone's arm: Def. To force someone to agree with you.
37.	Two heads are better. Def. In most cases this is correct, meaning two people can do better work than one person.
38.	Up to my ears: E.g. Sorry I didn't call, I've been up to my ears in work, said Lincoln.
39.	Uphill battle: E.g. Getting that project done, starts is an uphill battle.
40.	Use your head: E.g. Use your head, we're fifty feet underwater, you can't just swim to shore.
41.	Use your noodle: Def. Use your brain, the noodle being the brain.
42.	Walk on air. E.g. when things are so good, you feel lighter, so light you can practically walk on air.
43.	Walking off the meal: E.g. When you try to exercise off a recent weight gain.
44.	Walking on eggshells: Def. When a situation is very delicate.
45.	Weary bones: Def. To be tired. E.g. those seniors have weary bones, go easy on them.
46.	Weigh a ton: E.g. With all the dressing on it the salad is going to weigh a ton.
47.	What do you want from life? E.g. the guidance counselor would always ask, what do you want from life?
48.	What's the point? E.g. the student asked, what's the point in learning geometry?
49.	When life gives you lemons: E.g. When life gives you lemons, make lemonade (lem-uh-neyd).
50.	When pigs fly: Def. When an impossible task actually comes true.
51.	When the cats away the mice play. E.g. when authority is gone, the children misbehave.
52.	When wine is in, wit is out: Def. When intoxicated, wit or intelligence is gone.
53.	Whipped into shape: E.g. The trainer whipped me into shape.
54.	White as a ghost: E.g. He turned white as a ghost when they announced his name on TV.
55.	Who let the cat out of the bag? Def. When a secret is revealed by mistake.
56.	Win hands down: Def. To win something easily and decisively, without any question.

57. Word to wise:	E.g. Word to the wise, don't try that at home.
58. Words fail to express:	E.g. Sorry for your loss, words fail to express my sympathy.
59. Work your fingers to the bone:	E.g. At the new job, I worked my fingers to the bone.
60. Works like a charm:	Def. When something is easier than expected. E.g. the new skin cream works like a charm.
61. Writing on the wall:	E.g. The writings on the wall, they ran out of alcohol, so the party is over.
62. You get hired for skills and fired for behavior:	E.g. Good luck on the new job, but don't forget, you get hired for skills and fired for behavior.
63. Piss in my pocket and tell me it's raining:	E.g. You wrote the bad review, so, please don't piss in my pocket, and tell me it's raining.
64. You're pulling my leg.	Def. When you question the validity or truth of a statement.
65. You're the man:	E.g. You're the man, said the band leader to the soloist
66. Your fly is open:	E.g. I'm sorry to inform you that, your zipper is down, or your fly is open, zip up.

14.8   Dialogue: Playing Poker

There are many different card games, this is one example. This exercise will help explain card rank and interaction.

Exercise 1: Repeat aloud the following dialogue. Switch sides, repeat.

Dealer:	The four suits(soots) are: Clubs(kluhbz), Diamonds(dahy-muhndz), Hearts(hahrts) & Spades(speydz). With a wild card you can get a five of a kind.
Player:	I win with five Aces(eysez); here's a wild card and four Aces. I have a five of a kind.
Dealer:	Correct. After a five of a kind, which is very rare is a Royal flush. The odds of getting a Royal flush are 649,739 : 1. Here see Ace, King, Queen (kween), Jack, and Ten of Hearts.
Player:	Look a straight(streyt) flush: I have a straight flush, see King, Queen, Jack, Ten, Nine of Diamonds.
Dealer:	After that is a four of a kind. See four fours, I really thought you were the winner with a four of a kind.
Player:	I got a full house, here, I thought I had a good hand but whatever, look, two fives and three sevens, see a full house.
Dealer:	After the full house is a flush, look all hearts.

Player:	I usually win with a straight: Look, here's my straight, five, six, seven, eight, nine.
Dealer:	Not tonight. Look he's got a three of a kind that doesn't win.
Player:	Right, well I had tens and sixes, two pairs, guess I'm out.
Dealer:	So much for my one pair of twos.
Player:	That is correct.

14.9 Word Derivatives and Root forms

This is a reasonably tricky list. These derivatives are formed by adding suffixes and prefixes. Go slowly; many have complicated sounds. Try to figure out their meanings based on roots, prefixes, and suffixes.

Exercise 1: Review aloud the chart of roots and their derivatives. Go across and down.
Exercise 2: Create a sentence for each word.

Root form	Derivatives				
adorn(v)	adornment (n)	adorningly (adv)	adorner(n)	well adorned (adj)	unadorned (adj)
aggression (n)	aggressor(n)	aggressive (adj)	aggressively (adv)	aggressiveness(n)	
ambitious (adj) (am-bish-uhs)	ambitiously (adv)	ambitiousness(n)	overambitious(adj)	overambitiously (adv)	overambitiousness(n)
bolt (v, n,)	bolter(n)	boltless (adj)	bolted		
book(n)	bookless(adj)	booklike(adj)	bookie(n)	unbooked (adj)	
care(n) (kair)	carer(n)	noncaring (adj)	overcare (n.)	uncaring (adj)	
coarse(adj)	coarsely(adv)	coarseness(n)			
credulous (adj)	credulously (adv)	credulity(n)	incredulous (adj)	incredulously (adv)	incredulity (n)
defect(n)	defective (adj)	defectively (adv)			
define(v)	definable (adj)	definability (n)	definably(adv)	definement (n.)	definer(n)
delectable (dih-lek-tuh-buhl)	delectably (adv)	delectability (n)			
detest(v)	detestable (adj)	detestably (adv)	detestation(n)		
dexterous (adj) (dek-struhs)	dexterity(n)	ambidextrous(adj)	ambidextrously (adv)	ambidexterity(n) am-bi-dek-ster-i-tee	
economy (n) ih-kon-uh-mee	economical (adj) ek-uh-nom-i-kuh l	economically(adv) (ek-uh-nom-ik-lee)	economize(v) (ih-kon-uh-mahyz)		
erase(v) (ih-reys)	erased	erasable(adj)	erasing	erasability(n)	nonerasable (adj)
giant(n)	gigantic(adj) (jahy-gan-tik)	gigantically (adv)	giganticness (n)		
grievous (adj)	grievously (adv)	grievousness (n)			
happy	happier	happiest	happily(adv)	happiness(n)	
hunger(n)	hungry (huhng-gree)	hungrier	hungriest	hungrily	hungriness

humble(n)	humbly(adv)	humility(n)	humiliate(v)	humiliat-ing (adj)	humiliatingly (adv)
ideal(n) (ahy-dee-uhl)	idealness(n)	ideally(adv) (ahy-dee-uh-lee)			
impetus(n)	impetuous (adj)	impetuously (adv)	impetuousness(n)		
imply(v)	implied(adj)	implication (n)			
malign(adj) (muh-lahyn)	malign(v)	malignant (adj) (muh-lig-nuh nt)	malignantly (adv)	malignancy (n.)	
material	materialness (n)	prematerial (adj)	immaterial (adj)	quasimaterial(adj)	quasimaterially(a dv)
mock(v.) (adj)	mocker(n)	mockingly (adv)	mockery(n) (mok-uh-ree)		
partial(adj) (pahr-shuhl)	partially(adv)	partiality(n) (pahr-shee-al-i-tee)	partialness(n)		
impartial (adj) (im-pahr-shuhl)	impartially (adv)	impartiality (n)	nonpartial (adj)		
perplex (v.) (per-pleks)	perplexed (adj) (per-plekst)	perplexity(n) (per-plek-si-tee)			
reflect(v.) (ri-flekt)	reflection(n) (ri-flek-shuhn)				
restive(adj)	restively(adv)	restiveness(n)			
resume(v)	resumption (n)				
sad(n)	sadder(adj)	saddest(adj)	sadly(adv)	sadness (n)	
scarce(adj) (skairs)	scarcely(adv)	scarceness(n)			
scrutinize (n)	scrutiny(n)	inscrutable (adj)	inscrutably (adv.)	inscrutability (n)	
secure(adj) (si-kyoor)	securable (adj)	securely(n)	securer(n)	secure-ness	insecure
silly	sillier	silliest	sillies	silliness	unsilly
skeptic(n) (skep-tik)	skeptical (adj) (skep-ti-kuhl)	skeptically (adv)	skepticism(n) (skep-tuh-siz-uh m)		
surmount (v)	surmountable(adj)	insurmountable (adj)			
symbol(n)	symbolic (adj)	symbolical (adj)	symbolically (adv)	symbolism(n)	symbolize (v)
tantalize(v)	tantalizing (adj)	tantalizingly (adv)			
tentative (adj)	tentatively (adv)	tentativeness (n)			
thoughtful (adj)	thoughtfully (adv)	thoughtfulness(n)	overthoughtful(adj)		
wretch(n)	wretched (adj)	wretchedly (adv)	wretchedness (n)		
yearn(v) (yurn)	yearning(n) (yur-ning)	yearner(n)			
match(n,v)	matchable (adj)	matcher (n)	unmatchable (adj)	unmatched (adj)	unmatching (adj)

14.10 World list of 194 Countries

This list provides country name and population (2020).

Exercise 1: Review the following list of countries and populations.
Exercise 2: Add additional information such as, area of country, currency, type of government.
Exercise 3: Find your country of origin and include three additional personal observations.

Country (phonetic spelling)
Population
(2020)

1 Afghanistan (af-gan-uh-stan) 38,928,000	8 Armenia (ahr-mee-nee-uh) 2,963,000
2 Albania (al-bey-nee-uh) 2,877,000	9 Australia (aw-streyl-yuh) 25,499,000
3 Algeria (al-jeer-ee-uh) 43,851,000	10 Austria (aw-stree-uh) 9,006,000
4 Andorra (an-dawr-uh) 77,000	11 Azerbaijan (ah-zer-bahy-jahn) 10,139,000
5 Angola (ang-goh-luh) 32,866,000	12 Bahamas (buh-hah-muhz) 393,000
6 Antigua (an-tee-guh) and Barbuda (bahr-boo-duh) 97,000	13 Bahrain (bah-reyn) 1,701,000
7 Argentina (ahr-juh n-tee-nuh) 45,195,000	14 Bangladesh (bahng-gluh-desh) 164,689,000
	15

	Barbados (bahr-bey-dohz)	25	
	287,000		Brunei (broo-nahy)
16			437,000
	Belarus (byel-uh-roos)	26	
	9,449,000		Bulgaria (buhl-gair-ee-uh)
17			6,948,000
	Belgium (bel-juhm)	27	
	11,589,000		Burkina Faso (ber-kee-nuh fah-soh)
18			20,903,000
	Belize (buh-leez)	28	
	397,000		Burundi (boo-roo n-dee)
19			11,890,000
	Benin (be-neen)	29	
	12,123,000		Côte d'Ivoire (koht dee-vwar)
20			26,378,000
	Bhutan (boo-tahn)	30	
	771,000		Cabo Verde (ka-bo verdey)
21			555,000
	Bolivia (buh-liv-ee-uh)	31	
	11,673,000		Cambodia (kam-boh-dee-uh)
22			16,718,965
	Bosnia (boz-nee-uh) and Herzegovina (her-tsuh-goh-vee-nuh)	32	
	3,280,000		Cameroon (kam-uh-roon
23			26,545,000
	Botswana (bot-swah-nuh)	33	
	2,351,000		Canada (kuh n-yah-duh)
24			37,742,000
	Brazil (bruh-zil)	34	
	212,559,000		Central African (af-ri-kuhn) Republic

4,829,000	
35	
Chad (Chad)	
16,425,000	
36	
Chile (chil-ee)	
19,116,000	
37	
China (chahy-nuh)	
1,439,323,000	
38	
Colombia (kuh-luhm-bee-uh)	
50,882,000	
39	
Comoros (kom-uh-rohz)	
869,000	
40	
Congo (Congo-Brazzaville)	
5,518,000	
41	
Costa Rica (kos-tuh ree-kuh	
5,094,000	
42	
Croatia (kroh-ey-shuh)	
4,105,000	
43	
Cuba (kyoo-buh)	
11,326,000	
44	
Cyprus (sahy-pruhs)	

1,207,000	
45	
Czechia (Czech (chek) Republic)	
10,708,000	
46	
Democratic Republic of the Congo (kong-goh)	
89,561,000	
47	
Denmark (den-mahrk)	
5,792,000	
48	
Djibouti (ji-boo-tee)	
988,000	
49	
Dominica (dom-uh-nee-kuh)	
71,000	
50	
Dominican (duh-min-i-kuhn) Republic	
10,847,000	
51	
Ecuador (ek-wuh-dawr)	
17,643,000	
52	
Egypt (ee-jipt)	
102,334,000	
53	
El Salvador (el sal-vuh-dawr)	
6,486,000	

The Hollywood Tutor's AMERICAN ENGLISH © 2020 Mitch Rubman. All rights reserved. No part of this publication may be reproduced or distributed in any form or by any means without the written permission of the copyright owner

#	Country	#	Country
54	Equatorial (ee-kwuh-tawr-ee-uhl) Guinea (gin-ee) 1,402,000	64	Georgia (jawr-juh) 3,989,000
55	Eritrea (er-i-tree-uh) 3,546,000	65	Germany (jur-muh-nee) 83,783,000
56	Estonia (e-stoh-nee-uh) 1,326,000	66	Ghana (gah-nuh) 31,072,000
57	Eswatini (fmr. "Swaziland") 1,160,000	67	Greece (grees) 10,423,000
58	Ethiopia (ee-thee-oh-pee-uh) 114,963,000	68	Grenada (gri-ney-duh) 112,000
59	Fiji (fee-jee) 896,000	69	Guatemala (gwah-tuh-mah-luh) 17,915,000
60	Finland (fin-luh nd) 5,540,000	70	Guinea (gin-ee) 13,132,000
61	France (frans) 65,273,000	71	Guinea-Bissau (gin-ee-bi-sou) 1,968,000
62	Gabon (ga-bawn) 2,225,000	72	Guyana (gahy-an-uh) 786,000
63	Gambia (gam-bee-uh) 2,416,000	73	Haiti (hey-tee) 11,402,000

74		84	
	Holy See		Italy (it-l-ee)
	800		60,461,000
75		85	
	Honduras (hon-door-uhs)		Jamaica (juh-mey-kuh)
	9,904,000		2,961,000
76		86	
	Hungary (huhng-guh-ree)		Japan (juh-pan)
	9,660,000		126,476,000
77		87	
	Iceland (ahys-luh nd)		Jordan (jawr-dn)
	341,000		10,203,000
78		88	
	India (in-dee-uh)		Kazakhstan (kah-zahk-stahn)
	1,380,004,000		18,776,000
79		89	
	Indonesia (in-duh-nee-zhuh)		Kenya (ken-yuh)
	273,523,000		53,771,000
80		90	
	Iran (ih-ran)		Kiribati (keer-ee-bah-tee)
	83,992,000		119,000
81		91	
	Iraq (ih-rak)		Kuwait (koo-weyt)
	40,222,000		4,270,000
82		92	
	Ireland (ahyuh r-luhnd)		Kyrgyzstan (kir-gi-stahn)
	4,937,000		6,524,000
83		93	
	Israel (iz-ree-uhl)		Laos (lah-ohs)
	8,655,000		7,275,000

94	
	Latvia (lat-vee-uh)
	1,886,000
95	
	Lebanon (leb-uh-nuhn)
	6,825,000
96	
	Lesotho (luh-soo-too)
	2,142,000
97	
	Liberia (lahy-beer-ee-uh)
	5,057,000
98	
	Libya (lib-ee-uh)
	6,871,000
99	
	Liechtenstein (lik-tuh n-stahyn)
	38,000
100	
	Lithuania (lith-oo-ey-nee-uh)
	2,722,000
101	
	Luxembourg (luhk-suhm-burg)
	625,000
102	
	Madagascar (mad-uh-gas-ker)
	27,691,000
103	
	Malawi (muh-lah-wee)
	19,129,000

104	
	Malaysia (muh-ley-zhuh)
	32,365,000
105	
	Maldives (mawl-deevz)
	540,000
106	
	Mali (mah-lee)
	20,250,000
107	
	Malta (mawl-tuh)
	441,000
108	
	Marshall (mahr-shuhl) Islands
	59,000
109	
	Mauritania (mawr-i-tey-nee-uh)
	4,649,000
110	
	Mauritius (maw-rish-uhs)
	1,271,000
111	
	Mexico (mek-si-koh)
	128,932,000
112	
	Micronesia (mahy-kruh-nee-zhuh)
	115,000
113	
	Moldova (mawl-doh-vuh)
	4,033,000

114	
	Monaco (mon-uh-koh)
	39,000
115	
	Mongolia (mong-goh-lee-uh)
	3,278,000
116	
	Montenegro (mon-tuh-nee-groh)
	628,000
117	
	Morocco (muh-rok-oh)
	36,910,000
118	
	Mozambique (moh-zam-beek)
	31,255,000
119	
	Myanmar (mahy-ahn-mah)
	54,409,000
120	
	Namibia (nuh-mib-ee-uh)
	2,540,000
121	
	Nauru (nah-oo-roo)
	10,000
122	
	Nepal (nuh-pawl)
	29,136,000
123	
	Netherlands (neth-er-luhndz)
	17,134,000
124	

	New Zealand (zee-luh nd)
	4,822,000
125	
	Nicaragua (nik-uh-rah-gwuh)
	6,624,000
126	
	Niger (nahy-jer)
	24,206,000
127	
	Nigeria (nahy-jeer-ee-uh)
	206,139,000
128	
	North Korea (kuh-ree-uh)
	25,778,000
129	
	North Macedonia (mas-i-doh-nee-uh)
	2,083,000
130	
	Norway (nawr-wey)
	5,421,000
131	
	Oman (oh-mahn)
	5,106,000
132	
	Pakistan (pak-uh-stan)
	220,892,000
133	
	Palau (Pa-loo)
	18,000
134	

	Palestine (pal-uh-stahyn) State 5,101,000	144	Russia (ruhsh-uh 145,934,000
135	Panama (pan-uh-mah) 4,314,000	145	Rwanda (roo-ahn-duh) 12,952,000
136	Papua (pah-poo-ah) New Guinea (gin-ee) 8,947,000	146	Saint Kitts and Nevis (nee-vis) 53,000
137	Paraguay (par-uh-gwahy) 7,132,000	147	Saint Lucia (loo-shuh) 183,000
138	Peru (puh-roo) 32,971,000	148	Saint Vincent (vin-suhnt) and the Grenadines (gren-uh-deenz) 110,000
139	Philippines (fil-uh-peenz) 109,581,000	149	Samoa (suh-moh-uh) 198,000
140	Poland (poh-luhnd) 37,846,000	150	San Marino (san muh-ree-noh) 33,000
141	Portugal (pawr-chuh-guhl) 10,196,000	151	Sao Tome (sountoo-me) and Principe (prin-suh-puh) 219,000
142	Qatar (kah-tahr) 2,881,000	152	Saudi (saw-dee) Arabia (uh-rey-bee-uh) 34,813,000
143	Romania (roh-mey-nee-uh) 19,237,000	153	

	Senegal (sen-i-gawl)		South Korea (kuh-ree-uh)
	16,743,000		51,269,000
154		164	
	Serbia (sur-bee-uh)		South Sudan (soo-dan)
	8,737,000		11,193,000
155		165	
	Seychelles (sey-shelz)		Spain (speyn)
	98,000		46,754,000
156		166	
	Sierra Leone (lee-oh-nee)		Sri Lanka (sree-lahng-kuh)
	7,976,000		21,413,000
157		167	
	Singapore (sing-guh-pawr)		Sudan (soo-dan)
	5,850,000		43,849,000
158		168	
	Slovakia (sloh-vah-kee-uh)		Suriname (soor-uh-nahm)
	5,459,000		586,000
159		169	
	Slovenia (sloh-vee-nee-uh)		Sweden (sweed-n)
	2,078,000		10,099,000
160		170	
	Solomon (sol-uh-muhn) Islands		Switzerland (swit-ser-luhnd)
	686,000		8,654,000
161		171	
	Somalia (soh-mahl-yuh)		Syria (seer-ee-uh)
	15,893,000		17,500,000
162		172	
	South Africa (af-ri-kuh)		Tajikistan (tuh-jik-uh-stan)
	59,308,000		9,537,000
163		173	

The Hollywood Tutor's AMERICAN ENGLISH © 2020 Mitch Rubman. All rights reserved. No part of this publication may be reproduced or distributed in any form or by any means without the written permission of the copyright owner

	Tanzania (tan-zuh-nee-uh)	183	
	59,734,000		Uganda (yoo-gan-duh)
			45,741,000
174			
	Thailand (tahy-land)	184	
	69,799,000		Ukraine (yoo-kreyn)
			43,733,000
175			
	Timor(tee-mawr) -Leste(les)	185	
	1,318,000		United (yoo-nahy-tid) Arab (ar-uhb) Emirates (uh-meer-its)
			9,890,000
176			
	Togo (taw-gaw)	186	
	8,278,000		United (yoo-nahy-tid) Kingdom (king-duhm)
			67,886,000
177			
	Tonga (tong-guh)	187	
	105,000		United States of America
			331,002,000
178			
	Trinidad (trin-i-dad) and Tobago (tuh-bey-goh)	188	
	1,399,000		Uruguay (yoor-uh-gwey)
			3,473,000
179			
	Tunisia (too-nee-zhuh)	189	
	11,818,000		Uzbekistan (ooz-bek-uh-stan)
			33,469,000
180			
	Turkey (tur-kee)	190	
	84,339,000		Vanuatu (vah-noo-ah-too)
			307,000
181			
	Turkmenistan (turk-me-nuh-stan)	191	
	6,031,000		Venezuela (ven-uh-zwey-luh)
			28,435,000
182			
	Tuvalu (too-vuh-loo)	192	
	11,000		Vietnam (vee-et-nahm)

97,338,000	
193	
Yemen (yem-uhn)	
29,825,000	

	194
Zambia (zam-bee-uh)	
18,383,000	

14.11 Prefixes, Roots and Suffixes 4

The English language is created from many different roots and has many prefixes (at the front of the word) and suffixes (at the end of the word) or root (in the middle of the word) used in creating words.

By studying roots, prefixes, and suffixes American English will become more understandable. This is a fairly difficult list, have fun.

Exercise 1: Repeat aloud the name of the prefix and the sentences that follow.
Exercise 2: Research and write a sentence or two about the origins of a suffix, prefix, or root.

Arch (ruler): root	anarchy, archangel, architecture, archives, archetype, oligarchy, hierarchy (hahy-uh-rahr-kee).
Ambi (both): prefix	ambidextrous, ambient, ambivalent, ambiguous.
Anti, ant (opposed, against): prefix	antonym, antidote, antiaircraft, antibiotic, antics, anticipate, anticyclone, antecedent.
Bene, bon (good, well): root	benefit, benefactor, benedictory, beneficent, beneficiary, benevolent, benign.
Circ, circum (around): prefix	circumstance, circumvent, circumnavigate, circumference (ser-kuhm-fer-uhns).
Con (with, together): prefix	Congress, contraction, concave, conceal, conceive, concentrate.
Dyn, dynam (power): prefix	dynamics, dynamo, dynamic, dynasty, dynamite, dynamometer.
Dia (through): prefix	dialogue, diameter, diagram, diagonal, diacritic, dialectic, diagnose, dialysis(dahy-al-uh-sis).
Epi (upon, besides, among): prefix	epic, epicenter, epidemic, epilogue, ephemeral, epileptic (ep-uh-lep-tik), epicurean.
Fluc, flu, flux, fluv, (flowing): latin root	fluctuate, fluid, fluency, fluidity, flume, influence, affluent.
Gen (race, kind of): latin root	gender, genius, general, generic, genesis, genetics, genre, genuine.
Hyper (over, above, excessive): prefix	hyperbolize, Hyperion, hyperdimensional, hyperirritability, hyperkinesia.

Ish (origin, resembling): suffix	bookish, childish, foolish, ghoulish.
Jud (judge, lawyer): root	judge, judgement, judicator, judicial, prejudice.
Liber, liver(free): Latin root	liberal, liberate, liberator, deliver.
Meta (beyond):	metabolism, metaphysics, metamorphic, metal, metallic.
Nov(new): root	nova, novice, novelty, novel, novella, renovate, innovate.
Per (through): prefix	personal, persist, perception, perceive, perchance, percentage.
Parl (speak):	parley, parlance, parlor, parliament, parliamentary.
Psych (mind)	psychologist, psychic, psychiatrist, psychedelic, psycho, psychoanalytic.
Peri (around): prefix	perimeter, peril, perilous, period, peripheral (puh-rif-er-uhl), periscope (per-uh-skohp), perish.
Poly (many): root	polygon, pollster, polygraph, polyester, polymer, polyp, polyphonic, polygonal.
Rect (straight, right): root	rectangle, rectify, rectory, direct.
Syn, sys, syl, sym (with, together): prefix	synonyms, synopsis (si-nop-sis), sympathy, syndication, synthesizer (sin-thuh-sahy-zer).
Trans (across, through, over): prefix	transportation, transit, transition, transfer, transport.
Therm (heat)	thermostat, thermal, thermometer, isotherm.
Spec (watch, see, observe, look): root	spectacle, spectacles, introspect, prospectus, conspicuous (kuhn-spik-yoo-uhs).
Tang, tact (touch): root	tangible, tangent, tangled, tango, tangy.
Ultima(last): root	ultimate, ultimately, ultimatum.
Vir (man)	virile (vir-uhl), virtuous, viral, virgin, virologist, virtual, virus.
Vol (wish)	volatile(vol-uh-tl), volume, volcano, volleyball.
Zo (animal)	Zoo, zodiac, zoology, zoologist, zoom.

Bibliography

Azar, B. (1995). *Basic English Grammar.* White Plains, NY: Pearson Education.

Baldick, C. (1990). *The Concise Oxford Dictionary of Literary Terms.* Oxford: Oxford University Press.

Bayan, R. (1984). *Words that Sell.* Chicago: Contemporary Books.

Boyer, S. (2003). *Understanding Spoken English.* Glenbrook: Boyer Educational Resources.

Comstock, A. (1844). *A System of Elocution.* Philadelphia: Butler & Williams.

Duffy, P. (2003). *Chicago Manual of Style.* Chicago: The University of Chicago Press.

Ehrlich, I. (1968). *Instant Vocabulary.* New York: Simon & Schuster, Inc.

Glatzer, J. (2004). *Words You Thought You Knew.* Avon: Adams .

Hancock, E. L. (1972). *Techniques for Understanding Literature.* Belmont: Wadsworth Publishing Company, Inc.

Hart, A. (1942). *The Latin Key to Better English.* New York: E. P Dutton.

Houghton Mifflin. (1997). *The Essential Writer's Companion.* Boston: Houghton Mifflin.

Jespersen, O. (1938). *Growth and Structure of the English Language.* Leipzig: B.G. Teubner.

Kipfer, B. A. (2003). *Roget's Descriptive Word Finder.* Cincinnatti: Writer's Digest Books.

Krulik, D. (1989). *English with a Smile.* Chicago: National Textbook Company.

Lamperti, G. B. (1957). *Vocal Wisdom, Maxims of Giovanni Battista Lamperti.* New York: Taplinger Publishing Company.

Lederer, R. (2005). *Comma Sense.* New York: St. Martin's Press.

Longman Group Ltd. (1995). *Longman Dictionary of Contemporary English.* Essex: Longman .

Lynn, S. (2014). *Leaving This World.* East Hampton: Sondra Lynn.

Merida, K. (2017, February 9). *44 African Americans Who Shook up the World.* From The Undefeated 44: www.undefeated.com

Muschla, G. R. (1993). *Writing Workshop Survival Kit.* New Jersey: The Center For Applied Research in Education.

Rorabacher, L. (1956). *A Concise Guide to Composition.* New York: Harper & Brothers Publishers.

Ross, S. V. (1981). *Spelling Made Simple.* New York: Bantam Doubleday Dell Publishing Group, Inc.

Scholastic. (1965). *Dictionary of Synonyms, Antonyms, Homonyms.* New York: Scholastic Book Services.

Spruiell, W. (2001). *Writing and Grammar.* New York: McGraw Hill.

Sullivan, P. (2003). *Sullivan's Music Trivia.* London: Sanctuary.

Troyka, L. Q. (1999). *Simon & Schuster Workbook For Writers.* New Jersey: Prentice Hall.

Watkins, D. (1932). *Effective Speech.* London: Markus-Campbell Company.

Watkins, M. (2000). *Useful Formulae.* New York: Walker & Company.

Webster, N. (1908). *The Elementary Spelling Book.* New York: American Book Company.

INDEX

A

A. Philip Randolph · 317
Abbreviations, acronyms, and mnemonics · 417
Abrasions · 329
Adjectival suffixes · 351
Aileron · 431
Alvin Ailey · 316
American Football · 292
American Heroes · 316
Americano · 280
Ankle · 329
Antiseptic · 329
Antonio Vivaldi · 380
Antonyms 4 · 362
Aorta · 329
Aquarius · 354
Aretha Franklin · 316
Aries · 354
Artery · 329
Auditory · 329
August Wilson · 316
Aviation and aerospace · 431

B

Badminton · 294
Bandages · 329
Barack Obama · 316
Barbara · v
Bartender: Mixed drinks, and supplies · 407
Baseball · 295
Benjamin · 310
Benjamin O. Davis Sr · 317
Betsy Blank · v
Bicep · 329
Big Six · 317
Billie Holiday · 317
Bishops · 311
Black Lives Matter · 316
Blood moon · 421
Blue moon · 421
Booker T. Washington · 317
Boris Leskin · v
Boxing · 298
Breast · 329
Brewed · 280
Business English · 372

C

Café au lait · 280
Café caramel · 280
Café latte · 280
Café mocha · 280
Café vanilla · 280
Calf · 329
Cancer · 354
Capillary · 329
Cappuccino · 280
Capricorn · 354
Caramel latte · 280
Caramel mocha · 280
Cardiovascular · 329
Cartilage · 329
Catch-22 · 290
Chadwick Aaron Boseman · 317
Chai(chahy) · 280
Cheek · 329
Chemistry Laboratory · 430
Chess · 310
Chest · 329
Chuck Negron · 470
Claude Debussy · 380
Cliches, Idiomatic expressions and Proverbs 2 · 290
Cliches, Idiomatic expressions and Proverbs 4 · 453
Cliches, Idiomatic expressions and Proverbs 5 · 469
Clippers · 329
Cloud types · 426
Cockpit · 431
Compare and Contrast 3 · 275
Compare and Contrast 4 · 339
Compare and Contrast 5 · 370
Compare and Contrast 6 · 443
Complex Colors · 268
Composers and Musicians · 380
Conditional Sentences · 281
Contractions with sentences · 261
Cory Wells · 470
Cough · 330
COVID-19 and related terms · 284
COVID-19 Symptoms · 287
COVID-19 Warning signs · 288
Cuticle · 330

The Hollywood Tutor's AMERICAN ENGLISH © 2020 Mitch Rubman. All rights reserved. No part of this publication may be reproduced or distributed in any form or by any means without the written permission of the copyright owner

D

Danny Hutton · 248, 470
David · v
Dedications and Acknowledgments · v
Denzel Washington · 318
Dermatology · 330
Devin · v
Devorah · v
Dialogue : At the Post Office · 435
Dialogue : Buying a slice of Pizza · 270
Dialogue : Cover letter for Resume · 404
Dialogue : Grocery Shopping · 396
Dialogue : Ordering at a Delicatessen · 271
Dialogue : Playing Poker · 472
Dialogue : The Florist Shop · 401
Dialogue : Tony, the Car Mechanic · 279
Dialogue: A Job interview · 398
Dialogue: COVID-19 Emergency Room · 286
Dialogue: Visiting the Beauty, Hair & Nail Salon · 464
Difficult words and sentences 1 · 262
Difficult words and sentences 2 · 333
Difficult words and sentences 3 · 364
Difficult words and sentences 4 · 375
Difficult words and sentences 5 · 391
Difficult words and sentences 6 · 402
Difficult words and sentences 7 · 405
Difficult words and sentences 8 · 431
Difficult words and sentences 9 · 465
Dimples · 330
Double vision · 330
Dr. Charles Drew · 318
Dr. Martin Luther King Jr · 317
Dr. Martin Luther King Jr. · 323
Drooping · 330
Dude · 306
Duke Ellington · 318

E

Ear · 330
Elbow · 330
Electric and Hybrid Cars · 441
Electromagnetic · 431
Elevator · 431
Elie Wiesel · v
Ella Baker · 318
Endocrinology · 330
Esophagus · 330
Espresso · 280
Esthetician · 330
Eye · 330
Eye drops · 330

Eyebrow · 330

F

Farsighted · 330
Fashion: Styles, and Trends · 266
Finger · 330
Fitness, Workout and Nutrition terms · 299
Flaps · 431
Florence Price · 380
Foot · 330
Forehead · 330
Foreword by Danny Hutton · 248
Francis Johnson · 380
Francis Scott Key · 380
Frederic Francois Chopin · 380
Frederick Douglass · 318
French Defense · 312
Friday · 354
Fuselage · 431

G

Gas Internal Combustion Engine · 437
Gastroenterology · 331
Gemini · 354
Gene · 331
George Bridgetower · 380
George Gershwin · 380
George Walker · 381
Gordon Parks · 318
Gregg · v
Gustav Mahler · 381
Gymnastics, Track & Field · 303

H

Hair · 331
Hand · 331
Harriet Tubman · 319
Hazelnut · 280
Heart · 331
Heather · 310
Henrietta Lacks · 319
Hepatology · 331
Hot chocolate · 280
How is the weather? · 259
Human Anatomy · 329
Hypothermia · 331

I

Ida B. Wells · 319
Igor Stravinsky · 381
INDEX · 490
Ion · 431
Irregular plural nouns · 463
Itzhak Perlman · 381

J

Jackie Robinson · 319
Jakob Ludwig Felix Mendelssohn · 381
Jama · v
James Baldwin · 319
James Farmer · 317
Jay Z · 320
Jean-Michel Basquiat · 320
Jennifer · v
Jesse Jackson · 320
Jesse Owens · 320
Jimi Hendrix · 320
Jody Vanessa Watley · 320
Johann Sebastian Bach · 381
Johannes Brahms · 381
John Lewis · 317, 321
Joints · 331
Jonathan · v
Joseph Bologne · 381
Julie Ariola · v

K

Kamala Harris · 321
Katherine Johnson · 322
Kidney · 331
King · 311
King's Gambit · 311
Knee · 331
Knights · 311
Kobe Bryant · 321

L

LAC + USC Medical Center · v
Larynx · 331
Led Zeppelin · v
Leo · 354
Lesson 10 · 313
Lesson 11 · 355
Lesson 12 The Internet, Computers, Jobs, Cover letter · 383
Lesson 13 The Moon, Polygons, Prefixes, Hybrids · 415
Lesson 14
    Beauty Salon, Jazz, Cliches, Derivatives · 457
Lesson 8 Vowels, Weather and Difficult words · 254
Lesson 9 Covid-19, Sports, Cliches, Chess · 283
Libra · 354
Ligament · 331
Lips · 331
Liver · 331
Long and short vowels in words · 258
Lou · v
Louis Armstrong · 322
Ludwig van Beethoven · 381
Lung · 331

M

M. Cohen · v
Macchiato · 280
Madam C.J. Walker(waw-ker) · 322
Malcolm X · 322
March on Washington · 317
Mary McLeod Bethune · 323
Maureen · v, 310
Maurice Ravel · 381
Maya Angelou · 323
Menopause · 331
Metabolism · 331
Michael Jordan · 323
Michelle Obama · 323
Miles Davis · 324
Mocha · 281
Monday · 354
Moon idiomatic expressions · 421
Moon notes · 420
Moonbows · 421
Morgan Freeman · 324
Mouth · 331
Mr. Lutvak · v
Mucci · v, 364, 366
Muhammad Ali · 324
Muscle · 331

N

Nail polish · 331
Nails: · 331
Nearsighted · 332
Neck · 332
Nobel laureate · v

Nose · 332
Nostrils · 332
Noun suffixes · 350
Numbers 6: Polygons · 421

O

Obama · 322
Ointment · 332
Onomatopoeias: · 353
Oprah · 325
Organic · 332

P

P.S. 169 · v
Pawn · 311
Periodic Table of Elements · 424
Phil · 310
Physique · 332
Pierre Gustav · 325
Pisces · 354
Plasma · 431
Prefixes, Roots and Suffixes 2 · 344
Prefixes, Roots and Suffixes 3 · 411
Prof. W. Jeffrey Hughes · v
Pronunciation Key 12 · 254
Pronunciation Key 13 with sentences · 283
Pronunciation Key 14 · 313
Pronunciation Key 15 · 355
Pronunciation Key 16 · 358
Pronunciation Key 17 with sentences · 383
Pronunciation Key 18 with sentences · 415
Pronunciation Key 19 and sentences · 457
Pronunciation Key 20 and sentences · 461
Pyotr Ilyich Tchaikovsky · 381

Q

Queen · 311
Queen's Gambit · 311
Quincy Jones · 325

R

Ramjets · 431
Randee Sullivan · v
Razor · 332
Reba McEntire movie · 430
Red eye · 281

Richard Allen · 325
Richard Georg Strauss · 381
Richard Pryor · 325
Ridge · 332
Robert Abbott · 326
Rooks · 311
Roy Wilkins · 317
Rudder · 431

S

Sagittarius · 354
Sammy Davis Jr · 326
Samuel Coleridge-Taylor · 381
Saturday · 354
Scientific Terms · 427
Scissors · 332
Scorpio · 354
Scott Joplin · 382
Scramjets · 431
Serena Williams · 326
Sergei Rachmaninoff · 382
Shakespeare · 363
Shirley Chisholm · 326
Sicilian Defense · 312
Sidney Poitier · 326
Skin · 332
Skull · 332
Slang Spoken Contractions: · **469**
Slats · 431
Snickerdoodle · 281
Soap · 332
Sojourner Truth · 327
Sol and Sarah Rubman · v
Sondra Lynn · v
Spoiler · 431
Stabilizer · 431
Stethoscope · 332
Stevie Wonder · 327
Stomach · 332
Stroke · 332
Sunday · 354
Supermoon · 421
Surfing · 306
Swimming · 307
Synonyms 6 · 260
Synonyms 7 · 337
Synonyms 8 · 395

T

T. Tannenbaum · v

Taurus · 354
Technology · 385
Teeth · 332
Tendon · 333
Tennis · 309
The American English Alphabet · **254**
The Four Seasons of the Year · 420
The Internet: · 385
The Solar System · 426
Throat · 333
Thumb · 333
Thurgood Marshall · 327
Thursday · 354
Toes · 333
Tom · v
Tongue · 333
Tongue Twisters 5 · 336
Toni Morrison · 327
Travel · 333
Tuesday · 354
Turbine · 431
tutoring sessions · 431
Tympanic · 333

V

Vanilla chai · 281
Vein · 333
Verb suffixes · 350
Vertebra · 333

Virgo · 354

W

W. E. B. Du Bois · 328
Waist · 333
Wednesday · 354
White mocha latte · 281
Whitney Young · 317
Wilhelm Richard Wagner · 382
William Grant Still · 382
Willie Howard Mays Jr. · 327
Winglet · 431
Wings · 431
Wolfgang Amadeus Mozart · 382
Word Derivatives and Root forms · 473
World list of 194 Countries · 476
Wrist · 333
Wynton Marsalis · 382

Y

Yaw · 431
YM-YWHA · 316

Z

Zora Neale Hurston · 328

The Hollywood Tutor's AMERICAN ENGLISH © 2020 Mitch Rubman. All rights reserved. No part of this publication may be reproduced or distributed in any form or by any means without the written permission of the copyright owner

www.ingramcontent.com/pod-product-compliance
Lightning Source LLC
Chambersburg PA
CBHW081454040426
42446CB00016B/3241